D0475653

Female
TOMMIES

Female TOMMIES

THE FRONTLINE WOMEN OF THE FIRST WORLD WAR

Elisabeth Shipton

The History Press

In memory of my grandmother, Catherine O'Donnell, who
served in the WAAF from 9 April 1943 to 3 June 1946.

First published 2014

The History Press
The Mill, Brimscombe Port
Stroud, Gloucestershire, GL5 2QG
www.thehistorypress.co.uk

© Elisabeth Shipton, 2014

British Library Cataloguing in Publication Data.
A catalogue record for this book is available from the British
Library.

ISBN 978 0 7524 9143 1

Typesetting and origination by The History Press and Printed in Malta by Melita Press
Production managed by Jellyfish

Contents

Foreword

Today, the presence of women in war zones around the world causes little surprise. The tragic deaths of journalists Marie Colvin in Syria (2012) and Anja Niedringhaus in Afghanistan (2014) made international headlines, but the ability and suitability of both women to undertake the work they had chosen was unquestioned. Meanwhile, the deployment of female military personnel to Iraq, Afghanistan and elsewhere is taken for granted.

While women still form a minority within the armed forces of most nations, the range of roles they undertake has expanded. Servicewomen are encouraged to expect equal treatment in terms of pay and opportunities. The exclusion of women from close combat roles is gradually disappearing in countries such as Australia and the United States. In some nations, such as Israel, women are routinely conscripted to perform national service. Even in nations such as Afghanistan, where gender segregation is fundamental to national culture, women are encouraged to serve with the armed forces.

The origins of this contribution are rooted in the First World War, which served as a catalyst for change in virtually every field of life and on every continent. As we mark the centenary of the war, Elisabeth Shipton's book provides a timely and important reminder of the war's profound impact on the lives of women. For many, life would quite simply never be the same again. On the home front, widespread personal loss and privation were augmented by the terror of coming under fire from modern weapons delivered by long range aircraft, warships and artillery. While nursing remained an important option for women seeking an active role, the escalating demands of the war effort required many to undertake completely new roles, including service with the newly founded women's branches of the armed forces. Their experience would inform that of women during the Second World War and continues to reverberate today.

Hilary Roberts
Research Curator of Photography, Imperial War Museum

Acknowledgements

Writing and researching this book has been a great experience from start to finish, but I could not have done this without the help and support of others. My first thanks go to Jo DeVries for commissioning the project and for her encouragement and enthusiasm throughout. Also to Sophie Bradshaw, Rebecca Newton and all the hard-working team at The History Press.

My friends and family have been key, from reading early drafts, to assisting with foreign translations and allowing me to bounce ideas off them, not to mention making me countless cups of tea whilst I wrote. In particular I would like to thank my father Alyn for not only translating a series of French books but for always being there to talk things through with me and offering plenty of sound advice. Also my mother Siobhan for all her endless encouragement, and Tom for keeping me going. I am extremely grateful to Melanie Hall for helping me with further translations and to Daniel Bellissimo for going out of his way to find and digitise text for me in the Italian National Central Library in Florence. I would also like to mention Mike Gallacher, Tony Dougall, Eileen North and Doctor Simon Smith for first setting me on the path of historical research. I wish to say a special thank you to Lieutenant-General Sir Christopher Wallace for sharing his extensive military knowledge and for all his support.

The British Library became a second home to me and I will forever be indebted to their extensive resources and high level of service. I'd like to thank the staff at the Templer Study Centre at the National Army Museum for being so helpful and accommodating. The Army Medical Services Museum in Aldershot received me with great generosity and enthusiasm and followed up by posting copies of documents to me with further suggestions for more material of interest. These along with other individual regimental museums (including my former employers the Royal Green Jackets (Rifles) Museum) are a great national asset and retain remarkable archives available to the public. I am also grateful to the Liddle Collection at Leeds University and the archival staff at the Royal Air Force Museum in Hendon, London. Thanks also to Jane Naisbitt, Carol Reid and their colleagues at the Canadian War Museum in Ottawa for providing copies of Grace MacPherson's diaries and related material.

During my archival research, the most unforgettable experience was listening to the recorded interviews with individuals who lived through the First World War, courtesy of the Imperial War Museum's collections. After reading the diaries of Mairi Chisholm and Florence Farmborough, to hear their voices really brought home what this generation of women achieved and their bravery. In addition to thanking the Imperial War Museum, which kindly provided photographs for this publication, I am particularly grateful to Hilary Roberts, Research Curator of Photography at the museum, for taking the time to talk to me about the role of women and photographic journalism. Last, but by no means least, I would like to thank Rosalie Maggio, co-author of *Marie Marvingt – La Femme d'un Siecle* for generously giving me permission to use a photograph of Marvingt from her own collection.

Women and their Place in War

> The last half century has gained for women the right to the highest education and entrance to all professions and occupations, or nearly all. ... By what toil and fatigue and patience and strife and the beautiful law of growth has all this been wrought? These things have not come of themselves. They could not have occurred except as the great movement for women has brought them out and about. They are part of the eternal order, and they have come to stay. Now all we need is to continue to speak the truth fearlessly, and we shall add to our number those who will turn the scale of equal and full justice in all things.
>
> Lucy Stone, American suffragist, 1893.[1]

It took just four years, but the First World War saw one of the biggest ever changes in the demographics of warfare, as thousands of women donned uniforms and took an active part in conflict for the first time in history. When the First World War came to an end in 1918, both Britain and the United States had established women's auxiliary corps to support their armed services. In 1917, Russia had gone a step further and formed several women's combat units.

Nearly 200,000 women had, in one form or another, seen active service with British forces by 1918. At that date, over 57,000 women were serving in the Women's Army Auxiliary Corps, 9,000 women in the Women's Royal Air Force, and 5,450 in the Women's Royal Naval Service. Between 70,000 and 100,000 women had worked during the course of the war as members of voluntary aid detachments and over 19,000 women had been military nurses. In the United States, over 16,500 women served with the American Expeditionary Force overseas, of which 233 were 'Hello Girls' working for the Army Signal Corps. Meanwhile over 12,000 women worked in the United States Navy and Marine Corps as Yeomen (F) and Marines (F).[2] Furthermore, medical units (including a military hospital entirely staffed by women) were set up on both the Eastern and Western Fronts, and in Britain.

In 1918, the Canadian army proposed its own women's army auxiliary corps, but the war ended before it was put into effect. At the same time, in Germany, the army set about establishing a women's signal corps, women who would work as telephone, telegraph and radio operators. Whilst they did not see active service during the conflict, the idea was pursued over the following years, but the restrictions placed on Germany by the Treaty of Versailles ensured that all women were listed as civilian employees rather than being counted as military personnel.[3]

At the beginning of the twentieth century, it would have been inconceivable for women officially to enlist in the army or the navy of any of the participant countries, let alone take on a combative role. War was a man's world in which men fought to defend their monarchy, their government, their home country and their families, including their women. In the past, women had gone to theatres of war but not in an official military capacity. For example during the Peninsular and Napoleonic Wars in the early 1800s, the European armies had numerous camp followers, among whom soldiers' wives, mistresses and dependants (as well as prostitutes) would travel with the baggage train. Over time the term 'camp follower' became synonymous with a woman of loose morals. When the reporter Dorothy Lawrence acquired a uniform and managed to reach the Western Front trenches in 1915, she had to defend herself from accusations that she was a camp follower. In the Napoleonic era, some officers' wives would travel to the Continent to be closer to their husbands, usually living in nearby towns. Sometimes they would watch a battle unfold from a distance, but they were no more than spectators. Yet as the nineteenth century progressed, and large pitched battles on open plains were replaced with trench warfare and modern firepower, this changed.

It was generally felt at the end of the nineteenth century that women did not belong in conflict and that they would not be able to cope mentally or physically with the harsh reality and violence of war. Of course, during the previous hundred years there had been a number of women who had challenged this view. In the early 1800s, James Barry, a young Irishman, went to medical school in Edinburgh, qualifying in 1812, before joining the British army. He is thought to have served during the battle of Waterloo before working across the world, holding posts in Cape Town, the Caribbean, the West Indies and Canada, attaining the senior rank of Inspector-General of Hospitals. It was only after Barry's death in 1864 that it emerged he had been a woman, christened Margaret Ann Bulkley.[4] During the American Civil War (1861–65) a number of women were known to have fought in combat. One of these was Sarah Edmonds who posed as a Union soldier called Frank Thompson. Like the British woman Flora Sandes in the First World War, Edmonds began the war as a nurse. There was also Jennie Hodgers who called herself Albert Cashier and continued to live as a man after the war, enjoying the benefits of her military pension.[5]

Although their stories intrigued audiences, these women were considered exceptional, their actions only justifiable under unique circumstances, and therefore not to be repeated. Society was generally suspicious of women who wanted to be like men, to act like them, to dress like them and to cut their hair short. It contravened the very image of womanhood and raised questions about female sexuality.[6]

Nevertheless, during the late 1800s and early 1900s there was a general movement in Europe, Australasia and North America for female equality, through education, occupation and the fight for women's suffrage. It was not the case that all the women who took part in the First World War were educational reformers or political campaigners, but the movement created an environment in which women were able to take a significant step towards equality and go on to enlist in the armed forces. The war provided an opportunity for women to realise their potential, to demonstrate their capabilities and to use their skills on a grand scale.

The war also provided an opportunity for the suffragists to promote their cause, finally to persuade their governments that they, like men, should be allowed to vote. In the United States, the campaigners for women's suffrage and equality organised the first National Women's Rights Convention in 1850. In addition to suffrage, the attendees, both female and male, discussed a range of issues for women including education and employment opportunities, the right to earn the same as men and property law for married women. The conventions were held annually, except during the American Civil War, during which the campaign was suspended. Proponents of female suffrage had supported those arguing for the African-American vote, hoping that a new amendment could make both groups eligible. However the new legislation granting African-Americans the vote in 1866 referred to 'male' citizens, meaning that the wording excluded women. Two prominent suffragists, Susan B. Anthony and Elizabeth Cady Stanton, rejected the legislation and tried to encourage a petition for it to be reworded to grant universal suffrage, but to no avail.

It was at this point that a schism developed between America's female suffragists following a dispute on strategy. In 1869 Cady Stanton and Anthony formed the National Woman Suffrage Association, which campaigned for multiple issues, whilst Lucy Stone founded the American Woman Suffrage

Association. Unlike the National Association, Stone's organisation worked alongside men and focused solely on suffrage. It was also less militant. Stone had married into the Blackwell family, but significantly decided not to change her name. Her husband, Henry Browne Blackwell, co-founded the American Woman Suffrage Association with his wife. His sister, Elizabeth, was the first American woman to qualify as a medical doctor. In 1890 the separate organisations combined to form the National American Woman Suffrage Association. Importantly, by 1900, Wyoming, Utah, Colorado and Idaho had all granted women suffrage. Then in 1917, a new group was formed, the National Woman's Party, which saw the First World War as a significant opportunity to win federal legislation. The group believed that by suspending activity during the Civil War they had lost out in 1866, so this time they were determined to shout even louder, becoming more militant and even picketing outside the White House.[7]

The British suffrage movement also experienced a schism, resulting from a difference in approaches. In the later half of the 1800s, the main suffrage group in Britain was the National Union for Women's Suffrage Society (NUWSS) which had most in common with Lucy Stone's American Woman Suffrage Association. One of the most prominent figures in the NUWSS was Millicent Garrett Fawcett, whose husband Henry was a Liberal MP (as her father had been) and supported votes for women in a similar manner to Henry Browne Blackwell. In fact, it was Blackwell's sister Elizabeth who had inspired Garrett Fawcett's elder sister, Elizabeth Garrett Anderson, to study medicine, later becoming a British medical pioneer. Having grown up in an educated political household, Millicent Garrett Fawcett had a thorough understanding of the British political system and her approach was to use the law to support the emancipation of women.[8]

However there were others who were more impatient for change. The Women's Social and Political Union (WSPU) was formed in Manchester in 1903. Frustrated at how little women had achieved so far, Emmeline Pankhurst and her daughters Christabel and Sylvia led the WSPU, adopting a more militant approach like that of National Woman's Party in the United States. Yet unlike the NUWSS and the National Woman's Party, the WSPU focused solely on obtaining the vote for women. In the early years this saw an exciting change of pace, with the promise of action. It attracted many members and in 1906 the headquarters moved to London.[9] While the NUWSS members were typically working- and middle-class women, the WSPU appealed more to the upper classes.

Both the United States and Britain were still campaigning for suffrage when the First World War began. Yet women in New Zealand voted for the first time in 1893 and by 1902 Australia had granted women the federal vote followed by the state vote in 1911.[10]

While the actions of the suffragists helped bring women together and find a collective voice, at the same time it created outside resistance to these women, who were perceived as troublesome and demanding. When Field Marshal Lord Kitchener[11] (Secretary of State for War 1914–16) was serving as a General during the Boer War (1899–1902), he encountered the human rights activist Emily Hobhouse. She campaigned relentlessly about the poor condition of the women and children held in concentration camps, demanding that Kitchener took responsibility for the situation. Her campaign did a great deal to turn public opinion against the war. Hobhouse was a source of intense irritation to Kitchener and he referred to her as 'that bloody woman'. Her protests did little to convince Kitchener that women belonged in war. Men were seen to qualify for the vote as they were eligible to fight for their country, which entitled them to national citizenship. Therefore, when women campaigned to be militarised during the First World War, the state and military authorities were concerned that military service would promote their right to suffrage, prompting them to go to some lengths to explain their reluctance for women to become involved. When the shortage of manpower along the front became severe, the state and the military had to reconsider. In most cases it was made abundantly clear that women would only be employed as civilians, on contract. There was, however, no uniform policy: some women were enlisted and some were enrolled as civilians, while others worked for voluntary organisations brought under military control.

Education was another way in which women were attempting to close the gender gap and compete more fairly with men. Throughout the latter half of the 1800s, educational opportunities were expanding for women. As well as more investment and support from the government (particularly with elementary schooling), new academic schools were established, such as Queen's College, London, founded in 1848 by Frederick Denison Maurice, a professor at King's College, London. This was followed by the North London Collegiate School in 1850, Cheltenham Ladies' College in 1854 and a series of schools established in 1872, and governed by the Girls' Public Day School Trust. Yet 'most of the new white-collar jobs, such as clerking and elementary-school teaching, were only open to those who had continued in education until the age of sixteen, a commitment not all families were willing to make.'[12] In 1900 the majority of girls who were educated outside their homes attended small, privately-run schools rather than these new institutions. However the establishment of the grammar school system under the 1902 Education Act meant that by

1913 there were over 1,000 grammar schools making secondary education more readily available to the middle classes.[13]

By enabling women to obtain academic qualifications at school on a par with their male contemporaries, the education crusade naturally extended to gaining a wider acceptance of women at university. In Britain, new institutions of higher education began to be established, such as Bedford College, London, founded in 1849. Although Bedford was largely restricted to training middle-class women to be teachers and governesses, both of which were deemed suitable professions, it was a step in the right direction. By 1878, the University of London was accepting female students and by the early 1900s it had three women's colleges. 'In the mid-nineteenth century, women were permitted to take Local Examinations for entrance to Oxford, and Cambridge (tests that had been designed to help non-elite men qualify for admittance). They were not, however, permitted to matriculate or even to attend classes at first. Both universities resisted accepting female students long after other institutions had done so.'[14] Emily Davies, who established Girton College with Barbara Bodicon and Lady Stanley, successfully campaigned for women to attend lectures at Cambridge from 1870, and five years later Newnham Hall was founded, while Oxford's first two women's colleges, Lady Margaret Hall and Somerville, were founded in 1889 and 1879 respectively.

Helen Gwynne-Vaughan (née Fraser), who was destined to be the chief controller of the Women's Army Auxiliary Corps and then head of the Women's Royal Air Force, embarked on her university career in 1899. She was the niece of Lord Saltoun, a Scottish peer, and had to battle hard to gain her family's consent to study, as they 'adhered to the view that education spoilt a girl's chances of marriage'.[15] However if she insisted on going, they felt that either Oxford or Cambridge would be the most suitable choice. Having just turned twenty-one, Helen passed the Oxford entrance exam, but then discovered that the university would not award any woman a degree. Instead she became 'one of the first women students at King's College'[16] London, graduating with a degree in Botany in 1904. Continuing with her academic career and eventually earning a PhD, she became a vocal supporter of the women's suffrage movement. Although she did not join any of the national societies, she did befriend Dr Louisa Garrett Anderson, and together they founded the London Graduates' Union for Women's Suffrage in 1909.

In America, one of the first co-education colleges was Oberlin College founded in 1833. At first women were only allowed to take preparatory courses but within four years women were allowed to undertake a full bachelor's degree. The first women to do this graduated in 1841.[17] From then on the educational opportunities for women in the United States continued to grow.

As more women began to attend university, a new career path opened up to women: medicine. Louisa Garrett Anderson was a member of this new generation of skilled women. Along with Dr Flora Murray, she founded the first military hospital in London in 1915, to be entirely run by women. The entry of British women into medicine had begun in 1859 when Louisa's mother, Elizabeth Garrett (Millicent's elder sister), was in her mid-twenties and met Dr Elizabeth Blackwell. Having gained her qualifications in the United States, Blackwell was the first female to be entered onto Britain's General Medical Council Register when she returned to England to practise. Elizabeth Garrett was so inspired by this example that she was determined to qualify too. Her applications to the London teaching schools and universities in London and Scotland were rejected. Eventually she was accepted by the Society of Apothecaries, obtaining her licence in 1865. She was then entered onto the Medical Register and later earned an MD from the University of Paris in 1870. In 1871 she married, becoming Elizabeth Garrett Anderson, and established the New Hospital for Women in London, which was staffed solely by women, providing medical students and newly qualified doctors with the opportunity to practise.

Meanwhile, Sophia Jex-Blake led a small group of prospective medical students wanting to qualify in Scotland. In 1869, they succeeded in having female medical students admitted to Edinburgh University. However within four years the University overturned its decision. Whilst some of the students opted to go to Switzerland to finish their training, Jex-Blake herself responded by founding the London School of Medicine for Women in 1874. In 1883, Elizabeth Garret Anderson became dean of the school, forming close ties with the New Hospital and ultimately overseeing the school's incorporation into the University of London.[18] Jex-Blake later moved back to Edinburgh, where in 1886 she founded the Edinburgh School of Medicine for Women.[19] One of the first students was Elsie Inglis, who, within a few years, along with some of the other students, had a public falling-out with Jex-Blake, and they founded a new, separate school in Edinburgh, the Medical College for Women, in 1889.[20] Once qualified, Inglis took up the post of resident medical officer at Elizabeth Garrett Anderson's hospital in London.

Female physicians were not widely accepted in what was, like the military, a predominantly male world. Garrett Anderson's hospital was one of the few that offered women jobs and medical experience. Generally they found themselves specialising in women's healthcare, such as gynaecology, as female patients began to show a preference for female doctors.

It was more difficult for women to be accepted in other spheres of medicine such as surgery. Consequently, when war was declared in 1914, many female physicians offered their services to the army, because they were keen to have an opportunity to face new medical challenges and further their careers. They were flatly refused, however, and instead they looked to join one or another of the new voluntary organisations where their skills would be appreciated. One of these organisations was the Scottish Women's Hospital formed by Elsie Inglis, which was to send medical units to France, Serbia and Russia.

At the same time as the women's movement grew and developed, so did public philanthropy, resulting in many new voluntary organisations. One of the largest of these groups was the International Red Cross Organisation. The original concept had come from the Swiss Henry Dunant, who had been shocked by the large number of men who had died during the Battle of Solferino in Italy in 1859 owing to the lack of medical treatment. He proposed a humanitarian society to treat the wounded and a treaty in which governments recognised the neutrality of this society on the battlefield. This resulted in the founding of the International Red Cross Committee in Geneva in 1863 and the first Geneva Convention in 1864. After the formation of the International Red Cross, individual countries began to form their own national Red Cross organisations. Confusingly France had three separate branches. The first, the Society to Aid Wounded Soldiers (*Societé de Secours aux Blessés Militaires*) was formed following the Franco-Prussian war of 1870. However, members felt that it excluded women and, as it didn't offer nursing training, a second, more female-dominant group was formed in 1879, the Association of French Ladies (*Association des Dames Françaises*). Then, in 1881, the Union of Women in France (*Union des Femmes de France*) was established, the third such organisation under the Red Cross.[21] Other countries generally only had one national Red Cross service.

The mid-1800s also saw the formation of two other voluntary organisations that would have a major impact in the First World War, looking after the welfare of soldiers: the Young Men's Christian Association and the Salvation Army.

The growth of philanthropy during this period coincided with the expansion of nursing and by 1900 it had became a suitable occupation for women (excluding the upper classes). By the start of the First World War, nursing was one of the few avenues open to women wanting to work alongside the military. It was a logical extension of the traditional role of a caring mother, the doting daughter and the loving sister. It is therefore unsurprising that the majority of the female voluntary societies established by 1914 were medical organisations, using the nursing profession as a platform for women's war work. Yet compared to the typical female nurse, the members of these voluntary groups tended to be from the middle and upper classes, women who were used to supporting philanthropic projects and who were ladies of leisure, able to devote much of their spare time (and money) to supporting these ventures. Many of the women were unskilled and received basic first aid training. They did not consider themselves as nurses, but rather as trained volunteers.

In Britain the institution of military nursing had only developed over the last fifty years and was relatively new. Florence Nightingale, and the popularity of her story, was instrumental in establishing modern nursing. Having befriended Sidney Herbert, who was the Secretary for War during the Crimean War, Nightingale had succeeded in getting his permission to travel to the conflict zone with a group of thirty-eight female volunteer nurses in October 1854, where they remained until 1856. Nightingale was then appointed by the War Office to oversee the training of female nurses for the military and she established the first secular training institution for nurses at St Thomas's Hospital, London, in 1860. A year later the first female nurses were employed by the army at Woolwich, London. In 1881 the Army Nursing Service was established and in 1882 a small group of nurses was selected to support the army in Egypt and the Sudan.[22] Throughout the 1880s, the Nursing Service expanded and in 1902 it was replaced by Queen Alexandra's Imperial Military Nursing Service.[23]

Meanwhile, in America, during the American Civil War, Sally Louisa Tompkins established and worked in a hospital for Confederate soldiers in Richmond, Virginia. In recognition of her work, the Confederate President Jefferson Davis appointed Tompkins as a Cavalry Captain in the army and she was referred to as 'Captain Sally'. When she died she was buried with full military honours.[24] Tompkins' work helped remove the stigma associated with nursing as a female profession. A decade after the New England Hospital for Women and Children[25] was founded in 1862 it began to run a nurse training school, and in 1873 Linda Richards graduated as America's first officially trained nurse. Twenty years later, the author and journalist Mary Roberts Rinehart trained as a nurse, although she had originally considered a career in medicine, but was too young to attend medical school. Her training allowed her to join the Red Cross in 1915 and travel to France and Belgium during the First World War. In 1901 the United States Army Nurse Corps was established, followed by the United States Navy Nurse Corps in 1908. In addition, the American Red Cross was organised by Jane Arminda Delano, who, in anticipation of the United States joining the First World War, used the Red Cross to create a substantial nursing reserve that would support the Army Nurse Corps.[26] In Canada, the army had employed female nurses in the years before the formation of the official Canadian Army Nursing Corps in 1908.[27]

From 1868, the British Nightingale system of nursing was replicated in the United States and Australia. Certainly in Australia, towards the end of the nineteenth century, numbers of male orderlies in hospitals and institutions were increasingly being replaced by female nurses. Nursing became more popular, applicants became more competitive and hospitals became more selective. In 1900 the Australasian Trained Nurses' Association was established in order to standardise training and working conditions. In the same year the Australian Army Medical Corps was formed, followed by the Australian Army Nursing Service Reserve.[28]

In the early years of the First World War, it was up to a series of voluntary organisations and a set of enterprising individuals to carve out a role for women. In Britain there were several groups that were established before the war that would go on to have a major role in the forthcoming conflict.

At the same time as contending with the growing suffrage debate, the British Government was reforming its army. The Territorial and Reserve Forces Act of 1907 provided a platform to form new auxiliary organisations. Up until then, the reserve army had consisted of local militia, yeomanry and volunteer regiments. During the Boer War, the British army had found itself seriously overstretched in a long, protracted war for which it was heavily criticised. To supplement the regular forces in South Africa, the British Government raised three contingents of the Imperial Yeomanry and deployed 140,000 men from the reserves. This in turn raised fears over the weakened state of Britain's home defence and initiated campaigns for conscription.[29] The 1907 act reformed the current system and established a territorial force, organised in a similar way to the regular army, but only intended for home defence. Importantly there was a general recognition that in order to be ready in the event of war, the new organisations had to be properly trained in peacetime.

Significantly the act also established a territorial medical service, which included the Territorial Force Nursing Service. In 1909, the Voluntary Aid Detachment (VAD) scheme was launched, which was intended to supplement these new medical services. To oversee this new organisation, two separate voluntary societies were involved – the British Red Cross Society (BRCS) and the St John Ambulance Association. The VAD is generally remembered as a society of female volunteers, but initially the organisation was open to both men and women. As the war progressed, the number of women increased, and fewer men joined as they were called up. Originally the term VAD related to a unit of members, the men's units numbering approximately fifty-six, and the women's units approximately twenty-three; but within a few years the term VAD was being used to describe an individual member. The scheme was open to existing BRCS and St John Ambulance branches, as well as independent societies, provided that the members were adequately qualified (the examinations had to be awarded by institutions approved by the War Office).

The British branch of the Red Cross was originally dubbed 'The British National Society for Aid to the Sick and Wounded in War', but it was renamed 'The British Red Cross Society' in 1905, with a royal charter in 1908. From 1907, the BRCS established local branches to recruit members. The St John Ambulance Association had been formed in 1887 'to train men and women in First Aid to minister to the sick and wounded in war and for the benefit of the civil population in time of peace.'[30]

Should war be declared, the detachments had to be ready to go into action immediately as part of Britain's home defence. Along with regular meetings, first aid training and official inspections, they had to make preparations for hospitals and medical supplies. This typically involved securing the promise of bedding, clothes, furniture, hospital premises and anything else they considered essential, so that at short notice the detachment could provide an emergency hospital.

Katharine Furse joined Detachment 22 of the Westminster Division of the VAD in London around the beginning of 1910. Aged thirty-four, Furse was a mother of two young sons and had been widowed five years previously. She had been deeply affected by the loss of her husband and, while looking for a worthwhile occupation, she saw the scheme advertised in the newspaper. Furse devoted herself to her detachment and through it she made life-long friends:

> The first meeting I attended was at the London and Scottish Drill Hall where we were set to roll bandages and here I met Isabel and Rachel Crowdy and later their sisters Mary and Edith, all of whom became much beloved friends who have been a great stand-by throughout my life ever since. ... gradually I became absorbed in the work of the detachment and began to see light ahead in life.[31]

She had great admiration for Rachel Crowdy who had trained as a nurse at Guy's Hospital. Like Furse, Crowdy was a proactive member and, on joining the detachment, she applied through the Apothecaries' Hall so that she could work as the group's dispenser.

Furse was always enthusiastic, looking for ways to improve, and whilst the regulations stipulated members only had to attend a minimum of twelve meetings per year, she did not think this sufficient and encouraged more regular attendance. The level of commitment and standard of the different detachments varied across the country. The standard training included 'First Aid, Home Nursing, Cooking, Laundry, [and] Carpentry'[32] but the VADs found it difficult to get hospital experience as very few institutions were prepared to take them on. Each year the detachment was inspected by the War Office, for which the members became increasingly competitive:

> The Division of Westminster made most elaborate preparations for these occasions. For the first, we took over Epsom College and converted it into a hospital, where I was improvised into Quartermaster for the day, having no experience, but quite ready to pretend that I could give out stores, etc. Another year the inspection was in one of the Westminster drill halls and 22 London was given the Ambulance Train to improvise. The cotton dress and its starched adjuncts were most unsuitable for carpentry and rough work on a hot day, but we flung ourselves into the phantasy and produced a very creditable 'train' out of practically nothing. Later V.A.D.s 128 and 146 London actually 'converted' ordinary railway carriages on a siding at Paddington Station into an ambulance train, and here we produced a much more realistic effect.[33]

Increasingly the detachments were encouraged to improvise, something which would become a necessity during war to an unanticipated degree. The VADs also organised summer camps, but Furse says little about these other than mentioning the fact that she didn't particularly like camping. However she was keen to make amendments to the uniform:

> Regulations for V.A.D. uniform were particularly irksome as this consisted of washing cotton dresses with starched collars, cuffs and belts, and a Sister Dora cap perched on the head. For out of doors we had a full length coat of navy blue serge and what used to be called a 'motor cap', like a heavy flat plate made of serge with a peak; this one tried to balance on one's head, using 9-inch long hat-pins or special safety pins.
>
> Our Commandant being of practical and independent character, insisted on our being allowed to wear felt hats, and she prescribed a blue knitted cardigan as an unofficial extra. Living in Surrey, and travelling to London as I did, even this was not very suitable, so I had a coat and skirt made on the lines of a military tunic and, when other members of the Detachment approved this, we agreed to try to get it generally adopted as uniform. I don't remember consulting Mrs. Gray [the Commandant] before writing on 6th January, 1913, a separate letter to every member

of the Uniform Committee at 9 Victoria Street, not one of whom did I know personally at the time except Dr. Cantlie, to whom went a particularly touching appeal ... Members of the Committee told me later of their surprise when all those present reported that they had received a similar letter from this unknown but insistent lady. They granted her request, which was all that mattered to us and, after the war, I gave the original 'costume' to the War Museum.[34]

Such was Furse's reputation that within a few years of joining the Westminster Detachment, she and Rachel Crowdy were invited to establish new detachments in the Paddington area.

In 1907 Edward Baker founded an entirely separate organisation, the First Aid Nursing Yeomanry (FANY). While serving as a cavalry sergeant-major in the Sudan in the 1890s, Baker had witnessed dying men on the battlefield, and he knew that many lives would have been saved had medical assistance been able to reach them earlier. He proposed a nursing corps of women riding on horseback, arriving quickly at the scene and administering first aid, while the oxen carts and horse-drawn ambulances were still slowly and precariously navigating the rough terrain. Baker was to be the head of this organisation that would provide the 'missing link' in military medical care, and for this he assumed the rank of captain.[35] In addition to receiving first aid training, members would also ride regularly, train to drive horse-drawn ambulances, carry stretchers and hold summer camps.

Pat Beauchamp (née Waddell) joined the FANY in 1913 and described the summer camps in her memoirs:

Work was varied, sometimes we rode out with the regiments stationed at Bisley on their field days and looked after any casualties. (We had a horse ambulance in those days which followed on these occasions and was regarded as rather a dud job). Other days were detailed for work at the camp hospital near by to help the R.A.M.C. [Royal Army Medical Corps] men, others to exercise the horses, clean the officers' boots and belts, etc., and, added to these duties was all the everyday work of the camp, the grooming and watering of the horses, etc. ... The afternoons were spent doing stretcher drill: having lectures on First Aid and Nursing from a R.A.M.C. Sergeant-Major, and, when it was very hot, enjoying a splash in the tarpaulin-lined swimming bath the soldiers had kindly made for us. Rides usually took place in the evenings, and when bedtime came the weary troopers were only too ready to turn in! Our beds were on the floor ... we had brown army blankets, and it was no uncommon thing to find black earth beetles and earwigs crawling among them![36]

The women also went on marches with games and exercises designed to test their training. In one such game the members:

> Were lined up and divided into groups, some as stretcher bearers, some as 'wounded', some as nurses to help the 'doctor', etc. The wounded were given slips of paper, on which their particular 'wound' was described, and told to go off and make themselves scarce, till they were found and carried in (a coveted job). When they had selected nice soft dry spots they lay down and had a quiet well-earned nap until the stretcher bearers discovered them. Occasionally they were hard to find, and a panting bearer would call out 'I say, wounded, *give* a groan!' and they were located. First Aid bandages were applied to the 'wound' and, if necessary, impromptu splints made from the trees near by. The patient was then placed on the stretcher and taken back to the 'dressing station.'
>
> 'I'm slipping off the stretcher at this angle,' she would occasionally complain. 'Shut up,' the panting stretcher bearers would reply, 'you're unconscious!'[37]

The members of the FANY learned to shoot and took part in shooting competitions. Many of the women had learnt to ride on their family and friends' countryside estates, or had been hunting and were therefore familiar with guns. In 1910 an article in the FANY magazine argued that 'Every woman should be able to load and fire a revolver. In moments of danger there cannot always be one of the stronger sex at hand, and for our work especially, this would come in useful.'[38]

The FANY was a voluntary organisation and therefore its members had to be financially independent: paying an enrolment fee, buying uniforms, paying for courses and riding schools, and for the care and maintenance of their horses. Therefore the majority of its members were from the middle and upper classes.[39] The backlash against the suffrage movement, in particular the demonstrative Suffragettes, meant in general that British society was uncomfortable with women being different and taking on these masculine roles. Recognising this, the original uniform reflected the clothes typically worn by an Edwardian woman:

> A scarlet tunic with high collar and white braid facings, a navy blue bell-shaped skirt with three rows of white braid at the bottom, long enough to cover the feet, and a hard-topped scarlet hat with a shiny black peak. The women wore white gauntlet gloves & carried riding crops or small canes as well as white first aid haversacks (backpacks). The mess uni-

form for official occasions consisted of a short scarlet jacket with pale blue facings worn over a white muslin dress with a scarlet sash.[40]

An early recruit was Mabel St Clair Stobart, a widow in her late forties, who described herself as a feminist and became involved with Garrett Fawcett's suffrage campaign, but disagreed with the Suffragettes:

> My attention was drawn to an organization, the Women's First Aid Nursing Yeomanry, which was then being formed under the aegis of a Mr. B., who styled himself Captain B. It had a recruiting office in an upper room above Gamage's shop in the Kingsway, and I well remember standing on the pavement on the opposite side of the road, looking across at the window, making up my mind whether I should or should not cross the road and join the organization. I crossed, climbed the stairs and joined the Corps. Now, I don't want to be unloyal or ungrateful, but frankly the aims and efforts of the promoter, though well meaning, were absurdly unpractical.
>
> We were to be nurses mounted on horseback, yeomanry nurses, and we had visions of galloping bravely on to the battlefields and snatching the wounded from under the cannons' mouths and rendering them first aid. We rode horses, wore scarlet tunics, helmets, and divided skirts, and brandished whips, and were doubtless picturesque. But though it was a move in the right direction, it was all unpractical and would have led nowhere except to derision. The Corps was subsequently reorganized and has done excellent work on serviceable lines of its own. But at the time of which I speak there was no hope of reform from within.[41]

Stobart is describing the beginning of an internal dispute amongst the members of the FANY and Captain Baker, and by association, his daughter Katie. The members were dissatisfied with Baker as a leader, in particular his draft constitution for the corps and mismanagement of their finances. As a result of the dispute, Stobart resigned from the corps and took many of the other members with her.[42] At that point in 1909 there were nearly 100 members.[43] It was shortly afterwards, in January 1910, that Grace Ashley-Smith, a twenty-three-year-old Scot, joined the FANY, which was now much smaller in number. After leaving school, Ashley-Smith had 'spent a year at Aberdeen University, studying physical training, riding, and fencing, and then went to a convent in Brussels for two years to learn French'.[44] On seeing the newspaper advertisement for the FANY, as an accomplished horsewoman, she was captivated by the notion of a female yeomanry. She quickly established herself as a prospective leader and became focused on rebuilding the corps and ultimately removing the Bakers in 1912. As a fiery and energetic individual, Ashley-Smith's leadership was tempered by the more pragmatic Lillian Franklin who had joined early in the previous year. Ashley-Smith became secretary, with the rank of sergeant-major; Franklin became treasurer and second lieutenant.[45] Little more is known of Baker during the years after he left the FANY. Apparently one day 'he walked out of his home in Greater London and failed to return.'[46]

Ashley-Smith described those early years in her diary:

> I spent the next few months fighting for my own way in the office. Soon I had the girls in khaki astride skirts with tunics to match, and I wrote out a scheme of training based on the R.A.M.C. training manual. I laid down that we were to help the R.A.M.C. with the removal of wounded from dressing stations to clearing hospitals, and were to be mounted to save time in reaching our goal. Riding on battlefields was quietly dropped from our programme. (This did not prevent Franklin and myself riding in a pageant at the Crystal Palace. We had to come in at a full gallop, leap from our horses, bandage wounded men, pull one up on our saddles, and gallop off amid the shouts and spears of Zulus, and to the wild applause of thousands of spectators …)
>
> I hunted round for recruits and pestered all my friends to join. That was the first step. The second was to weed out the others, amongst them a soulful lady with peroxide hair, very fat and hearty, who insisted on wearing white drawers with frills under her khaki skirt. She also insisted on falling off at every parade and displaying them. She was so breezy and warm-hearted that it cost me a pang, but she had to go; no women's movement could have survived those white frilly drawers on parade. Within two months we had twelve recruits and Mr. Baker promoted Miss Franklin and myself to be sergeants.
>
> We had a full programme. Weekly riding drills at Savigears and Regents Park, driving once a fortnight on Saturdays when we could have the use of Gamage's van horses for our ambulance wagon, and classes in signalling. We all took Courses in First Aid and Home Nursing.[47]

The new khaki uniform introduced by Ashley-Smith also included riding breeches, puttees and boots. The design was more practical, with a shorter skirt allowing the women to ride astride rather than side-saddle. This was a bold and confident statement and affirmation that the corps wanted to be taken seriously. The choice of khaki was symbolic and identified the FANY as a military organisation. Ashley-Smith also worked hard to distance the FANY from the suffrage debate and to work with the current political system.

Meanwhile Stobart, having left Baker and the FANY, established a society of her own, the Women's Sick and Wounded Convoy Corps. While the FANY looked to provide transport between the dressing stations or regimental aid posts on the frontline and clearing stations or field hospitals, the Convoy Corps would provide transport and medical service between the clearing stations and the base hospitals. These were generally further behind the frontlines and the hospitals to which the patients were later transferred. Stobart appreciated the need for support from a recognised authority and, like Ashley-Smith, she forged ties with the RAMC. Stobart wanted the women to 'be allowed to form a supplementary Army Medical Corps with opportunities of training and discipline similar to those which were given to the Territorial R.A.M.C. men.'[48] She explained:

At this moment the 'Votes for Women' agitation was sadly upsetting social equilibriums. ... I knew from personal experience that women could do things of which tradition had supposed they were incapable. I viewed the situation from an angle of my own. My feeling was that if women desired to have a share in the government of the country, and this seemed a legitimate ambition, they ought to be capable of taking a share in the defence of their country.

I thought that in the present agitation women were putting the cart before the horse, and I made up my mind to try and provide proof of women's national worthiness, in the belief that reward of political enfranchisement would be the natural corollary. I want to lay stress on this point, for this was the secret motive power that initiated my War work. I don't remember speaking on any suffrage platforms, I contented myself with the secretly-held belief that in helping women to take a share in national defence I was working none the less effectively for the goal of women's enfranchisement.[49]

Taking an office in Westminster, Stobart organised first aid courses similar to those undertaken by the VAD and the FANY, as well as riding drills and horse management. As with the other societies, members learned to adapt buildings into hospitals and make carts and railway trucks suitable for the transport of patients. They also held summer camps in which they set up their own tents, did their own cooking and practised medical and riding drills, as well as digging trenches. What made the Women's Sick and Wounded Convoy Corps distinct was that all the members were women, even the doctors and the surgeons.

Wanting to expand the credibility of this women's corps, Stobart successfully registered it as a voluntary aid detachment in 1910. She also hoped
'that wider notions as to the work allotted to women might permeate Red
Cross circles.' Yet Stobart was to have a great falling out with the Red
Cross when it failed to acknowledge all of the corps' achievements, and
her biography is laced with bitterness. She says that despite her commitment and co-operation with the VAD scheme the Red Cross 'always looked
askance at me and regarded me as a dangerous and undesirable element.'[50]

Stobart's fallout with the BRCS started in the autumn of 1912, when
the First Balkan War began. The Ottoman (Turkish) Empire had been the
dominant power, with the smaller countries fighting for independence
throughout the late 1800s and all the countries looking to expand and con-
solidate their territories. Bulgaria, Greece, Montenegro and Serbia formed
a military alliance, the Balkan League, and in October 1912 went to war
against the Ottoman Empire. This was an opportunity for the Women's
Sick and Wounded Convoy Corps to demonstrate their effectiveness in an
actual conflict. Stobart met with Sir Frederick Treves, the chairman of the
British Red Cross, and requested permission to be sent out. She recalled,
'Sir Frederick smiled sarcastically and said that there "was no work fitted
for women in the Balkans".' Stobart was incredulous. Well aware of the
overcrowding in the hospitals and the acute shortage of qualified medical
staff, she knew that her female doctors and surgeons would be of great
assistance. However Sir Frederick Treves 'replied that the soldiers would
object to being nursed by women, and as to the women surgeons – a
woman would be incapable of operating in a hospital of war'.[51]

Stobart was determined to find some way of getting out to the Balkans.
In 1911 she had married for the second time, but unusually for the period
she retained the name of her first husband. Her second husband, John
Herbert Greenhalgh, supported her fully, and following her disagreement
with Treves, accompanied her to their London Club. It was there he saw
Noel Buxton, a Liberal MP with connections to Bulgaria, and suggested
that his wife approach him. After explaining everything to Buxton, Stobart
was invited to go with him to Bulgaria. He was due to travel in just a
few days' time. Of course Stobart accepted the invitation and immediately
began preparing a unit of the Women's Convoy Corps, which included
three female doctors and surgeons, and arranging the medical supplies
and equipment. She planned to travel ahead, and once she had organised
somewhere for them to work, she would send them a telegram instructing
them to set off. Within two days, Stobart and her loyal husband, as the
honorary treasurer of the corps, set off on the Orient Express with Noel
Buxton and his brother. The journey took four days.

Arriving in Sofia, the capital of Bulgaria, Stobart was introduced to the director of the Bulgarian Red Cross Society, Dr Radeff, who accepted the offer of the unit. However she needed the permission of Dr Kiranoff, head of Bulgaria's military medical services. He was at that time stationed in Stara Zagora with the Bulgarian army headquarters. Stobart urgently needed his permission so that she could cable her unit, and, dissatisfied with a set of vague telephone messages, she set off to Stara Zagora to speak to him in person. On arrival, Stobart and the Buxtons were given a reception with the mayor, Dr Kiranoff and other local officials. Stobart found herself giving the group an impromptu speech in German – their common language – about English women. This greatly impressed Dr Kiranoff, and he readily accepted the Women's Convoy Corps. He asked Stobart about the unit and where she would like them to operate, to which she replied: 'I want, please to go as near the front as possible.'[52]

It was arranged that the unit would be stationed in Kirk-Kilisse, a town to which the army headquarters was preparing to move, and which was likely to be in the middle of all the action. Dr Kiranoff said that he wanted a surgical team, so Stobart sent a telegram to her unit to set off immediately and bring the required surgical equipment. As the corps was a voluntary organisation, Noel Buxton, who was chairman of the Balkan War Relief Committee, paid for the unit to travel to and from Sofia. After that the Bulgarian Government paid for them, as they were attached to the Bulgarian army under the Bulgarian Red Cross. While waiting for her unit to join her, Stobart met Queen Eleanore of Bulgaria, who herself was working as a nurse, and she generously provided the Corps with gifts of bedding and clothing for their new hospital. Stobart wrote:

> The Unit numbers sixteen, and included, besides myself as Commandant and Directrice, two Sisters (Miss V. Adams and Miss P. Gadsden), four other fully qualified trained nurses, six members for general duty as cooks, dressers, nurses, etc., and the three women doctors: Dr. Alice Hutchinson, Dr. D. Tudor, and Dr. E. Ramsbotham.[53]

Miss Greg, a VAD, had volunteered as a probationer in the unit. Within six weeks of the outbreak of war, she found herself in Bulgaria with only three months' hospital training. Greg was nervous about the potential dangers ahead and concerned that the BRCS had issued statements discouraging women's organisations independently going to the Balkans. But despite this, Greg knew this was a 'unique opportunity to gain some war experience.'[54] The unit went slowly to Kirk-Kilisse as part of a convoy of fifty-three carts travelling across the mountainous countryside, haunted by the fear that the war might be over before they arrived and that they would return home humiliated. They passed through land that had recently been reclaimed from the Turks, and they had to cope with inadequate food supplies. While they were cooking what they had managed to throw together, they often found that the oxen drivers had taken the bedding straw as food for the animals. Once they arrived in Kirk-Kilisse the Buxton brothers secured them more bedding and they made their quarters in an old building. At night, however, they had to contend with rats running over them as they tried to sleep. They found their living conditions to be an extreme contrast to those they had left behind in England. However this was only the beginning of what was to be an enormous lesson in the realities of war. The women had to clean and sanitise the building that had been designated as their hospital while contending with the immediate arrival of fifty men whose wounds had been left unattended for a period of six days. Stobart proudly recalled that, despite Sir Frederick Treves' warnings, there were no objections to being treated by female medics and all who visited the hospital were greatly impressed. The unit arrived in Bulgaria at the end of November 1912, and following the armistice, returned to England in January 1913 after two months of hard work behind the frontlines.

Stobart then went to visit family in British Columbia for three months. When she returned, she discovered that her fellow members of the Women's Sick and Wounded Convoy Corps no longer wanted to be an organisation that acted independently of the BRCS. Instead they wanted to conform with other VAD units and follow the directives of Treves and his staff. Stobart was saddened that they were 'desirous of giving up their individuality as a Corps and throwing in their lot wholesale with the B.R.C. Society'[55] She felt that this decision meant the BRCS was unlikely to build on her achievements and experience in Bulgaria and thereby expand the role of its female members. The only units which the BRCS itself had sent to the Balkans were made up of men, and at the annual general meeting of the London branches, while these individuals were praised, Stobart and her corps were not mentioned. Stobart was deeply hurt. Standing down from her role of corps director, she and her husband returned to Canada.

At the same time, Grace Ashley-Smith was looking for an opportunity for the FANY to prove itself. The escalation of the Irish home rule debate and the rising militancy of Irish politics in 1913 led to fears of a rebellion and consequently a possible role for the women. The Ulster army accepted Ashley-Smith's offer of an ambulance unit should events develop into war. After demonstrating their capabilities to the Ulster army's principal medical officer, Ashley-Smith and another member, Cicely Mordaunt, were invited to Belfast for interview. Provided with a car and an officer, they were given a tour of the area and the buildings where their proposed hospital would be. They returned to England and held a camp at Pirbright, Surrey. There they were met by newspaper reporters who photographed them and publicised the ladies' plans to fight for Ulster.[56] However the idea of a group of ladies participating in a war did not sit well with the majority of the Ulster army and raised concerns that extra men would be required to guard them. Notwithstanding Ashley-Smith's efforts to emphasise the feminine virtues of her group through her writing, advertisements and interviews, because FANY members were more than simply nurses, some viewed the organisation as one that masculinised women. Over the next few months, relations with the Ulster army fizzled out and nothing came of it.[57]

Despite the FANY's setbacks, Katharine Furse thought that an Irish war could still provide 'a patriotic use' for the VADs, but later admitted, 'my main motive in wanting to help Ulster, was my wish to put my Red Cross work into practice.'[58] Unlike the FANY, the VADs were officially recognised by the War Office and their role in supporting the army's medical services was more traditional and they did not wear khaki. They were also protected by the Red Cross emblem – although on a trip to Ireland with Rachel Crowdy, Furse realised that not everyone respected this international symbol:

> [We] were motored round the country measuring barns and school houses with a view to determining how many beds they would hold, only hearing later on one of these excursions a number of rifles were carried in the car, our Red Cross uniform being looked on as sufficient guarantee to cover them. Had we realised this at the time we should have been shocked to the core, because we were absolute sticklers for the neutrality of the Red Cross.[59]

However, the declaration of war in Europe in the summer of 1914 meant that Furse's Irish plans, like Ashley-Smith's, came to nothing.

Notes

1 Lucy Stone giving a speech entitled 'The Progress of Fifty Years' at the World's Columbian Exposition in Chicago, 1893.
2 Zeiger, Susan *In Uncle Sam's Service: women workers in the American Expeditionary Force.*
3 'German Women Help to Win! Women and the German Military in the Age of the World Wars in *A Companion to Women's Military History* edited by Hacker, Barton C. and Vining, Margaret.
4 Holmes, Rachel *The Secret Life of Dr. James Barry: Victorian England's Most Eminent Surgeon.*

5 Tsui, Bonnie *She Went to the Field: Women Soldiers of the Civil War.*
6 Cook, Bernard A., *Women and War: A Historical Encylopedia from Antiquity to the Present* pp 237–8.
7 Frost, Elizabeth and Cullen-DuPont, Kathryn *Women's Suffrage in America – An Eyewitness History.*
8 Howarth, Janet, 'Millicent Garrett Fawcett' in *Dictionary of National Biography.*
9 Chandler, Malcolm, *Votes for Women, c.1900–28*, p.9.
10 Oldfield, Audrey *Woman Suffrage in Australia – A Gift or a Struggle?*
11 Kitchener was made a local general in December 1900 and was awarded the substantive rank of general in 1902.
12 Steinback, Susie, *Women in England, 1760–1914: A Social History*, p.173–4.
13 Ibid.
14 Ibid.
15 Izzard, Molly, *A Heroine in her Time – A life of Dame Helen Gwynne-Vaughan 1879–1967*, p.71.
16 Creese, Mary R.S., 'Dame Helen Gwynne-Vaughan' in *Dictionary of National Biography.*
17 Micheletti, Laura Marie, 'Co-education' in *Women in Higher Education: An Encyclopaedia*, edited by Martinez Aleman, Ana M. and Renn, Kristen.
18 Elston, M.A., 'Anderson, Elizabeth Garrett (1836–1917) in *Dictionary of National Biography.*
19 Leneman, Leah, *In the service of life.*
20 The Edinburgh School of Medicine which had been set up by Sophia Jex-Blake closed in 1898.
21 Darrow, Margaret H., *French Women and the First World War.*
22 http://www.scarletfinders.co.uk/8.html.
23 Piggott, Juliet, *Queen Alexandra's Royal Army Nursing Corps (Famous Regiments).*
24 Glazé, Robert L., 'Tompkins, Sally Louisa (1833–1916)' in *An Encyclopaedia of American Women at War: From the Home Front to the Battlefields*, ed., Tendrich Frank, Lisa.
25 The hospital was founded by and entirely staffed by women doctors.
26 Gavin, Lettie, *American Women in World War I.*
27 Bates, Christina; Dodd, Dianne and Rousseau, Nicole (ed.), *On all Frontiers – Four Centuries of Canadian Nursing.*
28 Harris, Kirsty, *More than Bombs and Bandages: Australian Army Nurses at Work in World War I.*
29 Becket, Ian F.W., *Territorials – A century of Service.*
30 Fletcher, Corbet, *The St. John Ambulance Association – its history and its part in the ambulance movement*, p.3.
31 Furse, Katharine, *Hearts and Pomegranates: The Story of Forty-five Years, 1875 to 1920*, p.287.
32 Ibid., p.290.
33 Ibid., p.293.
34 Ibid., pp.291–292.
35 Popham, Hugh, *FANY in peace and war*, p.1.
36 Beauchamp, Pat 'Fanny goes to war' pp.5–6.
37 Ibid., p.9.

38 From 'The training of women of war' in *Women and War*, July 1910 p.28, as cited in Lee, Janet, *War Girls: First Aid Nursing Yeomanry in the First World War*, p.35.

39 Lee, Janet, *War Girls: First Aid Nursing Yeomanry in the First World War*.

40 Ibid., p.33.

41 Stobart, Mabel, *Miracles and Adventures*, p.84.

42 Lee, Janet, *War Girls: First Aid Nursing Yeomanry in the First World War*, p.43.

43 McDougall, Grace, 'Brief Resume of Corps Works' Gazette, August 1916, p.17, as cited in Lee, Janet, *War Girls: First Aid Nursing Yeomanry in the First World War*, p.41.

44 Terry, Roy, 'McDougall [nee Smith], Grace Alexandra' in *Dictionary of National Biography*.

45 Lee, Janet, *War Girls: First Aid Nursing Yeomanry in the First World War*, p.47.

46 Ward, Irene, *F.A.N.Y. Invicta*, p.35.

47 Ashley-Smith's diary, as cited in Ward, Irene, *F.AN.Y. Invicta*, pp.34–5. Savigears was a school of riding in Earls Court, directed by Mr Savigear, formerly the riding instructor to officer cadets at Sandhurst. See Graham, Lt Col J. (ed.), *Savigear's Guide to Horsemanship and Horse-Training*, Farmer's, Kensington, 1899, pp.5–6.

48 Stobart, *Miracles and Adventures*, p.84.

49 Ibid., p.83.

50 Ibid., p.86.

51 Ibid., pp.86–7.

52 Ibid., p.91.

53 Ibid., p.95.

54 Greg, E.A., 'Getting Out', p.1 – personal memoirs, Imperial War Museum Collection, document 8337.

55 Stobart, Mabel, *Miracles and Adventures*, p.135.

56 Ward, Irene, *F.A.N.Y. Invicta*, p.36.

57 Lee, Janet, *War Girls: First Aid Nursing Yeomanry in the First World War*, p.54.

58 Furse, Katharine, *Hearts and Pomegranates*, p.296.

59 Ibid., p.297.

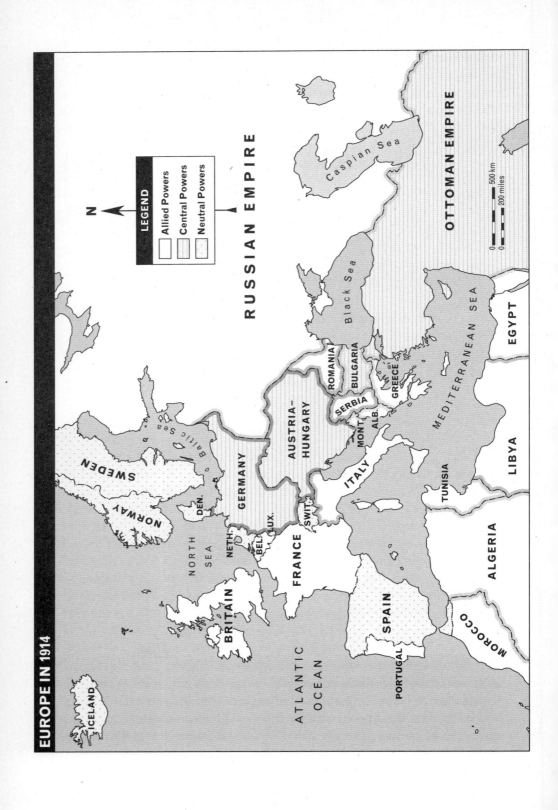

EUROPE IN 1914

LEGEND

N

Allied Powers
Central Powers
Neutral Powers

ICELAND

NORWAY

SWEDEN

Baltic Sea

NORTH
SEA

BRITAIN

ATLANTIC
OCEAN

NETH.
BEL.
LUX.
SWIT.

DEN.

GERMANY

AUSTRIA–
HUNGARY

RUSSIAN EMPIRE

Caspian Sea

ROMANIA

Black Sea

FRANCE

ITALY

MONT.
SERBIA
ALB.
BULGARIA

GREECE

OTTOMAN EMPIRE

PORTUGAL

SPAIN

MEDITERRANEAN SEA

MOROCCO

ALGERIA

TUNISIA

LIBYA

EGYPT

0   500 km
0   200 miles

2

1914: The Western Front

... all day long there came an endless procession of women wanting to help, some trained nurses, many – far too many – half-trained women; and a great many raw recruits, some anxious for adventure and clamouring 'to go to the front at once,' others willing and anxious to do the humblest service that would be of use in this time of crisis.

Violetta Thurstan[1]

Part 1: War is declared

As the movement for gender equality continued to progress within the spheres of education, employment and politics, the outbreak of war in Europe provided the opportunity for women to establish a new role in military matters.

During the nineteenth century Europe embraced industrialisation and the associated economic power it brought. Britain was the early industrial leader, but by 1913 it had been overtaken by Germany. During the latter half of the 1800s the balance of power in Europe shifted as each country attempted to assert itself politically and economically against the others. The Balkans were caught in the middle of this power struggle. The Austro-Hungarian Empire and its neighbours Italy and Germany lay to the north-west, and to the south-east were Greece and the Turkish Empire. Across the Black Sea to the north-east was Russia and across the Mediterranean to the south and west were Egypt (under British rule), Libya (Italian) and Tunisia and Algeria (French).

Russia had defeated the Ottoman Empire in the Russo-Turkish War of 1877–78 and declared Serbia, Montenegro and Romania independent of Turkish rule. However the other European countries were wary of a Russian treaty dictating the Balkan situation, in particular Austria–

Hungary, which wanted to prevent the Balkan countries within its own empire from declaring their independence. So Britain, France, Italy, Germany, Austria–Hungary, the Ottoman Empire and Russia collectively agreed on a new treaty at the Congress of Berlin in 1878. The key elements meant that the Balkan states of Serbia, Montenegro and Romania retained their new independence, but Austria–Hungary retained Bosnia-Herzegovina, and Turkey kept Macedonia. Russia resented international interference following its victory over Turkey and its relationships with Germany and Austria–Hungary remained hostile.

Throughout this period from 1878 onwards, Germany was emerging as a strong military power, and so other European countries began investing in arms so as not to be left behind and vulnerable. Over the next thirty years the European States formed alliances with one another, dividing into the two opposing sides of Britain, France and Russia (who would become the Allies) and Germany, Austria–Hungary and Turkey (who formed the Central powers). Each of these countries also faced their own internal problems; for example, the Russian Revolution of 1905 nearly succeeded in deposing the Tsar, while Austria–Hungary became increasingly concerned about the independence of Serbia and the growing nationalism amongst the Balkan states within its Empire. This tension in Eastern Europe led to the two Balkan wars, the first in the winter of 1912–13 (in which Stobart and the Women's Sick and Wounded Convoy Corps served), and the second in the summer months of 1913.

When the heir to the Austro-Hungarian Empire Archduke Ferdinand was visiting Bosnia-Herzegovina with his wife in June 1914, two attempts were made on his life by a Slav nationalist group. On the morning of 28 June 1914, the first attempt, a bomb, failed to harm the Archduke, but in the afternoon, an assassin succeeded in shooting and killing both Ferdinand and his wife. The situation escalated further when Austria–Hungary blamed Serbia for being involved in the assassination. Looking to reduce Serbian power and repress Slavic independence, Austria–Hungary issued Serbia with a series of ultimatums. However, Russia advised Serbia to protect its independence and not to concede on every single point, which led to a dissatisfied Austria–Hungary declaring war on Serbia on 28 July. Then the different European treaties one by one brought in the other European powers; within days Russia began mobilising to support Serbia while Austria–Hungary and her ally Germany also began to mobilise. A German field marshal called Graf Alfred von Schlieffen had devised a war plan for Germany, knowing that if France joined with Russia, they would have to fight on two fronts, with Russia in the east and France in the west. Due to the vast size of the Russian Empire, it would take longer to defeat Russia and so the plan was to secure the eastern border and not venture further until France had been neutralised in the west. Accordingly Germany began by issuing France with an ultimatum, demanding that she remained neutral during the conflict. France refused, however, and began to mobilise. So on 1 August Germany declared war on Russia and moved to occupy Luxembourg, which shared borders with both Germany and France. Germany then declared war on France on 3 August. Rather than make a direct attack on the French/German border, which the French had heavily reinforced, the Schlieffen plan proposed marching through Belgium and descending southwards into France and encircling Paris. Germany demanded that neutral Belgium allow its forces to pass through the country but it refused. Britain demanded that Germany respect Belgium's neutrality, and promptly issued its own ultimatums, which Germany ignored. On 4 August, as Germany marched on the Belgian city of Liège, Britain declared war.

In Britain, the war generated a wave of patriotism and a surge of eager volunteers keen to support their country in its time of need. In August 1914 there were already several different routes that women could take if they wanted to become an active part of the war effort. Firstly the official organisations overseen by the War Office included several of those whose emergence was discussed in the previous chapter, such as the military nursing services, the British Red Cross, the St John Ambulance Association or the Voluntary Aid Detachment scheme. Alternatively there were several independent voluntary societies, such as the well-established First Aid Nursing Yeomanry (FANY), and others which were swiftly founded in direct response to the declaration of war, such as the Women's National Service League[2], the Women's Emergency Corps, and a range of ambulance units. Most of these independent organisations were set up by middle- and upper-class women like Grace Ashley-Smith and Mabel St Clair Stobart, who either had sufficient personal wealth or friends wealthy enough to provide financial support. On the other hand, suffragists like Elsie Inglis, the founder of the Scottish Women's Hospital, relied on women's suffrage groups for funding.

Britain was not short of women declaring their desire to support their country who were eager to volunteer for whatever was needed. But while most of the organisations mentioned above provided medical services, each one was different in terms of its own mission and purpose. The VAD provided workers with basic medical training, the FANY offered a frontline ambulance service and the Scottish Women's Hospital employed skilled female physicians and surgeons. It was up to each organisation to convince Britain's military authorities to accept its services and to deploy them where they were needed the most.

In August 1914 the Queen Alexandra's Imperial Military Nursing Service (QAIMNS) consisted of 297 trained nurses. To be accepted in the QAIMNS a candidate had to be over twenty-five, single (or widowed), well-educated and to have successfully completed three years of training. This set of criteria made it difficult to recruit, and during the war the QAIMNS relied heavily on its reserves which ultimately provided nearly 11,000 nurses. This meant that after the war the size of the regular service would be maintained, with the reserves being easier to disband. There was also the Territorial Force Nursing Service, which had similar entry criteria. By 1918 there were 8,140 nurses who had enrolled for service and of these, 2,280 served overseas.[3] In addition the BRCS instructed qualified nurses to report to its headquarters in London and it began to deploy small parties of nurses overseas to support their sister Red Cross societies in Europe.

Established as part of Britain's home defence (should the country be invaded), the VAD was an appealing option for women with little or no medical training. Its members were tasked with setting up and helping to run hospitals for those wounded who were brought home. Active VAD members since 1910, Katharine Furse and her close friend Rachel Crowdy were to become commandants of two new London detachments. As the storm clouds gathered in Europe, Furse recalled:

> We did not want men to be sick or wounded, but we thought that, if men had to be sick and wounded, we would do our best to help them, so that, when war seemed to be imminent, we were boiling over with our desire to put into practice what we had learnt.[4]

At the declaration of war, the VAD reacted with enthusiasm and excitement, immediately calling in favours and collecting promised items, ready to serve their country. Furse explained that so many offers of help and support came flooding in that they could not all be taken up at once. There was also a sudden increase in volunteers, with an 'endless stream of women wanting to be sent to the front at once.'[5] So Furse, Crowdy and the other commandants organised 'First Aid and Home Nursing classes [which went on] … all over the country and working for examinations cooled everyone and gave them time to settle down.'[6]

What was significant was that the majority of the new volunteers in August 1914 didn't just want to be VADs, but also to be sent to work overseas, near the action. This was not what the VAD had been established for, but there was a lack of direction from the BRCS, and now that the country was at war, its role suddenly seemed less clear. The army's medical services initially overlooked the VAD, preferring qualified nurses.

An example of this early period of confusion is the story of Miss Cannan, who had joined the Oxford University VAD in 1911 when she had turned eighteen. A member for three years, she became the quartermaster, and as soon as war was declared, her detachment set up their hospital in a wing of Magdalen College School. Cannan complained that, rather than being congratulated for their quick response, the group was issued with so many orders and counter-orders that the members became demoralised, which undermined all their hard work. The military medical services refused the help of her detachment, and in the end the Oxford University VAD was ordered to close its hospital and the equipment was sent to a new military base hospital. Exasperated by the situation, Cannan resigned from her unit and took up paid employment. In addition to the new volunteers, there were approximately 54,000 trained VADs awaiting orders. Someone needed to take charge and give the VAD direction.

Katharine Furse was the person to step into this void. Edward Ridsdale, a former Liberal MP who had succeeded Sir Frederick Treves as chairman of the executive committee of the BRCS, invited Furse to run the London office. He had been greatly impressed by the preparations Furse and Crowdy had already made for VAD work in Ireland. Faced with the challenge of preventing further disillusionment and resignations amongst the members of the VAD, Furse immediately set to work, organising training for new recruits, finding them employment, and ultimately establishing the VAD service overseas. When the BRCS office proved too small to cope, Furse took on administrative staff, and worked from a new office situated on the ground floor of Devonshire House.[7] It was not until six weeks into the war that the joint committee of the VAD was established, a group made up of equal members of both parent societies, the BRCS and St John Ambulance Association.

The First Aid Nursing Yeomanry (FANY) also got off to a slow start, but unlike the VAD its members knew exactly what their role should be in war. The delay was down to the fact that at the beginning of August, the FANY's leader Grace Ashley-Smith was en route to South Africa for a holiday. She only heard that Britain was at war when her boat reached its refuelling stop at Gibraltar. Without hesitation she transferred to the next ship sailing back to England, but she did not arrive back until 5 September. In her absence, Lillian Franklin and other members of the FANY tried to organise meetings with the Army Medical Services. In the same way that they had appealed to the Medical Services regarding their deployment in Ireland, they now wanted to be sent to Belgium in an official capacity.

While the VAD reorganised themselves and the FANY awaited the return of Ashley-Smith, several of the new independent organisations were able to get off to a quicker start.

The president of the National Union of Women's Suffrage Societies (NUWSS), Millicent Garrett Fawcett, announced that the group would suspend all activities and support the British government for the duration of the conflict. By setting up the London Society for Women's Service to direct and find employment for women wanting to support the war effort, and by supporting other groups, Garrett Fawcett managed to maintain and redirect the energies of NUWSS. At the same time, the NUWSS earned the respect of the politicians who would be instrumental in awarding female suffrage. However the NUWSS did lose members who disagreed with this new role, in particular those who were pacifists. Under Christabel Pankhurst's leadership, the Women's Social and Political Union (WSPU) also agreed to support the war. Evelina Haverfield, who had been an ardent Suffragette and member of the WSPU, founded the Women's Emergency Corps at the beginning of August. Like the London Society for Women's Service, the Women's Emergency Corps was set up to co-ordinate women wanting to do war work, rather than have lots of overlapping societies 'with the view of safe-guarding the paid labour market.'[8] The Women's Emergency Corps reported that within its first two weeks, it had received 'over 10,000 offers of personal service … They were classified in professions and trades, and lists were sent to the heads of institutions, mayors and local bodies.'

Names and addresses of a large number of women 'skilled in the management of horses and motors and thoroughly competent to take charge of a remount camp were also registered to be ready if required.'[9]

Right from the beginning of the war, Haverfield channelled all her energies into organisations that promoted the principle of a new, stronger and more assertive woman. She became involved in the early debate over women bearing arms. Throughout the first month of the war, the WSPU newspaper *Votes for Women* received many letters from women anxious over whether or not they, as female non-combatants, should arm themselves with guns in case of invasion. On 28 August the paper published two opposing letters on the debate, with Haverfield in favour and fellow WSPU member Emmeline Pethwick Lawrence against. In the pre-war years, members of the FANY had trained with guns and taken part in shooting competitions. But outside the world of hunting and sporting competitions, British society was still deeply uncomfortable with the idea of armed women. So Haverfield was careful to argue the case for self-defence, rather than suggesting that women should actively identify and kill the enemy. She wisely anticipated that women would be needed and, therefore, they should be prepared:

It would appear very necessary at the present time to inform women who are desirous of learning to shoot for defensive purposes, that unless they are enrolled in an organised body that is recognised by headquarters, they stand the chance of being shot at sight by the enemy. According to the laws of war, non-combatants found with arms in their hands are liable to be shot. I am quite ready to form a Women's Volunteer Rifle Corps for home defence and shall be very glad if anyone will communicate with me on the question. As time goes on and more and more men are needed for the front, the authorities will be more inclined to accept our services. At the eleventh hour it will be too late to organise anything; whereas if strong and capable women accustomed to outdoor life, and any others whose hearts are burning to defend their country, will start drilling, rifle shooting, route marching now, we shall be able at the right moment to place at the disposal of the War Office a thoroughly useful, enthusiastic, and capable body of women. Numerous letters have been written to me by women who desire to learn to shoot in order to defend themselves; but I would point out to them that the wish of the Women's Volunteer Rifle Corps will be not so much to defend themselves as to defend those who are incapable of defending themselves.[10]

Pethwick Lawrence replied:

I feel the matter to be a difficult one, for of all things most distasteful to me, that of placing objections and obstacles in the path of high-hearted and courageous women, who desire to pioneer in hitherto untrodden paths, is the most disagreeable.

Yet if I am to speak from my inmost conviction, I have to say that I consider the moral immunity of all women in civilised nations from the terrible duty of organised murder is too great a boon to the whole world to be placed in jeopardy by the initiative of the women of any nation.

That women have a great and important part to play in the nation at all times, and especially when it is undergoing the stress of war, is so evident that at such a crisis as this no one dreams of questioning it. ... the essential work of women lies in giving, maintaining, and saving the life of their own people, while the main task of men, so long as war – that relic of barbarism — is tolerated in a civilised world, is to mutilate and destroy the enemy. For that differentiation of function let us be thankful, since it applies to the whole organisation of the civilised world.

The recognition of women as non-combatants is the one area of sanctuary redeemed from the field of universal slaughter.[11]

Although they were no longer partaking in militant demonstrations and openly campaigning for suffrage, the members of the WSPU were taking advantage of the war and the eager volunteers, to continue promoting women's rights and encouraging debate.

Mabel St Clair Stobart, also keen to give women the opportunity to prove themselves, returned to London in June 1914 from her latest holiday in Canada. As the Women's Sick and Wounded Convoy Corps was no more, Stobart set up a new organisation, the Women's National Service League, which would provide service on both the home front and overseas. The overseas unit would consist of 'women doctors, trained nurses, cooks, interpreters, and all workers essential for the independent working of a hospital of war.'[12] The Women's National Service League, like the FANY, was a much smaller organisation than the VAD (the overseas unit consisted of about eighteen members), and therefore it was much easier to mobilise. Drawing on her experience with the Women's Sick and Wounded Convoy in Bulgaria and her social connections, Stobart immediately made preparations for her new organisation. Within a fortnight, she had raised £1,200, received a donation of X-ray apparatus, and recruited a full complement of female staff. Although Stobart still felt aggrieved toward the BRCS over their failure to acknowledge her work in Bulgaria, she again went through the motions and offered them the Women's National Service League for service in Belgium. The BRCS turned Stobart down, as they had done in 1912, and they would not authorise her female medical team. But unlike Furse, who was obliged to work with the BRCS to negotiate the role of the VAD, Stobart was able to circumnavigate the British authorities. Instead, with the help of her friends, Lord and Lady Esher, she managed to secure an invitation directly from the Belgian Red Cross for the Women's National Service League to set up and run a hospital in the capital city of Brussels. In her rush to get to Belgium, it seems that Stobart did not heed warnings that the German army was advancing through the country and heading straight for the capital. In the early stages of the war, the frontline moved considerably and did not reach a position of relative stalemate until December. Alternatively it is possible she was well aware of the German advance, but took no heed, because she simply wanted to be as near the action as possible.

Part 2: Brussels

After entering Belgium on 4 August 1914, the German army took the town of Liège within forty-eight hours, but it took them until 16 August to secure the twelve surrounding forts. It was then that the Germans began to march on Brussels, which lay 60 miles to the west. Two days later, on Tuesday 18 August, Stobart sailed for Brussels via Ostend with her husband John Greenhalgh, as the Women's National Service League's honorary treasurer, and the Reverend Basil Bourchier as their chaplain. The trio intended to finalise arrangements and then cable instructions to the rest of the women to join them. Violetta Thurstan, a Red Cross nurse, travelled out to Brussels via Ostend on the same day. She had been asked to supervise a team of British Red Cross Nurses to work for the Belgian Red Cross, who were due to follow her out the next day. In comparison to Stobart's excitement at reaching Belgium, Thurstan looked around her and saw the early effects of war.

Ostend – normally a bustling port, and also the Belgian royal family's favourite seaside resort – was ominously silent for the height of summer and she heard conflicting rumours about the proximity of the German army that concerned her greatly. When Thurstan arrived in Brussels that evening, the local authorities confirmed that the Germans were expected to arrive any day. Immediately she cabled her nurses and told them not to come, but the telegram did not arrive. The following morning, on the Wednesday, the nurses left London as planned, arriving in Brussels that evening. Instead of the expected sixteen, however, Thurstan discovered she had been sent twenty-six nurses to look after. She found them accommodation in a hotel and planned to organise placements for them the following morning. Even if the Germans took Brussels, nurses would still be needed and Thurstan's group would, in theory, be protected under the neutrality of the Red Cross. During the day, Thurstan had gone out to inspect the city's defences for herself and was not filled with confidence:'It did not look very formidable – some barbed-wire entanglements, a great many stones lying about, and the Gardes Civiles in their quaint old-fashioned costume guarding various points. That was all.'[13]

Meanwhile Stobart continued with her work, seemingly oblivious to the impending danger and the city's inadequate defences. Although she was in Brussels at the invitation of the Belgian Red Cross, unlike Thurstan she was not technically a member of the Red Cross, nor was her hospital operational yet. So once the Germans arrived, she would be treated as a civilian, and therefore – as a Briton – an enemy of the German Empire. On the Wednesday, having viewed the university buildings which the Women's National Service League would occupy, she telegrammed her unit to join her and began preparations to transform the building into a hospital.

On the morning of Thursday 20 August, Thurstan quickly installed her nurses in a number of institutions across the city and two nurses went to an ambulance station just outside the city barriers. If Brussels were to be occupied, it was thought best that all the nurses should be stationed in hospitals on active duty to demonstrate their worth, rather than left idle. Later on that day, Stobart had lunch at her hotel and was returning to work when she met with great commotion on the city's streets:

> I was surprised to see the whole population of Brussels hurrying out of their shops and houses to run and gaze at something. I followed with J. [her husband John Greenhalgh] and B. [Reverend Bourchier] to the Boulevard des Jardins Botaniques and in a few moments we found ourselves gazing at an amazing spectacle – we were watching the German army making a triumphant entry into, and taking possession of, the capital of Belgium.
>
> The crowds lining both sides of the avenue, watching the continuous procession of the enemy, were dense ...
>
> But the picture upon which for some hours we gazed was indeed remarkable ... in all those streets the only sounds were the clamping of the boots of the marching infantry, the clattering of the hoofs of the horses of the proud Uhlans and Hussars, the merciless rumbling of the wagons carrying pontoons, and murderous guns.
>
> The gazing people were silent, as though stupefied; indeed, earth, air, sky, the whole world outside that never-ending procession seemed benumbed. No one noticed whether the rain fell or the sun shone, whilst in a continuous cinema that pitiless pageant of triumphant enmity passed, during three days and nights through the streets of the Belgian capital in silence that was unforgettable.[14]

In her autobiography, Stobart recalls her attempts to get out of Brussels as a desperate effort to send word to the rest of the Women's National Service League to stop them travelling out to join her. With the city's public buildings including the Post Office under German control, she was unable to send telegrams from Brussels. But her story is also that of a brash, somewhat naïve woman finding herself out of her depth and stuck behind enemy lines. Learning that the German general had ordered that no passports were to be issued, Stobart decided to appeal to him in person. Hiring a carriage, to 'look as important as possible' she set off to find him.[15] However the street was blocked by many groups of soldiers, so Stobart says that she had to get out of the carriage to persuade them to move out of her way, before eventually reaching the town hall:

> The entrance-hall was alive with self-important, excited and formidable-looking officers, all rushing about and tearing up and down the large

staircase excitedly. How was I to attack? For a few moments I hid myself behind one of the large pillars whilst I scanned the countenances of the incoming officers, to select one that might be sympathetic. The right countenance duly appeared and the owner ran up the staircase. I followed and half-way up caught him by the sleeve. He stopped in surprise, and before he could say anything I told him what I wanted – a passport from the General. I begged him to persuade his Chief to help me to get out of Brussels to go to the rescue of my Women's Unit.

My pyschology had not failed. I had made a good choice. For ... this officer was, he told me, married to an English-woman, and he was, as he explained, sympathetic to the English, and for his wife's sake he promised to do his best with the General. But after a few moments he returned, saying that the General would allow no one, and least of all an Englishwoman, to leave Brussels.[16]

As Stobart looked for alternative ways to leave, Thurstan anxiously waited to see what the occupation meant for her nurses and whether the Red Cross would be respected. Each day the nurses went to their hospitals and carried out their work, and each day Thurstan visited them to check that they were all right. Then:

At the end of the week the Germans put in eighty soldiers with sore feet, who had overmarched, and the glorious vision of nursing Tommy Atkins at the front faded into the prosaic reality of putting hundreds of cold compresses on German feet, that they might be ready all the sooner to go out and kill our men. War is a queer thing![17]

A week after the fall of Brussels, Thurstan was sent 37 miles south to a hospital in the occupied town of Charleroi where she was to remain for most of September. As they drove out, Thurstan looked sadly at the devastated Belgian countryside. Many buildings had been reduced to rubble by the heavy bombardments; homes were deserted and there were fragments of furniture and personal items visible in the ruins. The Charleroi hospital and its patients were in a terrible condition, few of the staff were adequately trained and there were shortages of both food and medical supplies. The majority of the patients were French and German, and Thurstan was appointed matron of the hospital. She explained that despite the circumstances, and cruel taunting by German surgeons, she worked hard, caring for all her patients whatever their nationality. At the end of September, the German authorities decided to remove non-German Red Cross nurses from Brussels. Thurstan and her nurses were put on an eastbound train, but rather than going directly to Holland, they were taken on a long journey through Germany and eventually to neutral Denmark.

Meanwhile, back in Brussels, after failing to speak to the German general, Stobart continued to plot her escape and recounts that she befriended a local cobbler who had been given permission to visit his son in nearby Alost. He was going to walk there, and it was proposed that Stobart would accompany him disguised as his peasant wife. It is unclear how her husband or the reverend fitted into this plan, suggesting Stobart was not being serious, but before they enacted their scheme, the general changed his mind and decided to issue passes. Hoping to retrace their journey out, and return to Ostend, Stobart's party was told that they could only get a passport to Venlo in neutral Holland, which meant travelling further into occupied Belgium. Conceding that it was better than nothing, their papers were marked with the German general's stamp. Needing transport, Stobart, her husband and the reverend commandeered a taxi offering the driver a large amount of money to drive them to Venlo, and they left on the evening of 24 August. Reaching Louvain a couple of hours later, they found a hotel, but after hearing gunfire during the night, they left at 5 a.m., not wanting to be caught up in any conflict. They were regularly stopped and their papers were checked. They also had to contend with a continuous flow of German army units on the roads.

Later that day they reached Hasslet, and were once again asked to show their papers. This time, instead of being allowed to continue, the officer claimed that the stamp was invalid and easy to forge, and that only the general's signature would make the passports legitimate. On this basis they were taken prisoner and, after their luggage was searched, they were marched to the town hall to see the local commandant who accused them of being spies. They were held in a room in the town hall for the whole afternoon, before joining a larger group of prisoners and being taken to the railway station and put into a dirty empty coal truck. At the time, the prisoners did not know where they were being taken, but as it turned out they went to Tongres, near Liège. Stobart's party of four was then split up and interrogated by an officer whom Stobart dubbed the 'Devil-Major'.

After a poor night's sleep, the group was once again taken to the station. This time they were transported to Aachen to be formally tried; they narrowly avoided being pulled off the train at Liège by what Stobart dramatically described as a 'lynching mob' of German soldiers, keen to get their hands on English spies. Arriving late in the evening, they were marched through the streets in front of jeering crowds and locked up in the local army barracks. In her cell, Stobart waited in fear that if found guilty they would be shot and if found innocent they would be imprisoned for the remainder of the war – neither prospect was appealing.

In the morning they were brought before a judge. Since being arrested, Stobart and her party had been unable to provide confirmation that they had been in Brussels to establish a hospital. The German military authorities had contacted the Belgian Red Cross in the city, but following the occupation and the fact that Stobart had been there less than forty-eight hours, no one was able to vouch for her party. As she went to speak with the judge, Stobart recalls that she found a newspaper cutting in her pocket, which detailed the whole premise of the Women's National Service League and their invitation to Brussels, which she submitted as evidence. Stobart was then returned to her cell and made to wait. The next day, at 5 p.m., she was let out and to her great surprise taken to a hotel, where she was delighted to find she could bathe for the first time in six days. They were free! Stobart believes that it was her husband who inadvertently secured their release. During his interview with the judge, Greenhalgh mentioned that he and Stobart lived in Hampstead Garden Surburb in London, and that he had been personally involved in the building of many of the properties there. The judge and Greenhalgh found that they knew people in common and the connection swayed the judge's decision in their favour. The taxi driver was allowed to return to Brussels, and with the correct paperwork Stobart, Greenhalgh and Reverend Bourchier returned to England via Holland. To their great relief, Stobart found out that some members of her unit had reached Ostend, but had been advised to turn back, and so they were all safe and well back in England. Allowing herself a short rest, Stobart began to plan her return to Belgium, even more determined to make a success of the Women's National Service League.

Part 3: Antwerp

With the loss of Brussels, the Belgian army had fallen back to the fortified town of Antwerp, which was a strategically important stronghold. Situated on the River Scheldt which opened onto the English Channel, the town was protected by a number of coastal fortresses. In addition it was surrounded by two rings of land fortresses, the first 5km from the town and the second about 10–15km. The Belgian army used its position to divert the full attention of the German forces, which were now focused on reaching Paris. The result was that from the second week of September the German army detached a division to lay siege and to take Antwerp.

Arriving back in England at the beginning of September, Grace Ashley-Smith immediately sought permission from the Army Medical Services to take a FANY unit to Belgium. Ashley-Smith discovered that some of her members had been impatient at the corps' apparent inertia in the first month, and doubting that the FANY would secure overseas work; they had resigned and become VADs or joined other organisations[18]. When the army turned her down, the ever-persistent Ashley-Smith decided on a different strategy. Managing to secure a place in a party of Red Cross nurses that were about to be sent to Antwerp, she planned to appeal in person to the Belgian authorities and secure FANY a direct invitation to work on the Belgian front. With each of the groups that she had founded, Stobart had been keen to maintain their independence from the BRCS (the Women's Sick and Wounded Convoy had been registered as a voluntary aid detachment). She did not believe that the BRCS would ever allow women to expand their role beyond nursing. Ashley-Smith was equally determined to maintain the FANY's independence and even though she was part of a Red Cross party, she wore her khaki FANY uniform instead of the Red Cross one. She had every intention of distinguishing herself and demonstrating the value of the FANY. Thus, in mid-September, she arrived at a field hospital on the Boulevard Leopold in Antwerp for what was to be an extremely steep learning curve in the reality of warfare.

Because the FANY was an auxiliary ambulance corps, once she was in Antwerp, Ashley-Smith took every opportunity to go out with the field hospital's ambulances to collect the wounded from behind the frontlines:

One afternoon I went out with a motor ambulance to just behind where fighting was. We met a cyclist who said he wanted help at a lonely trench to take men away and so we went. There was a little brick hut or stables, and there the car stopped, and before I got out from inside, the chauffeur and the cyclist and the owner, who was with us, were running hard along the road. It was a flat country, and the road was alongside a deep ditch; and a few little thin trees were along the roadside. Far away I could see cottages here and there, and there was a lot of noise all round. I was running after the men, when suddenly something made my heart stop and then thump hard. I slowed down and looked all round, and the sun glittered on the silver medal on my breast and held my eye. I put the medal into my pocket, and a feeling of awful loneliness came over me. I was alone, quite alone – there was nobody English near me. At that moment I longed for an Englishman. Then I looked behind – the ambulance looked safe and stolid, somehow; then I looked ahead. The men who had come with me were jumping down into a trench. I had never seen a trench, but I felt it was one, and into my heart and brain came something I had never felt before, I looked up at the little clouds of smoke breaking in the sky; I looked ahead and saw great clouds of smoke bursting from the ground; and I suddenly felt a great exultation, and I ran – ran my hardest – and stood on the edge of the trench and looked in. There were three or four figures there, very still, in big blue coats, but I hardly noticed them. Two men were lifting a man out and putting him across a third man's back, and a man wearing a heavy uniform coat, with a ragged, untidy moustache, and a white face was trying to climb out of the trench. One of his legs was all torn, – clothing and blood and bandage, and I leapt down beside him. Then, with his hand in mine and his arm drawn round my neck, I pulled and pushed and struggled, and we got out and slowly reached the road. In front of me two men were struggling along, each with an unconscious man hanging over his shoulders, and a group of soldiers who looked tired and were limping. Then suddenly came a terrific noise, so loud it dazed me, and all my sense of thought seemed gone. I stood quite still, and on my left a cloud of dark smoke rose, and a horrid smell. I looked all around – I was alone. My poor man with the shattered leg! – where was he? I wheeled slowly round, blinking my eyes, and there in the ditch was my sufferer, and all the other men. Then, in a flash, I knew! It was a shell that had burst close beside us. I dashed to the ditch and sat down. The men were looking at me with stolid unconcern, they were rising – going on, I went too. Along that bare road we ran at a sort of loping trot. Then through the cloud of deafness that still held me I seemed to hear a wailing scream, and the three soldiers nearest stopped and held on to a little thin tree. I stopped too, facing them, looking in their faces to question them. To me it was all new. I did not understand; I had had none of the horrors they had passed though. All I saw – three white scared faces, with fixed eyes, – in them a sort of dumb appeal. They were gasping, their lips were black, their clothes dirty and stained. A demon of mischief woke in me. I thought of a cinematograph, of what we must look like – four hefty people hanging on in fear to a little thin tree! I laughed; and their white faces and troubled eyes glared at me, but they ran on. I followed at their heels, and so we reached the ambulance and found the chauffeur already there.[19]

When she published an account of her experiences in *A Nurse at War: Nursing adventures in France and Belgium* in 1917, Ashley-Smith drew heavily on these trips to the front, focusing less on the regular nursing work in the hospital. The book was used publicly to promote the FANY and to gain recognition and funding. Ashley-Smith presents herself as a 'militarized woman' who is actively contributing to the war effort, in contrast to female observers or war tourists, while still retaining her traditional feminine qualities of caring and compassion.[20] An example of this was when she went with an ambulance to a church in Malines, which was just north of occupied Brussels, where a doctor was treating a serious casualty:

[The patient] was a big, strong man about five and thirty; he was tenderly laid on a table, his feet and legs propped up with chairs, his shirt cut off as gently as possible. One arm hung by a thread of flesh from the shoulder, and bled – always bled – though the tourniquet was as tight as possible; the dark blood oozed through steadily and fell with a constant drip, drip. He was shot through the diaphragm, too, and, although I was not well acquainted with death then, even I could tell his days were numbered. His face, livid and twisted with pain, looked towards us; he cried in a strange voice and a strange tongue, for in those days I knew no Flemish. A surgeon was there, a tall, clever Englishman, and he injected saline. His quick, deft movements fascinated me – I longed to help. … A nurse was there, an English nurse. She was crying as she held the man down, for he was struggling – and to me that, too, was strange; and suddenly she ran away sobbing, so I slipped up and took her place. The surgeon glanced at me keenly and was apparently satisfied, and so, as the poor fellow struggled and twisted, we held him. I had one arm and side; a priest held the other, and two Belgian women, in white overalls and caps with big red crosses on them, stroked his face and bent over him, speaking to him soothingly in his mother tongue. He shouted and writhed, and at last his head fell back: then, with a mighty effort he raised himself and opened his mouth to speak; but only a stream of blood rushed forth, and a brave soul had gone to its God!

The chapel was empty as I knelt to whisper a prayer for the dead, and passed on into the outer chapel, where, to my horror, I saw three English women in weird and wonderful costumes having tea, laughing and talking; it was like a tourist party attending a funeral. Something of what I felt was, perhaps, shared by an English doctor. He looked at the women inside; he took a long breath of fresh air and gasped out: 'My God, there's too much joy-riding about this to please me!'[21]

As Grace Ashley-Smith threw herself into her work, Mabel Stobart lost no time in returning to Belgium, arriving on 22 September after a particularly rough and delayed crossing. This time she succeeded in installing the Women's National Service League in Antwerp's Philharmonic Concert

Hall, which the league converted into a hospital. The entire group numbered eighteen, including six female doctors, and their accommodation was divided between rooms at the concert hall and a convent situated opposite. They were only a short distance from where Ashley-Smith was stationed. Within a week, all 130 beds were full and the group had to borrow camp beds from other hospitals and place straw mattresses directly on the ground to accommodate the growing number of patients. Sarah Macnaughtan was a probationer with the group and in her letters home she described the determination with which the women worked:

> We are fearfully busy, and it seems a queer side of war to cook and race around and make doctors as comfortable as possible. We have a capital staff, who are made up of zeal and muscle. I do not know how long it can last. We breakfast at 7.30, which means that most of the orderlies are up at 5.45 to prepare and do everything. The fare is very plain and terribly wholesome, but hardly anyone grumbles. I am trying to get girls to take two hours off duty in the day, but they won't do it.[22]

On 24 September, another small independent organisation departed for Belgium: Dr Hector Munro's Flying Ambulance Unit. The founder, Dr Munro, was an enthusiastic, if eccentric, Scot, described as a man:

> One of whose primary objects seemed to be leadership of a feminist crusade, for he was far keener on women's rights than most of the women he recruited. He was a likeable man and a brilliant impresario, but wonderfully vague in matters of detail, and in appearance the very essence of the absent-minded professor.[23]

While advertising for volunteers to join his group, he saw a lady driving through the streets of London on a motorbike. He found out that her name was Mrs Elsie Knocker, and that she was working for the Women's Emergency Corps as a messenger. In the same way that the yeomanry aspect of the FANY had appealed to the horse-mad Ashley-Smith, Knocker, a great motorbike enthusiast and a qualified nurse, leapt at the chance to drive a bike and do war work. Dr Munro invited Knocker to join him and assist with the recruitment of the other members, convinced that she was exactly the type of woman needed to work behind the frontlines in Belgium. However vague and eccentric Dr Munro was, in Elsie Knocker he succeeded in finding a dynamic individual who, along with her friend Mairi Chisholm, would go on to make headlines and they would be decorated for their war work.

Aged thirty, Knocker was a divorced mother of one who in 1913 moved to the New Forest to live with her ailing brother. Using the opportunity to purchase a motorbike with a sidecar she began to take part in competitions. Frequently mentioned in motor cycling publications, she was one of only about fifty female riders in the country.[24] As a teenager Mairi Chisholm joined the competitive circuit as a mechanic for her brother and in the autumn of 1913 became good friends with Knocker. Supporting her obvious talent, Chisholm's father saw that by the end of the year, she had her own bike.

Elsie Knocker brought Mairi with her to Hector Munro's unit. Unlike the FANY or many of the pre-war VADs who had trained regularly together, Munro put together an assortment of men and women with different backgrounds and qualifications. One member was Lady Dorothie Feilding[25], who had very nearly joined Stobart's Women's National Service League and gone to Antwerp with them. This is how she described the other members of Munro's group at the beginning:

> Our party is a dozen: Mrs Knocker A1 thank God, Miss Chisholm a strong buxom colonial wench pal of hers & capable, an American lady hanger on & quite useless tho' most obliging, Miss Sinclair ditto & Mr Wakefield ditto, two young doctors – sports & good souls & will get a move on, a Mr Gurney an engineer & car mechanic – not a gentleman but a good soul & knows his job, Then a boy scout person about 35 (not a child) a well meaning ass.[26]

The American woman was Helen Gleason, 'a pretty American woman whose husband was already in Belgium as a war correspondent. Neither she nor Mairi Chisholm was trained in any way, but they were strong, healthy, and willing to learn: Mairi was an excellent driver and mechanic. Lady Dorothie Feilding, though only twenty-two, had had considerable Red Cross experience, and was a most capable organiser.'[27] Knocker says that May Sinclair, a novelist, (whose real name was Mary St Clair) was 'highly strung' and proved to be ill-suited for ambulance work. She speculated that Munro had employed Sinclair as a secretary, but he had hoped that she would write articles about their work and help generate valuable funds. As it was, Knocker appears to have had little time or respect for Sinclair.

Knocker and Chisholm adopted their own uniform consisting of 'big khaki overcoats, high lace-up leather boots, and riding breeches'[28] which they proudly wore to Victoria Station in London, from where the group began their journey. Based in Ghent, about 35 miles south-west of Antwerp, Munro's unit was attached to a Belgian field hospital and the women went out in one of its two ambulances to fetch patients in much the same way as Ashley-Smith. Knocker and Chisholm would later separate from Munro's unit and become famous for running a dressing station from a cellar in a house in Pervyse, on the Belgian front, but it was through Munro that they first went to Belgium and in the beginning they worked under his direction.

As the Germans drew closer to Antwerp, they also drew closer to Ghent, and the ambulance trips to the frontline became increasingly dangerous. In her memoirs, Knocker recalled one particular outing:

> The weather had broken, and it was pouring with rain when we drove towards the noise of shelling and rifle-fire which was beginning to ring the city of Ghent. We stopped the ambulance, and had to walk about three miles to a river which had high breastworks thrown up on either bank. We searched for casualties in the boggy water-meadows, with our box of dressings and stretchers getting damper and heavier every minute. We had to bend double to keep below the level of the earthworks (and so avoid the rifle-fire which the Germans had opened up on us) while carrying two horribly wounded men on stretchers. One man's foot had been shot away and his back badly gashed; the other had a shattered thigh. The blood kept oozing through our bandages, but we got the men back to the ambulance.[29]

While Chisholm's father supported his daughter's efforts, her mother did not. As a result he travelled out to Belgium to bring her home, but he was so impressed by her work that he regretted that he himself was not enjoying the adventure and let her stay.

Part 4: Retreat

On 28 September the Germans began firing their artillery on the outer defences of Antwerp, and the city's authorities made plans to evacuate. The Belgians did not think they could hold on to the city for much longer without additional support. The British consul-general informed Stobart that there was a boat for British subjects scheduled to leave Antwerp imminently, because two of the forts outside the city had fallen and they expected the Germans to start shelling. Stobart was adamant that she would remain with her patients and oversee the evacuation of the hospital. She told the members of the Women's League that if they wanted to leave they could, but she proudly recalled that they unanimously chose to remain. In her letters home, Sarah Macnaughtan admits that one or two did decide to go, but Macnaughtan declared to her family that she would remain with the patients in Belgium, even if it meant leaving the Women's League and becoming an independent nurse.

Grace Ashley-Smith recalled that many times during her three weeks at the field hospital the staff were ordered to evacuate, only then to be ordered to return to the hospital. An evacuation was a terrible ordeal. When the patients arrived, their dirty uniforms were removed and their bodies were cleaned and they were dressed in fresh pyjamas. Any uniforms that were salvageable were sent off to be washed and repaired. When evacuated, the men had to be dressed in their uniforms (or whatever clothes they could find), and then they were moved – which in many cases caused further pain and suffering. On one occasion when Ashley-Smith's hospital was ordered to evacuate:

> [The] men's faces would turn white with horror and with fear, women would tremble and turn faint and we, who had to work, would spend every ounce of strength in dressing those poor fellows – pulling shirts over their shattered bodies, wrapping dressing gowns or coats or what we could round them in their weakness and suffering. We carried them down long stairs on stretchers, even on camp beds if there were not enough stretchers; we ran down stairs with mattresses and lifted them off the stretchers to bring down others; and to some of these men each movement meant agony. This used to happen once a week at least! And then very often, after having been taken to the station on a tramcar, the men would all be brought back and have to be carried upstairs again and put back to bed.[30]

Then at the beginning of October came a few days of respite. As First Lord of the Admiralty, Winston Churchill responded to Belgium's fears that it was about to lose Antwerp by visiting in person. He was there to assess how many men would be needed to hold the town. His arrival, followed by his deployment of British marines on 4 October, generated renewed optimism amongst the army and occupants of Antwerp. The Women's League was told that it was safe to remain for the time being, but Macnaughtan recalls that another four members chose to leave. Despite the reinforcements the situation was uncertain and so Stobart's women prepared their patients for an imminent evacuation. It was while they were doing this that on 4 October, Macnaughtan recorded a visit from Dr Munro and members of his ambulance unit:

Dr. Hector Munro and Miss St. Clair [Mary Sinclair] and Lady Dorothy Fielding [sic] came over to-day from Ghent, where all is quiet. They wanted me to return with them to take a rest, which was absurd, of course.[31]

Under siege, Antwerp was plunged into darkness. Any lights were forbidden so as to make it more difficult for the German artillery to hit their targets. Even the hospital had to work in the dark, which was made all the more difficult by the fact that patients generally arrived at night. Macnaughtan explained that 'as it got later, all the lights in the huge ward were put out, and we went about with little torches amongst the sleeping men, putting things in order and moving on tip-toe in the dark.'[32] Stobart says that she slept in her clothes, ready for immediate action and to organise new arrivals. Macnaughtan remarked, 'Mrs Stobart never rests. I think she must be made of some substance that the rest of us have not discovered. At 5 a.m. I discovered her curled up on a bench in her office, the doors wide open and the dawn breaking.'[33]

As the guns got closer to Antwerp they fired through the night, which made it difficult for those off duty to sleep and caused the ground to shake. The patients taught Stobart and her staff how to differentiate between the sounds of the guns, so that they were able to recognise the sound of the Belgian guns, which were no match for the powerful German siege artillery. Antwerp had one British gun, a Long Tom which had a distinctive 'boom-boom' sound, but even this was not sufficient to withstand the advance.

The respite did not last long, as the Germans began to bombard Malines, the nearby town where Grace Ashley-Smith had been only days before. By 5 October the Germans made an attempt to cross the River Scheldt south of Antwerp and encircle the town. This meant that the only way left for the Belgian army and the different hospital units to evacuate was via a set of pontoon bridges which the Allies had constructed nearer to the mouth of the river.

On the morning of Wednesday 7 October, Stobart's hospital was ordered to prepare all those able to travel for evacuation and for the unit to remain with the worst cases, only for the evacuation once again to be postponed. That morning the locals who had been working with the women as orderlies and interpreters left the city. Cars drove at great speeds along the road outside the concert hall, as all who could went. Stobart says that the staff of some of the other hospitals abandoned their patients and fled. Meanwhile more and more men began arriving at her hospital needing medical care. Macnaughtan suspected that there were many deserters passing through the town and although all hope of saving

Antwerp was gone, the majority of the members of the Women's League remained with their patients. That night, the shelling of the city began. Stobart recalled:

> No one was surprised, therefore, when at midnight we were all awakened by a sound we had never heard before. Through the air, just over our heads, a shell came screaming – wh-r-r – and dropped with a terrific crash on the roof of the house next to us. Another shell followed within a few seconds, and fell on the house on the other side of the road, splitting it in two and setting fire to it.
>
> Thereafter, at the average rate of four a minute, shells continued to drop promiscuously around us. But I never saw any of the staff take the slightest notice. Their coolness was marvellous.[34]

Macnaughtan agreed. She wrote, 'The staff are doing well. They are generally too busy to be frightened but one has to speak once or twice to them before they hear.'[35] Along with the others who had been sleeping in the convent, Macnaughtan got dressed and they made their way to the hospital:

> The shells began to scream overhead; it was a bright moonlight night, and we walked without haste – a small body of women – across the road to the hospital. Here we found the wounded all yelling like mad things, thinking they were going to be left behind.[36]

As planned, once the bombardment started, the women began moving their patients into a set of cellars under the concert hall, which had been prepared in advance. Many of the patients who were able to walk chose to leave and make their own way, leaving the women to look after the more serious cases, which made it easier for everyone to fit into the cellars. They could not remain there long, as they had no food, and sanitation would soon become an issue. Compared to the glass ceiling of the concert hall, its cellars offered 'comparative safety', but Stobart knew 'that if a shell had hit the building, we should have been no better off there than elsewhere, but the removal conveyed a sense of safety and rescue, and had a good psychological effect.'[37]

Once installed, Macnaughtan recalled:

> We laid the men on mattresses which we fetched from the hospital overhead, and then Mrs. Stobart's mild voice said, 'Everything is to go on as usual. The night nurses and orderlies will take their places. Breakfast will be at the usual hour.' … We came in for some most severe shelling

at first, either because we flew the Red Cross flag or because we were in the line of fire with a powder magazine which the Germans wished to destroy. We sat in the cellars with one night-light burning in each, and with seventy wounded men to take care of. Two of them were dying. There was only one line of bricks between us and the shells. ... The danger was two-fold, for we knew our hospital, which was a cardboard sort of thing, would ignite like matchwood, and if it fell we should not be able to get out of the cellars.[38]

That night was a long night, as the staff expected a direct hit on the hospital at any moment. The next morning, Thursday 8 October, the shelling continued. As Stobart's unit began to prepare breakfast, several of the less seriously wounded patients left, leaving them with between thirty and forty men. With defeat now a certainty, the Allied forces had begun the retreat across the pontoon bridges over the River Scheldt. The women decided that they had to leave and work out how to get the men out of Antwerp. Stobart visited the neighbouring hospitals and anyone else she thought could help. Outside the concert hall the remaining women managed to flag down an ambulance on the road, and persuaded the drivers to take six patients, including the two dying men. About three hours later, Stobart managed to stop another motor ambulance that was able to take twenty patients, along with one of the unit's doctors, Dr Mabel Ramsay, and four other staff. Stobart implored them to take the men as far as the bridge and send the ambulance back for the others, but it did not return. Stobart and the other women waited and waited for them to come back or for another ambulance to drive by, but the roads that had been so busy the previous day were deserted. Macnaughtan said that they felt abandoned. The American Vice-Consul had offered them protection under his own neutrality, but when Stobart went to see him that morning, she had found him leaving and learned that the General-Consul had already gone. A nearby field hospital which had secured a boat had declared it would not leave without the Women's National Service League and its patients, but it did. As the afternoon passed and it began to get dark, the Women's National Service League felt that it was 'Up against a dead end'[39.]

Meanwhile, Grace Ashley-Smith was still at the field hospital nearby to the convent. She had succeeded in securing provisional invitations for two FANY units to come out and work in Antwerp, but the German advance prevented anything further from happening. Ashley-Smith recalls that on the Thursday morning after the direct bombardment began, Stobart had called by, requesting help with the evacuation. However she had found the hospital overwhelmed with patients, and during her visit yet more wounded were being brought in so she left. In the afternoon, the field hospital somehow secured a number of buses, onto which they loaded their patients. Ashley-Smith boarded one of the last buses, which then drove up the boulevard towards the concert hall to assist Stobart, only to find she had already gone, so they set off for Antwerp's quayside:

> Down by the quai the crowd was appalling – men and women and children; 'buses, carts, barrows, limousines, taxicabs marked 'Service Militaire' or protected by Red Cross flags: everywhere people pushing and shoving or waiting stolidly; women sobbing and women calm and smiling; babies, dozens of them, piled on to carts and barrows – the parents doubtless somewhere in that dense throng of humanity. The guns were booming in the distance – shrapnel falling on the town. Thank God! they had not yet got the range of the quai – a shell falling in the midst of that crowd did not bear thinking of. Then at last, after an hour or an hour and a half of weary waiting, whilst officers restrained and controlled the people and kept their own irritation in check – and it must have been intense! – the order came to move, and slowly the four 'buses, packed with sufferers, rolled over the pontoon bridge, and all around the yellow sky and the setting sun seemed to cast a halo on the forsaken town.[40]

Stobart and the Women's National Service League, despairing that they would be left behind, had taken the remaining patients, of which there were about seven, to the convent and placed them in the care of the nuns. Stobart then decided to look for ambulances on the Chaussée de Malines, one of the main roads in Antwerp, explaining why they were no longer at the concert hall when Ashley-Smith came looking for them:

> There was nothing living in sight down that long length of street. It was like a bad dream. But suddenly I saw tearing along towards me, at breakneck pace, three London motor buses – a dream-like touch of incongruity. But I ran out into the road and, risking being run down, spread out my arms to stop them. Would they heed? Thank God they did, and I asked the drivers, English Tommies, if they could help me and my nurses to the frontier. 'If you're quick as lightning,' they replied, 'but we have to get over the bridge of boats with our loads of ammunition, before it is blown up.'
> I ran back to the staff, and in a few minutes we had collected our handbags which were waiting piled up on the road, and were all seated, sixteen of us, on the boxes of ammunition inside those motor buses which tore along the streets, dodging or bumping in and out of great

holes excavated by the shells. We laughed merrily at the thought of what fine fireworks we should be in the middle of, if a shell dropped our way. We were certainly, I believe, the last of the hospital staffs, and probably of the inhabitants, to leave the town and cross that bridge of boats.[41]

Once Stobart and the remnants of the Women's National Service League had crossed the pontoon bridge it was to be blown up to prevent the German army following them. They were driven by Red Cross Ambulances to a convent in St Gilles. However they were woken at 3 a.m. and told to leave immediately. This time they travelled via train to Ostend, a journey which took nineteen hours and saw them arrive at midnight. The following day, 10 October, having found Dr Ramsay and the others, Mrs Stobart took her party back to England, but Macnaughtan found a room and stayed in Ostend. Stobart says that she heard there were opportunities to set up hospitals in Ostend, so as soon as she got her women safely back to England, she says that she jumped straight back on a boat returning to Ostend to investigate. But on finding the situation in Ostend to be chaotic, she returned to London and immediately began planning her next hospital unit.

While Stobart's group made its way to the coast, Ashley-Smith remained with her buses, which were travelling to Ghent. They crawled along the heavily congested roads, alongside other cars, carts and people on foot. Ashley-Smith recalls the pained faces amongst the refugees, the sad-eyed children and the screams of the wounded as they were jostled by their transport. The roads were muddy, and the buses would frequently become stuck in the ruts. Ashley-Smith and the others on board had to get out and help push. It was her second night of no sleep:

> I was too tired to feel almost; and I was strong, very strong. What that night of hell meant to some of the nurses and to the wounded God alone could witness. Better to let the veils of silence drop … To me in the past War had meant romance and heroic deeds, not the awful hell of agony that it is.[42]

In this statement, Ashley-Smith declares that she is no longer an inexperienced volunteer, but a woman who truly understands the reality of modern warfare, and therefore an ideal candidate to lead groups of women on future expeditions behind the frontlines.

Driving through the night, the buses arrived in Ghent in the early hours of dawn and stopped at the Hotel Flandria. While the doctors began to unload some of the patients for Dr Munro's unit to take care of, Grace Ashley-Smith and an English nurse went to the hotel's kitchen. They quickly set about heating milk to take to the men waiting in the buses. They then continued on to the nearby convent, where thirty-two patients were given accommodation. As none of the nuns could speak English, nor did they have any medical training, they requested that an English nurse stay with them. Ashley-Smith volunteered. But first she helped to install the rest of the patients at the Hospital Civile, the town hospital. Towards the end of the afternoon she returned to the Convent and fell into a deep sleep, only to be awoken within hours. The buses had returned for the patients. That morning, Friday 9 October, the Germans had marched into Antwerp and now they had turned and were advancing on Ghent. Ashley-Smith apparently took so long to get ready that the buses left without her. However it seems that, faced with the choice of staying or going, Ashley-Smith preferred to be in the middle of all the action. She found employment assisting a doctor in his rounds who had a 'fair bevy of fair lady helpers'[43] but it is not clear if this was Munro or not.

On the afternoon of Sunday 11 October, Ashley-Smith went to the Hotel Flandria to visit one of the male patients whom she had accompanied from Antwerp. There she met with Miss Sinclair, who that evening visited Ashley-Smith at the convent. Sinclair told her that because all the Allied troops had left Ghent, Dr Munro's unit was planning on leaving before dawn and invited her to join them. Setting off from the Hotel Flandria in the small hours, in a car with Sinclair, Lady Feilding, Mairi Chisholm, Mrs Gleason and Dr Munro, an exhausted Ashley-Smith fell back to sleep. In the early morning the group managed to find accommodation in a countryside house owned by an acquaintance of Dr Munro. It was here that Ashley-Smith saw that:

> Miss Sinclair seemed to be in great distress; she was half-crying. A handsome woman was fiercely arguing some point with her. It appeared that they had left an English officer in Ghent, at the Flandria, as he was too ill to move. I went outside and was joined by Miss Sinclair and the parson, and to them I explained I was going back to Ghent to try and find the officer, who was dying, and to stay with him till the end. They tried to dissuade me, as I would have to go alone.[44]

The patient was Lieutenant Foote, whom Elsie Knocker had spent a great deal of time caring for. Mairi Chisholm recalls that it was all she could do to stop Knocker returning to Ghent with Ashley-Smith as well. Ashley-Smith says that Sinclair went with her to the railway station and that she arrived back at the Hotel Flandria later that morning as the Germans, unopposed, entered Ghent. For two days Ashley-Smith nursed Lieutenant

Foote before he died. After the funeral Ashley-Smith, still in her khaki uniform, was instructed to report to the German general of the occupying force. She recalled with amusement the mixed reactions of the German soldiers to her uniform and how they exchanged salutes. Clarifying that she was indeed a nurse, Ashley-Smith was repatriated to England via Holland. On her return to London, Ashley-Smith proudly presented the Admiralty with a list of the British dead and wounded, which she had got from a cemetery caretaker and a German military hospital while dressed as a Belgian woman.[45] As a result of her presenting this valuable information, Sir Arthur Slogget, head of the British army's medical services, who had turned down the FANY only a month before, arranged for Ashley-Smith to meet with Arthur Stanley, who had just become chairman of the British Red Cross Society. Later on, Miss Sinclair would claim that Ashley-Smith had abandoned Lieutenant Foote during their initial evacuation from Ghent, something which Ashley-Smith vehemently denied, and this escalated into a public war of words between the women.

Meanwhile, Munro's ambulance unit continued without Ashley-Smith, leaving the country house later that day and arriving in Bruges in the afternoon. Having been informed that Ghent had fallen that morning, they were advised to leave immediately and head to the coast:

> The nearer we got to Ostend, the greater was the crush – an inextricable jam of ambulances, troops, peasants, guns, lorries, carts, dogs, cattle, and perambulators filled with household goods as well as babies. Ostend was packed to the point of suffocation and hysteria. Grown-ups were carrying children on their backs, and cows, pigs, and poultry were roaming the streets.
>
> We got our wounded on to a small ship into which nearly seven thousand casualties were somehow crammed. People were embarking on trawlers, fishing-smacks, even rowing-boats. I think it must have been far worse than Dunkirk in 1940. When the mail boats arrived hundreds jumped from the landing stages on to the decks in order to secure a place. Some fell into the water and were crushed or drowned, the old and infirm were trampled in a frenzy of fear. Three hundred people sardined into a paddle steamer which normally took no more than fifty.[46]

The German advance was now progressing towards Ostend, so the ambulance unit continued on to Malo-les-Bains, beyond Dunkirk, arriving there on Thursday 15 October. From here, Munro returned to England to raise more funds, while Gleason and Chisholm ran into Macnaughtan who, having left the Women's National Service League, joined Munro's group.

Part 5: France

While the Women's National Service League, Grace Ashley-Smith and Dr Munro's hospital unit were busy in Belgium, Katharine Furse was hard at work organising the VAD. As it was a much larger organisation compared to an independent unit of around twenty people, Furse had to comply with directives from the War Office and work with the official channels. Yet by mid-September, frustrated by the unfair way in which the War Office was allocating war work, she chose to appeal directly 'to someone whose husband was in a high place at the War Office.'[47] In this letter she expressed her fears that being idle would destroy any semblance of discipline that the VADs had. She then approached members of the BRCS committee and managed to secure work for a local detachment at a Kent hospital for wounded Belgians, and for several London detachments at a hostel for Belgian refugees. However, Furse became focused on establishing an overseas role for VADs to supplement the understaffed hospitals in France that were overwhelmed with wounded from the front. Once the joint committee for the VAD was established, things began to develop more quickly. The new chairman of the British Red Cross Committee, Arthur Stanley, agreed with Furse's proposal of overseas service and on 24 September, under his instruction, Furse went to France to meet with Sir Alfred Keogh, the acting Red Cross commissioner who was based in Rouen. In her memoirs she admits that in her excitement she packed for every eventuality:

> With my 1910–14 V.A.D. thoroughness, I had provided myself with all sorts of apparently unnecessary articles in a knapsack, such as folding lantern, Tommy's cooker, compass, map, folding measure, Field Pocket Manual, First Aid equipment, etc., and also with stores of hard food which I looked on as the 'iron ration' about which we had learnt.[48]

As Furse was a member of a BRCS detachment, she travelled with Lady Oliver, who had been chosen to represent the detachments affiliated with the St John Ambulance Association. On arrival in Le Havre the women were given a tour of the No.1 General Hospital by the matron, which was Furse's first experience of a war hospital. Seeing the wounded and the extent of their suffering had a profound effect upon her and hardened her resolve to deploy VADs in France. The following day, Furse and Lady Oliver had a meeting with Keogh in Rouen, which, although encouraging, proved to Furse she still had much to learn. She recalled:

I heard from Colonel Wake, one of his Assistant Commissioners afterwards, that Keogh said to him: 'There's a woman called Furse downstairs. Get rid of her.' As a matter of fact he received us kindly and showed great interest in the possibility of V.A.D.s forming Rest Stations on the Lines of Communication, giving me a list of the places where they might work which I immediately marked on my map. He also told me to prepare a list of necessary equipment and then talked about several of his problems; for instance, the difficulty of obtaining suitable carriages for ambulance trains, which were much needed, and I asked why he did not ask Switzerland for some of their third-class carriages, which were so made that they could immediately be turned into ambulance carriages. His reply gave me another of my lessons regarding the real meaning of war; Switzerland being a neutral country could not supply rolling-stock to either side. Then I asked about wagon-lits, and he told us that these had all been collected hastily by their owners and were parked somewhere, and that anyway they were unsuitable, which is of course obvious to anyone who knows the facts of loading and unloading wounded. Finally I asked why English railway carriages could not be got over and Keogh told me that there was a difference between the gauges of railways in England and in France. One of my bibles of V.A.D. days was the Field Pocket Manual and I knew that the difference in gauge was very slight, so in the afternoon I went down to the station and measured the line. This taught me another war lesson, when the officials came to ask my business, and I was probably lucky to escape being arrested as a spy.[49]

After visiting the BRCS stores in Paris, and agreeing on an equipment list with Keogh, Furse returned to London and awaited further instruction. In the second week of October, Furse finally received orders to prepare to go to Ostend, but this proved to be a false start as the German advance, following the fall of Antwerp, succeeded in taking the coastal town. Then, on 16 October, Furse was ordered to take a party of twenty VADs to Paris:

[T]he Crowdys and I set to work to collect a party. A large proportion of the women who had joined our Detachments and on whom we had depended were, when the time came, unavailable because other duties held them; some had to do the work of their husbands who had been called up, some could not leave their homes, and others, having got tired of waiting for V.A.D. work for the British, had taken French leave and crossed to France to help the Red Cross there. We felt rather like Alice and her croquet party in Wonderland, but we collected those on whom we could depend and invited two or three individuals from other Detachments to join us. Everything had to be done in such a rush that there was no chance of doing it on a more representative basis or through official channels. Besides which I had definite instructions from Sir Alfred Keogh: 'Do it without fuss and don't make a Press matter of it. Let it be done quietly.' My memo of an interview with him states: 'I begged to be allowed to prepare units, but was promised plenty of time before a demand would be made for us.'[50]

From Paris, the party was sent to Boulogne. Eleonora Pemberton was a member of this detachment, and wrote home, saying that the journey had been interesting despite the fact it had taken thirty-nine hours to reach Boulogne from London rather than the usual four hour journey.

Finding that there was not any specific work for them to do, Furse used the opportunity to return to England and collect more supplies. While back in London, Furse visited Stanley at the Red Cross Office. While she updated him on events in Boulogne, Grace Ashley-Smith arrived for her meeting with Stanley, as arranged by Sloggett on her return from Belgium. In her memoirs Ashley-Smith says she recognized the VAD commandant, whom she believed 'had attempted to usurp FANY authority during negotiations for their attachment with the Ulster army'[51] although she doesn't name her. Ashley-Smith was dismissive of Furse's work behind the lines in Boulogne, in comparison to her own experience in Antwerp and her determination to secure work for the FANY at the front. That day Stanley gave Ashley-Smith permission to acquire an ambulance and take the first FANY unit across to France, but under the authority of the BRCS. Arriving in Calais on 27 October the unit consisted of twelve members. After meeting with Belgian military officials, Ashley-Smith arranged for the unit to take over Lamarck, an empty convent school in Calais, and they began converting it into a hospital for Belgian soldiers.

Meanwhile Furse had returned to Boulogne with Rachel Crowdy (who had remained in London) to find that the VADs were working at the No. 7 Hospital, which was understaffed and overwhelmed with wounded. This is how VAD Pemberton described the hospital:

It was of course v. different fr. a London hospital as it is a hotel with heaps of small rooms in a regular rabbit warren all leading out of one another but luckily plenty of bathrooms and lavatories. There was no lift big enough to take a stretcher so they had all to be carried up – 7 floors altogether – you can imagine that the orderlies were pretty hard worked –- most of the cases were very bad indeed with terrible wounds but most of them when they were conscious were quite cheerful.[52]

As the frontline was still moving position significantly and stalemate had yet to set in, the Army Medical Service was hesitant when deciding where best to place its medical staff. This was why the No. 7 Hospital was under-staffed and provided work for Furse's VADs. But shortly after they began there, the medical service decided to make Boulogne a hospital base at which point trained nurses were sent to the hospital and the VADs were no longer needed. They were referred to as 'Untrained Women', which hurt Furse deeply, for all the hard work they had done and were willing to do. Yet at this point in the war, the Voluntary Aid Detachment scheme and its members were not widely known, but Furse seized this chance Keogh had given her to establish their reputation and to make an impact. Keogh was soon appointed the director general of the War Office's medical services, and he was replaced as the Red Cross Commissioner by Colonel Wake. As they were no longer at the hospital, Wake requested that the VADs estab-lish a rest station at Boulogne's railway station. However all the rooms at the station were occupied by the military, including the Radio Telephone Operators (RTO):

> [W]e looked about among houses and warehouses, but could find noth-ing suitable, and the A.D.M.S. [Assistant Director Medical Services] office was too busy in other directions to help an unknown quantity like our party. They could not make us out – women were such nui-sance in war time and who were these odd women in uniform, anyway? There was a good deal of chilliness to face and not possessing charm or grace I probably had my full share of it. Luckily, patient pertinacity will sometimes win as far as charm on such occasions, and there can be no question but that the free use of 'Sir' and respectful standing at attention gradually won our way. Besides which, Rachel could contribute to the qualities I lacked and, as we were evidently backed by authority, on the 26th [October] the R.T.O. asked us whether three trucks and two sec-ond-class coaches on a siding would be of any use. We eagerly accepted them and 'just the thing', hoping that, when once we were installed in trucks, we might be rolled off to some new sphere.[53]

Before the war, the women had devised their own ambulance trains for the annual inspection of their detachment. Now they found themselves in France having to do it for real. The years of improvisation would pay off and imme-diately the VADs set about cleaning, disinfecting and whitewashing the carriages and the trucks. Using the water supply at the station, they converted the three trucks into a kitchen (with two or three primus stoves), a dispensary and a staff room. The two coaches were used for accommodation.

Hospital trains pulled into the station throughout the day and night, and on 27 October, the VADs received their first patients. For trains that did not have kitchens, the VADs prepared hot drinks such as tea and cocoa and made soup, which they served with lots of bread. With only a few small stoves it took organisation to get everything ready, and a great deal of patience when the trains arrived hours later than expected.

Right from the beginning, Furse wanted the VAD to run like a formal military organisation:

> Being in charge of the Rest Station, I used to go to it at any hour, day or night, and often wonder at the friendly welcome given to me as, when inspecting, I used at first to expect parade-ground manners and was very upset if everyone did not stand at attention and show respect for their Commandant. So much of it was play-acting and very unnecessary but, pompous and boring as it was, I believe that it started us on the right lines; it could not outlive the real pressure of work when we got busy. As a start off, it gave us the right tone and we soon settled down to a more simple way of life in which the leaders took their share of the drudgery together with all the other members, which I believe to be one of the most important factors in leadership.[54]

Indeed, life became extremely busy very quickly for the VADs. Always looking for jobs for her detachment, Furse saw that the overworked medical officers attending the patients on the trains were worn down and did not have any orderlies helping them. On arriving in Boulogne, many of the wounded needed fresh bandages, so Furse offered the service of two trained nurses in her party to change their dressings. Throughout November the VAD rest station expanded its services by treating the wounded as well as feeding them. Colonel Wake, the Red Cross Commissioner, organised for two surgeons and another three qualified nurses to join the group. With the surgeons treating the worst cases on the station platforms, Furse recalls that on the day the surgeons arrived they 'fed 2,300 men and did over 200 dressings'[55]. The reputation of the VADs grew and they were visited by Maud McCarthy, the Principal Matron in France, who would later be made a dame for her services to nursing. The VADs began organising laundry on behalf of the nurses working on the trains, looked after lost property at the stations and had locals coming to them asking for medical care and requesting home visits. Furse's detachment gladly undertook the extra work and they were given five more trucks and two ambulances. By the end of November they set up a second rest station. Even with the growing workload and responsibilities, Furse remained a strict disciplinarian:

Our great dread was that if we were too idle we should get into mischief. So we forbade smoking, and forbade association with men, with the result that our nickname was 'the Starched Brigade'. Poor Preston, our very fine ambulance driver, was a great anxiety to us, because she could not adapt herself to the rigid rules. This reminds me that one of the interesting things I learnt in the war was that women who drive cars are much less easy to control than the other women. Whether this is because being able to manage a car gives them greater self-dependence, or whether only very independent women volunteered to drive cars, I don't know, but the fact remains that both in VADs and in the W.R.N.S. [Women's Royal Naval Service which Furse later commanded] I found the self-dependence of our motor drivers baffling at times. As the war went on, however, I learnt to respect them immensely because they were not only independent but also indefatigable. Their conditions of service were hard and a great strain, as there was a good deal of night work and a girl alone driving an ambulance across country with four patients, one or two who may have been in great pain and possibly in danger of death, had a nervy task, increased by the fact that there were scamps wandering about who were not always trustworthy. But our drivers faced every sort of discomfort and danger, and always emerged grinning.[56]

However in April 1915, when Preston became engaged to a doctor, Furse explained that:

I imagined that our reputation might be ruined and that we might all be sent home in disgrace, so I took time by the forelock and sent Preston home. She was furious and several other people thought me ridiculous, but there it was – I had to make an example of a V.A.D. who so far forgot herself as to get engaged whilst on active service.

However, Sir Alfred Keogh, as he showed in the following note, thought us too severe:

'How dreadful! What an irreparable disgrace to the Red Cruisers! It is your fault, you take out a charming Eve and she meets Adam. I don't mind tackling a fashionable London, but I can't take Cupid on. I give it up. But is it not cruel to send her home, poor girl? She couldn't help it.'

Preston married Dr Graham Jones later and had a family and forgave me, so all came right in the end. It was not narrow prudishness which made me so severe. I knew enough about men and women and their relationships to be tolerant of perfectly natural behaviour and I did not read immorality into every love affair or mutual attraction. But I was sure that for uniformed women sent out to pioneer in new work it was essential, if they were to be successful and pave the way to an extension of their employment, that they should establish a reputation for almost exaggerated seriousness, and that this was safer than too great leniency at first. It is always easy to relax rules and far more difficult to impose them when people have become accustomed to freedom. All of which may seem to be autocratic now but was, I believe, in 1914–15 one of the foundations on which we built our good reputation.[57]

Although both women had a military outlook, relationships between the women and the men was something on which Furse and Ashley-Smith differed. Ms Warner, a commandant of another Red Cross VAD from London, saw the dynamic this created between the two organisations. Describing the members of the FANY she said:

They were all fashionable young women, and very sure whatever they wanted to do they could do and I had to occasionally step in and say I'm awfully sorry … if they were working for the Red Cross, and if they wanted to go abroad, which they very much did, for Red Cross work, they must I'm afraid conform with certain rules we laid down, but no, they were alright, the FANYs. They got a rather bad name because, of course, one of the silly things, and this will make you smile this, was that the poor Red Cross VADs were never allowed to even look at a man, whereas the FANYs of course had lots of boyfriends, and at their mess there would be lots of boyfriends, whereas at our place well …[58]

Despite their differences, Furse and Ashley-Smith were equally determined, and by November 1914 both women had succeeded in establishing each of their organisations in France. From that point on, both the VADs and the FANY grew in number and took on more challenges and more responsibilities. In Sir Alfred Keogh and Arthur Stanley, Furse and Ashley-Smith had found two men willing to take a chance with them. Meanwhile Stobart continued her war work with the Women's National Service League taking charge of a hospital in Cherbourg, France, while Dr Munro's flying ambulance unit returned to the frontlines in Belgium. Each of these groups had broken new ground and provided women, most of whom only had basic training, the opportunity to work abroad and support the war effort.

Notes

1 Thurstan, Violetta, *Field Hospital and Flying Column: Being the Journal of an English Nursing Sister in Belgium and Russia*, p.3.

2 'The Women's National Service League' is also referred to as 'The Women's Imperial Service League' in Stobart's *The Flaming Sword in Serbia and Elsewhere* and in several documents held in the Imperial War Museum, with respect to the work done by the overseas division. For continuity I shall refer to it as 'The Women's National Service League' as Stobart does in her biography *Miracles and Adventures*.

3 Light, Sue, http://www.scarletfinders.co.uk/8.html. Accessed 1 November 2012.

4 Furse, Katharine, *Hearts and Pomegranates*, p.298.

5 Ibid., p.299.

6 Ibid., p.299.

7 Ibid., p.300.

8 'Women and the War, work of the Emergency Corps' in *The Times* 4 September 1914, p.5.

9 'Emergency Women – Aiding the Nation in Many Ways' published in the *Daily Chronicle*, 9 March 1915 (Women at Work Collection, Imperial War Museum).

10 Haverfield, Evelina 'Letter to the Editor' in *Votes for Women* 28 August 1914 p.713.

11 Pethwick Lawrence, Emmeline 'Letter to the Editor' in *Votes for Women*, 28 August 1914, p.713.

12 Stobart, Mabel, *Miracles and Adventures*, p.148.

13 Thurstan, *Violetta, Field Hospital and Flying Column*, p.9.

14 Stobart, Mabel, *Miracles and Adventures*, p.149.

15 Ibid., p.149.

16 Ibid., p.150–1.

17 Thurstan, Violetta, *Field Hospital and Flying Column*, p.20.

18 Lee, Janet, *War Girls: First Aid Nursing Yeomanry in the First World War*, p.63.

19 McDougall, Grace, *Nursing Adventures*, p.3–6.

20 Lee, Janet *War Girls*, p.74

21 McDougall, Grace, *Nursing Adventures*, pp.13–5

22 Macnaughtan, Sarah, *My War Experiences in Two Continents*, p.4.

23 T'Serclaes, Baroness de, *Flanders and other Fields: Memoirs of the Baroness de T'Serclaes*, p.37.

24 Atkinson, Diane, *Elsie and Mairi Go To War: Two Extraordinary Women on the Western Front*.

25 Dorothie Feilding spelt her name this way, although in some memoirs and letters, others spell her name as you would expect it, 'Dorothy Fielding'.

26 Feilding, Dorothie – letter written to her mother Saturday 26 September 1914, as reproduced in Hallam, Andrew and Hallam, Nicola (eds), *Lady Under Fire on the Western Front: The Great War Letters of Lady Dorothie Feilding MM*, pp.5–6.

27 T'Serclaes, Baroness de, *Flanders and other Fields*, pp.37–8.

28 Ibid., p.37.

29 Ibid., pp.42–43.

30 Macdougall, Grace, *Nursing Adventures*, pp.2–3.

31 Macnaughtan, Sarah, *My War Experiences in Two Continents*, p.17.

32 Ibid., p.5.

33 Ibid., p.7.

34 Stobart, Mabel, *Miracles and Adventures*, p.175.

35 Macnaughtan, Sarah, *My War Experiences in Two Continents*, p.17.
36 Ibid., p.18.
37 Stobart, Mabel, *Miracles and Adventures*, p.175.
38 Macnaughtan, Sarah, *My War Experiences in Two Continents*, p.19.
39 Stobart, *Miracles and Adventures*, p.176.
40 Macdougall, Grace, *Nursing Adventures*, pp.51–2.
41 Stobart, *Miracles and Adventures*, p.177.
42 Macdougall, Grace, *Nursing Adventures*, p.55.
43 Ibid., p.60.
44 Ibid., p.68.
45 Lee, Janet, *War Girls: The First Aid Nursing Yeomanry in the First World War*, p.88.
46 T'Serclaes, Baroness de, *Flanders and other fields*, p.50.
47 Furse, Katharine, *Hearts and Pomegranates*, p.301.
48 Ibid., p.303.
49 Ibid., pp.304–5.
50 Ibid., p.307.
51 Lee, Janet, *War Girls: The First Aid Nursing Yeomanry in the First World War*, p.89.
52 Pemberton, E., 'Transcript of memoirs', p.3, Imperial War Museum Collection, document 3684.
53 Furse, Katharine, *Hearts and Pomegranates*, p.309.
54 Ibid., p.311.
55 Ibid., p.313.
56 Ibid., pp.319–20.
57 Ibid., pp.320–21.
58 Warner, J., interviewed in 1977, Imperial War Museum, document 997.

3

Women Working in the Trenches

When all was ready, we were given our instructions – we were to keep together till we had passed through the village when the doctor would be there to meet us and, with a guide, conduct us to the trenches; we were all to proceed twenty paces one after the other, no word was to be spoken, and if a Verey light showed up were to drop down flat. I hoped fervently it might not be in a foot of mud!

Pat Beauchamp, First Aid Nursing Yeomanry[1]

Britain, France and Belgium hoped to contain the women who wanted to participate in the war within the nursing service. It was an acceptable profession and provided a feminine role for women in war. Significantly, nursing would not qualify the women for citizenship and thus denied the campaigners for women's suffrage a powerful justification for being awarded the vote. Even at a time of war, the Allied governments were reluctant to make concessions which might compromise their stance on the suffrage debate. For as long as women were working either as military nurses, for the Red Cross or for the Voluntary Aid Detachment scheme as a VAD, the military authorities could oversee their work and deployment. Yet Katharine Furse had still found it necessary to take charge of the VAD scheme in order to turn it into a more effective organisation. The independent women's groups operating on the Western Front, in particular the First Aid Nursing Yeomanry (FANY) and Munro's Ambulance Corps, were a matter of concern for the British authorities, as they were working outside its authority, having secured invitations from Britain's allies. Even though the services they provided were invaluable, they were operating far beyond the remit of hospital nurses, working close to the front and even venturing into the trenches. Towards the end of 1914 the British army actively tried to ban women from the front, but these groups remained undeterred. When the British army tried to take control of them, the women proved unwilling to surrender their independence. Over the next four years, circumstances would force the military authorities in both Britain and France to change their attitudes towards women. 1914 saw the beginning of a highly mechanised war on an unprecedented scale. General opinion had been that like the recent Balkan wars, this European war would be over in a matter of months, certainly by Christmas. As the conflict dragged on, the desperate need for more men to take up combat roles opened up opportunities for women in general. Their supportive role became more widely accepted, but only out of necessity.

Trench warfare was not new, but it had never been experienced on this scale before. The opening manoeuvres of each army in 1914 had resulted in a mismatch of military strength along the Western Front. In anticipation of a German invasion, the French had chosen to concentrate their strength on the French-German border of the Alsace-Lorraine region. They had not foreseen the main German offensive sweeping through central Belgium and Luxembourg and on into France from the north. The speed of the German advance was alarming. The Belgian army was overwhelmed and, as covered in the previous chapter, it was pushed further and further back towards the northern coast. After the Germans took Brussels on 20 August, their main army turned westwards towards Paris but they left behind a significant number of troops to advance on Antwerp.

By 2 September, the Germans were only about 25 miles from Paris and so the French government relocated to Bordeaux, over 330 miles away on the west coast. Yet, with the Belgians determined to hold on to Antwerp, the Germans had to divert more troops to Belgium to secure the country's occupation. Consequently the remaining forces did not have sufficient strength to take Paris. On 6 September, the British and the French managed to halt the German advance on the French capital and within a week they had succeeded in pushing the Germans back behind the River Aisne. Soon after this, the Western Front quickly developed into stalemate as all the armies began to entrench themselves. In mid-September, the northern section of the line remained effectively open-ended. Wanting to take advantage of this, each side tried to outflank the other. Neither succeeded, and instead the Western Front extended further up towards the northern coast in what was called the 'Race to the Sea'.

After the Germans took Antwerp on 10 October, followed by Ostend, their attention turned westwards to the Yser region of Belgium, close to the French border. It was here that the Belgian army chose to make a stand, in the Battle of the Yser, which began on 16 October and continued until the end of the month. It was also here that, following their evacuation in the face of the German advance on Ghent, Dr Hector Munro's Flying Ambulance Corps re-established itself in Belgium. This time they had a new and highly influential member, Robert de Broqueville, whose father was both the Belgian prime minister and the country's minister for war. This new relationship helped to strengthen the position of the corps in the Belgian sector of the Western Front, and they formed strong ties with the Belgian army, operating independently of the British authorities.It quickly became apparent that there were not enough field ambulances to remove casualties from the front. With its small fleet of ambulances and drivers, Dr Munro's unit provided a hugely important service. After the evacuation from Antwerp, Sarah Macnaughtan had left Mabel Stobart's corps and joined Munro's group of 'oddly dressed ladies' with their khaki uniforms. She was instantly impressed by the women and their assertiveness. 'The girls rule the company, carry maps and find roads, see about provisions and carry wounded.'[2] Munro's group was attached to a field hospital in Furnes, a desolate town abandoned by most of its inhabitants, only about 8 miles from the trenches and in the midst of the Battle of the Yser. Meanwhile the First Battle of Ypres[3] had also begun only 20 miles south of Furnes. Munro's corps was indeed 'right at the heart and pulse of things.'[4]

The field hospital at Furnes was situated in an empty ecclesiastical school. In the morning everyone would gather in the courtyard next to the ambulances, smoking cigarettes and preparing themselves to head out into the cold winter air. The ambulance corps relied on messengers to tell them where they were needed. Most of these messengers rode push-bikes as petrol was scarce.[5] With a shortage of male drivers, the women found themselves in great demand. Elsie Knocker explained that straight away she was given one of the larger ambulances to drive, which were generally heavy and difficult to handle. Driving the ambulances so close to the front was highly dangerous: the land was open and flat, exposing them to enemy artillery. Once in range, the drivers could see the flash of the guns as they fired and the noise could be overwhelming. Knocker recalled that the continuous shelling broke the nerve of one of the male drivers attached to the corps leaving him 'sick with fear'. She reflects gratefully that somehow she possessed the nerve required to go out day after day, night after night.[6] The roads were uneven, littered with large shell craters, car wreckages and animal corpses. Shrapnel from the shells rained down on the ambulances and around the women as they worked.

As well as being extremely risky, the women's work could be unpredictable. One time while they were out, Knocker and Chisholm were approached by an armoured car which had a burst tyre. Unable to continue any further, the Belgian soldiers driving it handed over five, extremely young, German prisoners to Knocker and Chisholm, and asked them to take them to Furnes. Knocker explained that for the entire journey:

> I had something of the sensation you get when you offer strangers a lift on a long and lonely road. A prickling on the back of your head that makes you want to look around. However, there were too many shell-holes and other obstacles to negotiate for me to work up any real anxiety, and the young prisoners behaved quite correctly.[7]

Exhaustion was another serious issue the women faced. The work of lifting and carrying patients on stretchers, driving heavy vehicles, and the extensive hours they worked, were physically demanding. After a long day spent loading patients onto trains in Avecapelle, Knocker was asked to take medical supplies to a town called Dixmude:

> I was told that it would be madness to obey the order, since it meant using a road which was being particularly heavily shelled, and going through Dixmude itself, which was being battered from all sides.
>
> It was an emergency, and I could not refuse. So I drove off into the dark, drizzly, cold night, my head stuck out at the side because the fixed windscreen was blurred and there were no lights, except from star shells and an occasional conflagration. The doctor at Dixmude was overjoyed to get his supplies, and asked me to take back a load of wounded. There were four stretcher cases and two sitting cases inside the ambulance, with its flapping canvas cover, and two sitting cases on the front seat with me.

Knocker drove back to Avecapelle with the American journalist Arthur Gleason (husband of Helen who was also in Munro's ambulance corps) riding on the outside of the ambulance to help navigate. The journey was arduous. At one point they had to stop to negotiate a large crater which had appeared since Knocker had last driven past. Because of the deep mud either side of the road, Knocker was unable to go around it. So, placing blankets down on the ground, Knocker and Arthur Gleason unloaded the patients to make the ambulance lighter. They only just made it across. Knocker was by now shattered: 'my arms seemed to be coming out of their sockets and my eyes were not focusing properly, and all the time shells were screaming and whistling so that it was hard to think straight.'[8] Finding that they were no longer able to use the railway station at Avecapelle to send the patients on, they had to continue on for a further 12 miles to Furnes. Exhausted, Knocker despaired, but in her biography she says that as she stood with her head in her hands, a British soldier came over and told her to cheer up. He said that she wasn't doing herself or her patients any favours. Pulling herself together, she continued driving through the night. Throughout her biography, Knocker puts the women's work in Belgium into perspective, always reminding the reader that whatever they had to deal with, the men in the trenches had it much worse and relied on the women for their support.

Munro's corps was privately funded and it depended on newspaper articles for publicity and to help raise money back home. The articles applauded their work and many focused on Lady Dorothie Feilding, an aristocrat, roughing it on the Western Front. Nevertheless, however exciting the newspapers made it sound, working at the front was far from glamorous. Most of the women cut their hair short (it was more practical and helped prevent the spread of lice) and they often slept in their clothes. Baths were a rare luxury and food was limited. One night, when members of the ambulance corps were out collecting wounded, heavy fighting made it unsafe for them to return to the hospital. The women spent the night in an abandoned cottage, sharing a room with a group of French soldiers until it was safe to go back.[9] Feilding's mother wrote to her, asking her to find a position for the daughter of some family friends who was keen to join in the adventure, but Feilding was reluctant to make any promises. She wrote home, explaining how the allied authorities were trying to impose restrictions on women at the front.[10] Having heard that her brother's regiment was nearby in Ypres, Feilding had tried on several occasions to find him, driving behind the lines and seeking out the regimental headquarters. She was stopped near Ypres and sent back by English officers 'on account of being female'. So on subsequent searches for her brother, she would park the ambulance out of sight, put on her large khaki overcoat and try to get close enough to overhear news of the regiment.[11] Within a few days of this first incident, Feilding was working in the Ypres sector on behalf of Munro's corps and yet again faced the disdain of the British army:

> After our cars had been getting in masses and masses of wounded from far up while all the army ambulances stayed in the Grande Place at Ypres, a Captain Fitzpatrick dashed up, was frightfully rude to us & Broqueville & tried to arrest us for working in the English lines without being 'army'. He turned us out of Ypres ... It was disgusting too because we were doing work that no one else was.[12]

Certainly the Belgian army was much happier to accept the help of these women and to permit them near the trenches than the British were. It may be that having lost most of their country to the German advance, they were grateful for any help. Had it been Belgian women wearing khaki and working in the trenches, they may have objected strongly, but if foreign women wanted to act against their accepted gender roles, it was not Belgium's concern. Munro did not help the situation. After visiting England for funds, he returned with more female recruits, to the great annoyance of the original members of the corps. It appeared that Munro was choosing women based on their social connections in a bid to promote the corps, rather than women with the aptitude and physical strength which the work required. Knocker and Chisholm became increasingly dissatisfied with Munro's leadership.

Towards the end of October, the Belgian army made the tactical decision to flood the canalised Yser valley. By creating 'a lake eight miles long and five miles wide'[13] the Belgians succeeded in bringing the Battle of Yser to an end. However both sides continued to shell one another in the attempt to break through the line.

The field hospital at Furnes was 'pitifully inadequate'.[14] It could not cope with the large number of casualties, further hampered by the shortage of doctors. There were not enough beds, with men lying on the floor, the dying amongst the dead. The women had to help clear the bodies to make space for the new arrivals, and during the worst times, the military ambulances would leave wounded in the street outside the hospital. Observing these terrible conditions, Knocker realised the urgent need for these men to receive more medical attention nearer the trenches, far earlier on in the evacuation process. In particular she identified the impact of shock which largely went untreated and contributed significantly to the rapid decline of the patients. Taking the initiative, Knocker formulated the idea of the women running their own first aid post, closer to the front. She began to look for a suitable location and settled on the cellar of a ruined building in the village of Pervyse, approximately 6 miles from Furnes and next to the Belgian trenches. Like many of the villages in the area, the residents had long gone and the buildings were in ruins. Most of them were without roofs, what walls remained were crumbling and all the glass windows had been shattered.

Despite the hostile situation, on the third week of November 1914, Knocker, Chisholm, Helen Gleason and Feilding set up a first aid post and a soup kitchen in Pervyse. They provided hot soup and hot chocolate to those who came to the cellar, and when it was dark they would take the hot drinks out to the men in the trenches. On several occasions, Knocker offered hot chocolate to the German sentries, shouting across no-man's-land.[15] The women's reputation for bravery and kindness quickly spread

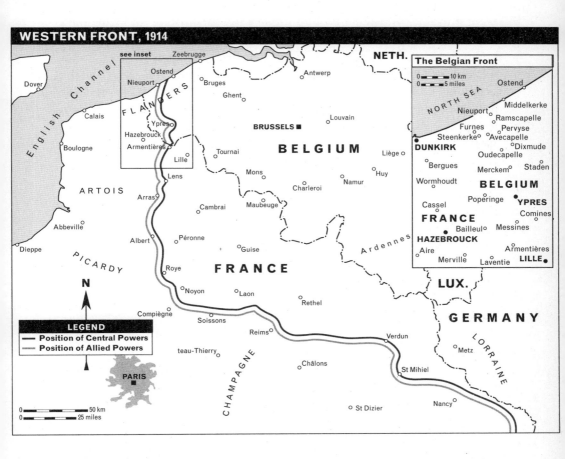

amongst the 3rd Division of the Belgian army which was stationed in
Pervyse. In gratitude a number of Belgian engineers helped the women to
reinforce what remained of their building and to make use of the ground
floor. Initially the women cooked the food, treated the wounded and
slept in the cellar, which measured 12 by 10ft with less than 6ft standing room[16]. Yet shortly after their arrival it was decided that it was too
dangerous to sleep there, so when the engineers, who had been so helpful, vacated another building in Pervyse, which was further back from the
front, the women moved their accommodation in there. They maintained
the first aid post in the cellar and regularly welcomed visitors, including
politicians and military personnel, all of whom had either heard or read
about the Women of Pervyse.

Feilding and Gleason continued to drive ambulances for Munro, working in the cellar whenever they could, but it was Knocker and Chisholm who undertook the majority of the work in Pervyse. During January they were forced to move their entire operation to the engineers' house as heavy rain had caused the cellar to flood and the shelling had become more intense. Knocker, strong willed and outspoken, had assumed the role of leader in Pervyse and was happier having put some distance between herself and Munro, as their relationship had become increasingly strained. The fact that the Corps was short on funds created an underlying tension within the group and the women disagreed with the way in which Munro managed them and their resources. With Munro being inconsistent in his decision-making, the women found it difficult to accept his authority and Knocker was not one to hold back on voicing her opinions.[17] Knocker and Chisholm loved their work and were resolved to remain in Pervyse, however close the enemy got.

At Christmas, Knocker went home to England for a few days to see her son, but she was excited to return, having missed the challenge of the front. At the end of the following January, Knocker and Chisholm were awarded the Belgian Order of Leopold in recognition of everything that they had done. The awards were presented by the King of Belgium at a ceremony on 1 February 1915. Although Knocker and Chisholm remained modest, the accolade created resentment within Munro's corps. Shortly afterwards it was organised that Feilding and Gleason received the same awards.

Life at Pervyse continued, until heavy bombardment in March forced Knocker and Chisholm, with deep regret, to leave. With Furnes unsafe, Munro's corps regrouped in La Panne on the Belgian coast. It was here that they received official confirmation that the corps was to be attached to the Belgian army's third division. The decree also said that women on the frontline would no longer be permitted, with the exception of Knocker and Chisholm. However, before they could return to the front, both women were obliged to go home and undertake a large scale fundraising tour.

The women continued their work near the trenches in Steenkerke, but in July 1915 they were able to move back to Pervyse. They had both formed a strong emotional attachment to the town and managed to remain there until 1918. The status that the women held amongst the men on both sides of the trenches was remarkable, as demonstrated by their forays into no-man's-land. As the war progressed, so did the use of aviation for tactical observation and bombing raids. With an increasing number of aircraft flying over the military lines, the armies used anti-aircraft guns to bring the planes down before they completed their missions, and a number crash-landed in the no-man's-land near Pervyse. The planes were expensive and took time to build, so when they crashed, the respective armies endeavoured to retrieve them and salvage what they could. Whenever they witnessed a crash, Knocker and Chisholm would go out into no-man's-land to try and rescue the pilot, whatever his nationality. Knocker recalled that, early on in the war, the Germans based at Pervyse sent them a message. Provided the women wore their nurse's wimples and did not try to move the planes, they would not fire on them.

One evening in about 1916, after the women had recovered the body of a British pilot, a rescue party arrived at the post intending to reclaim the aircraft. Knocker took pains to explain to the men the agreement that they had with the Germans. She also warned them that as soldiers they would be shot at, and that it would be particularly dangerous to go across in the dark. However the officer leading the party responded with a dismissive laugh: 'If a woman can go out to the machine I'm damned sure I can, especially in the dark.'[18] Knocker despaired that the officer was foolish enough to 'muddle a shooting war with the sex war.'[19] Within an hour the men returned. The major had been killed and his captain had been badly wounded.

Despite medals, despite mentions in the Belgian army's despatches and despite their hard work, the British army was still uncomfortable with women being in the trenches. When the British took over control of the Pervyse sector in 1917, an officer was incredulous when he came across Knocker sitting in the trenches, enjoying the sunshine and sewing. He demanded to know what she was doing there, and ordered her to leave before the main assault began. According to Knocker she replied that she 'had no intention whatever of leaving except at the end of a bayonet.'[20] Flummoxed by her defiance, the officer returned the following day with the commander of the Fourth Army, a general. Knocker maintained her position, declaring that she and Chisholm had permission to be there, and supported by several senior officials the women were allowed to remain.

Knocker and Chisholm would have continued at the front until the end of the war, but the side effects of a gas attack in March 1918 eventually forced them to leave and return to England to recuperate. Chisholm did return, only to be caught up in another gas attack. The Belgian army then officially closed the post.[21] The women's success was down to their sheer determination as well as their dedication and their ability to do their jobs. Yet the neutrality with which they were treated by the Germans was due to respect for their medical role and their gender: provided they did not take up arms they were 'safe'.

During this time, the First Aid Nursing Yeomanry (FANY) had been busy forging a role for themselves on the Western Front. After arriving in France at the end of October 1914, Grace Ashley-Smith and the

FANY had settled into work at the Lamarck Hospital in Calais. Aside from treating the wounded in the hospital, they were also asked to take on a convalescent hospital for typhoid patients. In addition to the horrific injuries the soldiers suffered, disease was a serious problem. Significantly, like Knocker and Chisholm, the FANY were also given charge of a regimental first aid post from which they visited the trenches. The post was in Oostkerk which was in between Pervyse and Dixmude and about one mile behind the trenches. It consisted of a dressing station situated in a building with a couple of small rooms and a bedroom loft which could accommodate forty to fifty wounded. The women worked with several male doctors and routinely made trips to the trenches with donations of cigarettes and clothes. Pat Waddell made the journey from Calais to the dressing station with the latest donations. She said that when she got within earshot of the guns she felt an unexpected thrill. Yet as the group she was travelling with got closer and a shell exploded over their heads and Waddell saw the wounded, her excitement was replaced by nervous anxiety.

To reach the trenches, the doctors preferred to wade through the 'thick and clayey and particularly gluey'[22] mud rather than stick too close to the railway line – an inviting target for artillery and enemy aircraft. They generally only went across to the trenches in the dark. The women would tuck their skirts up and wade across. One time Ashley-Smith lost her field boots in the mud and her buckskin breeches were soaked through. Another time, making her way back to the post in the dark, she slipped and fell into the mud, falling against the body of dead soldier. It was a nasty moment and the incident left her shaken.

On 11 January 1915, Cicely Mordaunt and her fellow FANY member Lillian Franklin visited Knocker and Chisholm in Pervyse.[23] Aside from each group working for the Belgian army in close proximity, it appears that for the most part they operated separately, reflecting the independence of their organisations. About a month after Knocker and Chisholm were awarded the Order of Leopold, three FANY members found themselves caught in the trenches when an attack started. Muriel Thompson, Mary White and Margaret Waite were in the rear trenches and as it was fairly quiet, they were invited to make their way up closer to the front. When the attack began, they were ordered back, but instead they used what supplies they had to treat the wounded. As a result of their actions they too were awarded the Order of Leopold. Yet despite the official recognition of what these women had done in the trenches, the British military maintained their stance against women working near the front.

The FANY was always looking for new opportunities for war work and in May 1915 Beryl Hutchinson was put in charge of a kitchen unit which was attached to the 7th Belgian Division, which was about to join the English at Ypres. After travelling to the Ypres area with one of the regiment's batterys, the FANY set up in a building on the Furnes/Ypres road:

> After a few days, the British woke up to the awful truth that two women had come with the Belgians and must be spies! The liaison officer was charming and regretful but said that we must leave the next day, and B Battery must make their own coffee.[24]

Until they received an official order to leave, the kitchen unit carried on with their work, only to be caught up in the aftermath of an early gas attack. Out on the road, a stream of walking wounded appeared, all suffering badly from the effects of the gas. Immediately the women ran out demanding that the men stopped so that they could treat them. Anticipating three months on the road, they had a large quantity of medical supplies available. Later on, the women received awards for their quick response, but the British were still not comfortable with them being so close to the front. The liaison officer returned and took them to the British General Headquarters where they were interviewed and then sent back to Calais where they re-joined the other members of the FANY.[25]

The Lamarck Hospital in Calais had become an unofficial headquarters for the FANY while it was in France. Throughout 1915 members of the FANY continued to look for more employment opportunities, and by January 1916 the British army agreed to employ them as an ambulance convoy based in Calais, to transport the sick and wounded as directed by the British Red Cross. This was a great feat for the FANY, to be the first women's convoy to be employed by the British army. However, the British Red Cross and the British army wanted to bring the FANY under their jurisdiction. They both became increasingly uncomfortable that the FANY, an independent organisation, proceeded effectively to create a monopoly with regards to convoy and military driving in Calais. They also disliked the FANY's strong association with its allies, in particular Belgium, and the 'unfeminine' behaviour of the women. According to 'FANY legend', as the BRCS tried to enforce more restrictions on them with a view to closing them down (save for the convoy which it would direct), Grace Ashley-Smith appealed directly to the Belgian army. Ashley-Smith organised for one of the smaller FANY units which was operating in Belgium and most under threat of closure to be officially enlisted in the Belgian army.[26] The defiant nature of this act was apparently enough to check future hostile take-overs.

The women volunteering in the war zone tried hard to gain acceptance and to be allowed to work behind the frontline and to go into the trenches in an official capacity. They were met with resistance, but their justification was that they wanted to support the medical services, not take up arms. The notion of a woman firing a weapon and taking lives was truly a step too far. In November 1914 an incident happened in Paris which caught the interest of newspapers in both France and the USA, and which provides an insight into the popular reaction to the idea of women in the military in the early days of the war. On 16 November 'a trimly uniformed titian-haired youth, of somewhat effeminate bearing, … presented himself to the recruiting officer for enlistment in the army.'[27] Suspicious that he was a German spy, the officer reported the young man to his general. An examination quickly revealed that the young man was actually a woman, and not just any woman, but the Scottish-American opera singer Mary Garden. General Gallieni, the French Minister for War and Military Governor of Paris was called, and interviewed Garden in private. At the beginning of the war, Garden had returned to Paris to work as a Red Cross nurse, donating her personal car for use as an ambulance. Concluding his interview with Garden, Gallieni advised the famous singer to return to work as a nurse. When asked about the affair she said, 'Yes, I tried to enlist in the French army … Why not? I owe France more than I can ever repay, even by giving her my life, and I am sure that I could fight as well as any man if they would only let me.'[28]

The more cynical view of this episode would be that this was a publicity stunt. The idea that a woman (an international celebrity no less) was so devoted to her country that she would risk everything to fight at the front, conveys a strong sense of patriotism and, it was hoped, would sufficiently embarrass more men into enlisting. It is significant that, after this, Garden was content to return to the more 'appropriate' womanly occupation of nursing, thus preventing any further debate about women in the army.

In the summer of 1915, a British woman succeeded in reaching the front in France and managed to impersonate a British soldier for ten days. Dorothy Lawrence, aged 18 years, was determined to find employment as a war correspondent, but she was repeatedly turned down by newspapers, who were unwilling to send a woman to the war zone. Lawrence was not interested in being a soldier; she simply wanted to be a journalist. Her intention was to create a sensational story with herself at the centre and to demonstrate to the newspaper editors that they had underestimated her. The military authorities prohibited most journalists from going to the front unless they had special permission, which is why Lawrence set her sights on reaching the trenches. Lawrence's account of her experiences focuses on the implementation and success of her plan rather than the time she actually spent in the trenches. At the time Lawrence did little to advance the debate about women and war in favour of her sex; instead the incident was a huge embarrassment to the British army and she was forbidden from telling anyone about it for the duration of the war. However the episode provides another insight into how women were viewed by the military.

Looking for a way to get closer to the front, Lawrence travelled to Creil in France, where there was a French army base. Finding a room above a café frequented by the soldiers she struck up conversations with the men, innocently asking questions, gathering information and carefully watching their body language. The men were amused by this young woman alone in a predominantly male environment, but her papers were in order and they were pleased to have female company. Most were happy to talk, many telling Lawrence about their families and the lives they hoped to return to. Lawrence says that it was one of these men who first suggested she impersonate a soldier. Yet this admission may have been Lawrence's attempt at making herself seem less reproachable to her readers for her actions.

After Creil, Lawrence went to the Senlis Forest area, chatting with soldiers en route and getting impromptu rifle lessons. In preparation for life at the front, she spent two rather uncomfortable nights sleeping out in the open. Finding no obvious way to get to the trenches, Lawrence returned to Paris and continued observing soldiers. There she had to brush off misunderstandings that she was a prostitute. Lawrence seems to have found accomplices relatively easily. She was successful because she played on their sense of fun and only asked them to help with one element of her plan, finding new accomplices at each stage. In Paris she quickly chose two British soldiers to whom she confided her plans. Rather than being aghast at the idea, Lawrence says the pair offered to get her a uniform, seeing the task as an 'adventure' and not believing that she would manage to get very far.

Lawrence arranged to meet the soldiers one evening while wearing her uniform so that they could teach her how to march, walk and drill properly. Using the cover of darkness she would walk past groups of soldiers in the city and practise everything she had learnt, building her confidence. The two soldiers suggested that Lawrence go to Bethune from where she could easily reach the front. Christening her alter ego Private Denis Smith, she managed to get the necessary paperwork and set off. Lawrence says she even persuaded a pair of Scottish military policemen to give her the required military-style haircut. If true, it is probable that, like the soldiers in Paris, they were amused by this eccentric young woman, seeing her venture as harmless fun. Dressed in her women's clothing, hiding her haircut under a large hat and with her uniform wrapped up in a parcel, Lawrence continued her journey. Cycling from Amiens to Bethune, however, she became lost:'I knew that as a woman, I certainly looked suspicious in proximity to the zone of fire.'[29]

Lawrence was in fact near the town of Albert, where she was given lodgings for the night. The next morning she set off once more for Bethune but came across a Royal Engineer. Tom Dunn was a sapper who came from Lancashire and in a very short time Lawrence had found an ally in the last stage of her plan. By now it was September and the Battle of Loos had begun nearby. Lawrence occupied an abandoned building near no-man's-land rather than sharing accommodation with the men. The plan was that, once again using darkness to aid her disguise, Dunn would collect her in the evening and take her to join the night-time shift. The Royal Engineers were tasked with laying mines, which required them to work in pairs. In her memoir Lawrence is keen to point out that she did not light the fuse as she did not wish to be complicit in murder.

Lawrence then confided in a sergeant who seemed to take the revelation well, only to return later with two men in order to arrest her. Once in custody, Lawrence faced a series of interrogations. She claims that at one point she was interviewed by six generals, which she thought ridiculous as they were in the middle of a large battle and she felt inclined to laugh out loud. Yet in her account, Lawrence makes little apology for her actions and for wasting everyone's time. Instead she was convinced that she held the upper hand in the situation because she had 'beaten' the system and they knew it.[30] Forbidden to disclose details of her adventure, Lawrence was sent back to England and interviewed further at Scotland Yard. If anything, the embarrassment surrounding Lawrence meant that the British army was inclined to be even more against women at the front and involved in military matters. Yet at the same time, circumstances began to bring about a change of opinion on the role of women in wartime, albeit a temporary change borne from necessity.

In Britain throughout 1915 it became increasingly apparent that the army needed more men, and the argument for conscription gathered pace. In support of conscription the British government began to promote the idea of women taking men's work at home to free up more men for military roles. By doing this, the British had to accept that this was a step towards women earning citizenship and that suffrage would inevitably follow. In January 1916, conscription in Britain came into force, at first only for single men between the ages of eighteen to forty-one, but by the summer this was extended to married men.

The French, on the other hand, already had conscription and were determined to avoid advancing women's suffrage through war work. Historian Margaret Darrow explains that at first the French government was taken aback by the number of women's voluntary organisations formed in response to the war. The government officials dealing with requests to authorise the organisations saw them as 'distracting, if not positively destructive to the war effort.' While the majority of French women's involvement in war remained confined to private voluntary organisations, by 1915 the French Government began 'to concede that women's active support was sometimes necessary.'[31] Like Britain, France began to face a severe shortage of manpower in 1915, which reopened a public pre-war debate in France about the degree to which women could play an active role within the armed services. Darrow shows that ultimately the public did not mind women being in the back of the war zone, where they risked death, but that they could not contemplate women taking lives. This is echoed in Dorothy Lawrence's account when she says that she could not bring herself to light the fuse and be complicit in killing someone.

Marthe Richer was one of a handful of French women who had obtained their pilot's licence prior to the war. She founded an organisation called the 'Patriotic Union of Aviatrices' that would undertake routine flights behind the frontlines. Richer 'tirelessly lobbied the Ministry of War, the Undersecretary of State for Aeronautics and even the Service of Aeronautical Manufacture' to support the Union. Her campaign included interviews in the national papers promoting women in the military, but by the end of the Autumn 1915 she had to concede that the Union had failed to achieve anything.[32] One of the other aviatrices who had been interviewed in the national papers was the competitive pilot Marie Marvingt, a very dynamic woman with a national reputation thanks to her many sporting achievements. These ranged from becoming the first woman to cross the English Channel in a hot-air balloon in 1909 to becoming the women's world bobsleigh champion in 1910. In 1908 she tried to enter the Tour de France but was turned down on account of being a woman, so she completed the course by herself.

Marvingt began the war as a journalist. Living in the town of Nancy, she felt compelled to write about her experiences of the attack on the town which were published in the local evening paper, the *Samedi Soir*. Like Richer, because she had a pilot's licence, Marvingt wanted to fly. The military airforce was in its infancy compared to the army and the navy and its pilots were not awarded officer rank. Instead they were considered to be the equivalent of infantrymen instructed by officers based on the ground.

Like Richer, Marvingt's attempts to be accepted as a pilot all failed. Instead, having trained as a nurse before the war, she became a Red Cross nurse in a field hospital. While working as a nurse, Marvingt tended to a pilot and asked him many questions. The severity of his injuries meant that he would not be able to fly his next mission and without another pilot to take his place, his plane would be left idle on the airfield. On hearing this, Marvingt immediately became excited, for surely she as a fully accomplished pilot was the perfect solution. She succeeded in persuading the pilot that the scheme would work, and then with a forceful determination, Marvingt set off to convince the commander of the air base. Perhaps Marvingt's famous reputation preceded her, for the commander agreed to her request and it wasn't long before Marvingt found herself in the pilot's seat of a bomber. The mission was a bombing raid on a German aerodrome at Frescaty. Although there are few details, later towards the end of the war, Marvingt went on to fly a series of solo missions on the Italian front. Her participation in military flights was viewed as highly irregular and certainly would not be allowed to set a precedent of other female pilots to follow, but she did receive official commendations for her role. Officially Marvingt was always referred to as a volunteer nurse rather than a serving pilot. Before she went to the Italian front, however, Marvingt's military career was postponed due to her father being diagnosed with a terminal illness. From May 1915 until the summer of 1916, she tended her father at his home until he died.

In 1917, Marvingt was interested to hear that infantrymen in the trenches felt that the pilots were not as brave as them as they did not experience face-to-face combat and were accommodated in airfields a comfortable distance from the front. In order to weigh in on this discussion, Marvingt decided that she needed to experience both. Marvingt succeeded in becoming a full fighting member of the 42nd BCP (*Battalion de Chasseurs a Pied Territoriaux*), an infantry regiment, for approximately three to six weeks. It is unclear how she managed to get into the battalion, but she posed as a man. During her time as a soldier she carried out regular duties, manning a listening post for German frontline activity and taking turns in the trenches. It was only during a regimental inspection, when some of her red hair fell loose around her face under her helmet, that she was discovered: she had not gone so far as to cut her hair short. Yet she managed to avoid the reprimands and subsequent interrogation that Dorothy Lawrence had received. Recently Georges Clemenceau had become the French prime minister and General Foch the new commander-in-chief of the army. Marvingt's biographer suspects that both men admired her and that it was their intervention that saved her and subsequently got her posted to the Italian front in the Dolomites as a member of the 3rd BCA regiment. In the same way as when she flew the bombing mission, Marvingt was technically classified as a nurse, but she climbed and skied with the men. Marvingt even sent photographic postcards to her cousin showing her using ropes to manage the descent of a wounded soldier from a high mountain pass. While in Italy she wore an Alpine infantry uniform, complete with a plumed hat, white collar, high boots and a cape that came down to her knees.

Remaining on the Italian front, Marvingt once again became a war correspondent, although she ran into trouble with her visa. Because her father's family came from Metz, the Italian authorities suspected her of being a German spy, but she managed to convince them otherwise. After the war, Marvingt was revered as a patriotic heroine and was awarded the *Croix de Guerre*.[33]

While women were using the logical route of medicine and healthcare to establish a place for themselves in the war machine, some, like Knocker and Chisholm, and the FANY, were always pushing beyond what was deemed acceptable, striving to work as close to the front as possible while the majority of women remained further behind the lines in the hospital cities on the coast. Having been driven out of their own country, the Belgians were certainly more accepting of the women and grateful for the invaluable assistance that they provided. The English were much more uncomfortable with the idea of women at the front and responded by trying to control the situation and restrict their activity. Dorothy Lawrence's adventure did little to promote the women's war effort; if anything, it made the British army more suspicious of women. In France, Mary Garden and Marie Marvingt demonstrated the different ways in which celebrity could be used. Garden's demonstration was intended to shame men who hadn't into enlisting, while at the same time promoting the idea that women should remain in their 'proper' place. Marvingt, on the other hand, a famous sportswoman, was heralded as a national hero for her role in the trenches and in the air, rather than condemned for acting against her sex.

As the war took its toll, it placed considerable strain on each nation's resources of manpower. Women began to fill the roles on the home front left behind by men who were released for military service, but something more was required. The achievements of the women who had gone over-seas, and the spirit that they embodied, led the way for the British to set up the Women's Army Auxiliary Corps, the Women's Royal Naval Service, and the Women's Royal Air Force, and for the French to employ women as civilians within the army. In turn it shaped how the USA employed women when it entered the war in 1917.

Notes

1 Beauchamp, Pat, *Fanny Goes to War*, pp.35–6.
2 Macnaughtan, Sarah, *My War Experiences in Two Continents*, p.29.

3 This was an attempt by the German army to push through the Allied line which ultimately failed. The battle was to last over four weeks from 18 October to 22 November, with an extremely high casualty rate on both sides.

4 Feilding, Dorothie. Letter dated 26 June 1915 written to her mother, as reproduced in Hallam, Andrew and Hallam, Nicola (eds), *Lady Under Fire on the Western Front: The Great War Letters of Lady Dorothie Feilding MM*, p.81.

5 Atkinson, Diane, *Elsie and Mairi go to War*.

6 T'Serclaes, Baroness de, *Flanders and other Fields*, p.56.

7 Ibid., p.53.

8 Ibid., p.58.

9 Atkinson, Diane, *Elsie and Mairi go to War*.

10 Feilding, Dorothie, letter dated 26 November 1914, as reproduced in Hallam, Andrew and Hallam, Nicola (eds), *Lady Under Fire on the Western Front: The Great War Letters of Lady Dorothie Feilding MM*.

11 Feilding, Dorothie, letter dated 2 November 1914, from Feilding to her mother, as reproduced in Hallam, Andrew and Hallam, Nicola (eds), *Lady Under Fire on the Western Front: The Great War Letters of Lady Dorothie Feilding MM*, p.26.

12 Feilding, Dorothie, letter dated 4 November 1914, from Feilding to her family, as reproduced in Hallam, Andrew and Hallam, Nicola (eds), *Lady Under Fire on the Western Front: The Great War Letters of Lady Dorothie Feilding MM*, p.28.

13 Atkinson, Diane, *Elsie and Mairi go to War*.

14 Baroness de T'Serclaes, *Flanders and other Fields*, p.61.

15 Atkinson, Diane, *Elsie and Mairi go to War*.

16 T'Serclaes, Baroness de, *Flanders and other Fields*, p.64.

17 Atkinson, Diane, *Elsie and Mairi go to War*.

18 Ibid., p.88.

19 Ibid., p.88.

20 Ibid., p.93.

21 Atkinson, Diane, *Elsie and Mairi go to War*.

22 Beauchamp, Pat, *Fanny goes to War*, p.22.

23 Lee, Janet, *War Girls: The First Aid Nursing Yeomanry in the First World War*, p.106.

24 Hutchinson, Beryl, first set of memoirs, p.8, Liddle Collection, document LIDDLE/WW1/WO/057.

25 Hutchinson, Beryl, first set of memoirs, p.9, and Lee, Janet, *War Girls: The First Aid Nursing Yeomanry in the First World War*.

26 Lee, Janet, *War Girls: The First Aid Nursing Yeomanry in the First World War*, p.116.

27 Turnbull, Michael, *Mary Garden*, pp.118–9.

28 Ibid., p.119.

29 Lawrence, Dorothy, *Sapper Dorothy*, p.40.

30 Ibid., p.77.

31 Darrow, Margaret, *French Women and the First World War*, p.74.

32 Ibid., p.241.

33 Cordier, Marcel and Maggio, Rosalie, *Marie Marvingt – La femme d'un siecle*.

4

Women Doctors and the Military

Women who had been trained in medicine and in surgery knew instinctively that the time had come when great and novel demands would be made upon them, and that a hitherto unlooked-for occasion for service was at their feet.[1]

Doctor Flora Murray

The main vocation of a doctor is to heal, to save lives and to relieve suffering. It was only natural in a time of war, particularly one in which their own country was involved, that doctors would want to enlist or volunteer. But at the start of the First World War, women were still a long way off being fully accepted as practitioners in the medical world as a whole, let alone in the military.

Having won the right to medical training, the next challenge that women faced was to achieve professional equality with their male peers. Since the first female pioneers qualified as doctors in the mid-1800s, the number of female physicians in Europe, Australasia and North America grew. It is difficult to get an exact number of how many women actually worked as doctors once they qualified, but it is possible to get an approximate idea. In Britain, the 1911 census recorded that there were 610 active female doctors and in 1921, 1,500 were recorded.[2] In 1914 there were about 1,000 women on the British Medical Register.[3] Before the war there were about 200 Canadian female doctors and by 1918 the number in both France and Italy was approximately 300[4]. In the USA, meanwhile, in 1916 the number of active women doctors was just under 6,000.[5] In Russia there were approximately 1,600 female doctors in 1914.[6]

The majority built their careers on treating women and children as there were few opportunities for them to pursue other fields of medicine. Graduates tended to look to all-women hospitals for employment, such as the New Hospital for Women founded by Elizabeth Garrett Anderson in 1871,[7] or to join the teaching staff at women's medical schools such as the Women's Medical College of Pennsylvania, founded in 1850.[8] Those with sufficient money or financial support followed Garrett Anderson's example and set up their own hospitals, whereas others hoped to practise privately. Dr Rosalie Slaughter Morton was welcomed when she set up premises in Washington DC in the early 1900s, but some faced a struggle for acceptance within their local communities. Agnes Bennett, an Australian, qualified from Edinburgh in 1899. Disappointed by the limited job opportunities in Britain, she decided to return to Australia, optimistic that she would have more success there. Bennett set up a private practice in Sydney, but after six months she was losing money and had to admit defeat. Her student debt forced her to take a salaried position at a mental hospital, which offered little means of career development. Bennett's big chance came when a fellow Edinburgh student invited her to take over her own, successful practice in Wellington, New Zealand, which she was giving up to get married.[9] Because of the limited number of institutions that accepted women, female medical students came from across the globe. After graduation, the strong friendships they had formed as students created a supportive international network of medical women.

Dr Elsie Inglis of Edinburgh, Scotland, was one of the many female physicians who wanted to enlist in 1914. Her biographer Leah Leneman says that for Inglis this was a combination of patriotism, an opportunity to show what women doctors could do, and a chance to promote suffrage. All the female physicians who wanted to do war work shared these same motives in varying degrees. When Inglis applied to the Royal Army Medical Corps she was immediately turned down, with the officer saying 'My good lady, go home and sit still'.[10] Applications from female doctors hit upon a sensitive area in the RAMC as male doctors had only just secured their own position within the British army.

Following the publicity surrounding Florence Nightingale and the Crimea in the 1850s, the army began to acknowledge the importance of medical care in maintaining soldiers' morale, and most significantly, in sustaining the level of active manpower. Nevertheless, there was tension between regular officers and the medical officers whom they viewed as inferior. The first factor was a class division; the army typically attracted doctors from the lower-middle class, who did not have the social connections needed to obtain senior civilian roles. The regular officers – who often hailed from upper-class backgrounds – were keen to distinguish themselves from this group and regarded them as second-rate doctors, unable to find alternative employment. The second factor was that the medical officers were doctors first and officers second, rather than trained

combatants. It was felt that they did not fully comprehend military operations. As a result, medical officers had relatively little command authority,
which made it difficult to do their work. It did not help that the emphasis
on sanitation and cleanliness meant that critics would 'point to similarities
between the caring role of the physician and the domestic work traditionally performed by women.'[11] In the 1890s, supported by the British
Medical Association, the medical officers campaigned for equal rank and
status to the combatant officers. In 1898 the RAMC was created and
the doctors were awarded 'substantive rank and limited command', but
little if any responsibility for operational matters.[12] Tensions remained,
but over the next sixteen years, the RAMC worked hard to establish its
authority and became a recognised contributor to international medical
research.[13] Therefore in 1914, a sudden influx of female medics threatened
to undermine everything that they had achieved.

Away from the particular concerns of the British army, the story of Draga
Liocic, the first Serbian woman to qualify as a doctor, illustrates how war
could provide an opportunity for professional advancement. Liocic graduated from Zurich in 1879, but her education had been interrupted by the
Serbian-Turkish war of 1876–78 in which she volunteered as a medical
assistant and was awarded the rank of second lieutenant by the Serbian
army. Once qualified, Liocic had to wait two years until she was allowed to
practise privately. Until then, she continued to work as a medical assistant.
When Liocic volunteered in subsequent wars, the Serbian-Bulgarian War of
1885, the Balkan Wars of 1912–13 and the First World War, she was allowed
to work as a doctor; although she was confined to hospitals far behind the
frontline.[14] The successive Balkan conflicts gave Liocic a great range of medical experience that would most likely have been closed to her in peacetime.
However, it took her several wars and a number of years to reach this position, and even then she was not allowed to work on the frontline.

During the Balkan Wars, under the Women's Sick and Wounded Convoy
Corps, Mabel St Clair Stobart had led a small party of female doctors
to Bulgaria. As well as demonstrating what women doctors could do,
Stobart's intention had been to use the conflict to champion her own feminist agenda. While the Bulgarians had been extremely grateful, the British
authorities barely acknowledged what the female doctors had done. It was
evident that it would take more to persuade the British authorities fully
to accept women as medics. Now the First World War presented female
physicians with the opportunity to replicate Liocic's achievements and
advance women's place in medicine on a much larger scale. As medical
professionals, the women doctors had high hopes that their skills would
be readily accepted in a time of war, regardless of their sex.

Unlike Britain, Russia was generally more accepting of its women doctors because the medical profession was not overcrowded. Even so, the women were underpaid and not allowed to use their MD title because that would immediately command higher pay, and in civilian life the women were only allowed to treat other women and children.[15] Yet in wartime the need for doctors was greater than any gender bias. Russia allowed women doctors to treat soldiers in hospitals near the front during the Russo-Turkish war of 1877–78, and in 1897 the Tsar financed the first medical college for women, the Russian Medical Institute for Women, in St Petersburg.[16] During the First World War, women doctors were again employed in Russia's military hospitals, and all female students with a minimum of two years' training were liable for service.[17] In August 1914, the Russian authorities asked Dr Elsa Winokurow to set up and run a military hospital in Moscow. As head physician she worked there for three years until the Russian Revolution of 1917. She recalled, 'My hospital was run by women. Two women surgeons and women specialists in internal medicine volunteered to work with me. The staff of nurses consisted of twelve female students in their first year at the newly founded medical college for women.'[18]

After the war, Winokurow went to work in Germany, her parents' native country, and she reflected that 'an educated woman was shown more comradeship and courtesy in Russia than in Germany.'[19] The Russian Women's Rights Society also financed a hospital, which was run by its president Dr Schischkina Yavein, and it also helped to train female nurses.[20] In 1914 Russian women had not yet been awarded the vote and they hoped that their war service would strengthen their argument.

In both France and Great Britain there was a fundamental reluctance to assign any civic duty to women because even in wartime that may constitute suitable grounds for full citizenship and qualification to vote. It is ironic, therefore, that the first all-female organisation to be given charge of a British Military Hospital was the Women's Hospital Corps (WHC), which was managed by two ardent Suffragettes.

Many female physicians were supporters of women's suffrage, and the more dedicated activists saw the war as an unmissable opportunity to demonstrate their right to political equality and citizenship. As members of the Women's Social and Political Union (WSPU), Louisa Garrett Anderson[21] and Flora Murray were both active Suffragettes. Garrett Anderson had spent one month in Holloway Prison in 1912 after breaking a window during a political demonstration. Murray had formed first aid units to tend WSPU members injured during protests and those recovering from hunger strikes. When the WSPU suspended activities during the war, Garrett Anderson and Murray needed an alternative organisation into which they could channel all their political energy, furthering the campaign and advancing the role of women in medicine. By 1914, both women were in their early forties, and, following the declaration of war, Garrett Anderson and Murray set up the WHC, a hospital unit complete with female surgeons, that could be established wherever it was needed. In 1920 Murray published an account of the WHC which heralded the achievements of the unit as a key component in the success of the suffrage campaign, declaring:

> The long years of struggle for the Enfranchisement of Women which had preceded the outbreak of war had done much to educate women in citizenship and in public duty. The militant movement had taught them discipline and organisation; it had shown them new possibilities in themselves, and had inspired them with confidence in each other. ... It was inconceivable that in a war of such magnitude women doctors should not join in the care of the sick and wounded, but it was obvious that prejudice would stand in their way. Their training and their sympathies fitted them for such work; they knew and could trust their own capacity; but they had yet to make their opportunity.[22]

Following the WSPU's previous dealings with the Home Office during its militant political campaigns, Murray believed that if she were to offer the WHC to the War Office, they would be met by the same 'cherished prejudices and stereotyped outlook of officials.'[23] Instead, on 12 August 1914, Garrett Anderson and Murray offered the WHC to France and were accepted by the French Red Cross. As well as raising funds and buying equipment, Garrett Anderson and Murray designed a uniform for the WHC. Murray proudly recalled a uniform that promoted authority, with a nod to the insignia of different military ranks, and a design which was practical yet feminine:

> The uniform of the Corps had been chosen carefully. It consisted of a short skirt with a loose, well-buttoned-up tunic, and was made of covert coating of a greenish-grey colour. The material was light and durable, and stood wear and weather well. The medical officers had red shoulder straps with the Corps initials, 'W.H.C.,' worked on them in white, and the orderlies had white collars and shoulder straps with red letters. The white was not serviceable, and at a later date blue was substituted for it. Small cloth hats with veils and overcoats to match made a very comfortable and useful outfit.

… Feminine, graceful, business-like, it was invaluable as an introduction to the character of the Corps.[24]

On 14 September 1914, the WHC left London to take charge of the Hotel Claridge on the Champs Elysées in Paris, and to convert it into a hospital. Garrett Anderson's mother Elizabeth came to see them off. Regretting she could not go with them (she was now seventy-eight years old) she proudly declared that the WHC would advance women's medicine by 100 years.[25]

After the WHC arrived in Paris, it soon became apparent that the French Red Cross did not have much of a plan for it, beyond selecting a building for its hospital and providing it with an attachment of British Red Cross nurses. So the WHC took the initiative. While converting the Hotel Claridge, 'a gorgeous shell of marble and gilt without heating or crockery or anything practical'[26] into an efficient working hospital in under a week, the women rapidly ingratiated themselves with Paris's wartime medical community. Garrett Anderson spent time with staff from other hospitals seeing how they worked, and she regularly ventured out with them in their ambulances.

The WHC worked hard and quickly earned respect from both the French and British military authorities. Murray declared its hospital:

A haven of peace and security. It was heavenly to lie in clean beds, to be cared for by Englishwomen, to be rid of regimental discipline and for the moment of responsibility too. … Probably none of them had been in contact with women doctors before; but that did not make any difference. They trusted the women as they would have trusted men – passing the bullets which had been extracted from their persons from bed to bed and pronouncing the surgeon to be 'wonderfully clever!'[27]

As doctor in charge of the hospital, Murray received many visitors (both official and social) who were eager to see this French military hospital run by women and she would provide them with a tour of the wards. It was an important part of building their public reputation, and in time the British began to treat the hospital as if it was one of theirs.[28]

In mid-October the position of the Western Front became more static and the Allied medical services organised for the majority of the wounded to be taken by train to established base hospitals, most of which were concentrated in Boulogne, Rouen and Le Havre. As the 'Race to the Sea' developed, more and more wounded were sent to Boulogne. In response to this, the hospitals in Paris formed a contingent of doctors and nurses (including three WHC doctors) and went to the city to offer help. 'When they reached Boulogne they found the hospitals and stations seriously overcrowded, and approximately three thousand casualties were coming in daily.'[29] Boulogne was 'a city of hospitals, every hotel a hospital, every road thronged with troops and nurses' and it was where Katherine Furse brought her first group of voluntary aid detachments.[30] Dr Rosalie Jobson and Dr Marjorie Blandy, both of the WHC, were attached immediately to a British hospital that was desperately understaffed and went on to serve under the RAMC for six months as contract employees. Meanwhile the WHC's Dr Gadzar approached the RAMC directly, offering them a new WHC hospital, which, based on the WHC's work in Paris, was accepted. Selecting a château in the nearby town of Wimereux, they were officially attached to the British Military Hospital situated in the Grand Hotel in Boulogne. By 6 November the new Wimereux hospital was ready for its first patients. Kate John Finzi, a Red Cross nurse who worked at the hospital in Boulogne where Jobson and Blandy were stationed, recalled the WHC in her memoirs:

> Everyone is exhausted … but they say the Army Nursing Service will be here in sufficient numbers soon. The lady doctors have been invaluable, their zeal unflagging. They are splendid operators, and in the midst of the worst rushes never careless. Besides their work here they spend much time at the 'Women's Hospital' at a chateau some three miles out of Boulogne, where everything is run by volunteer women workers, who act as doctors, nurses, orderlies and quartermasters.[31]

The WHC ran its hospital in Paris until 18 January 1915 when it closed due to issues with the building lease and winter fuel shortages. The RAMC was looking to establish more military hospitals in Britain and Alfred Keogh (in his role as director-general of the British army's medical services) agreed to allow the WHC to manage a new military hospital in Endell Street, London. They closed Wimereux and diverted all their staff and resources to London. Although the women were medical officers in a British military hospital, they were not given commissions, but they were graded from lieutenant through to lieutenant-colonel and awarded the appropriate pay and allowances.[32] They were not permitted to wear badges denoting their rank[33], yet the WHC women found themselves in an exceptional position, unprecedented in British military history.

The commandant of a VAD unit in Edinburgh, Dr Elsie Inglis – whose RAMC interview experience was recounted earlier – applied to join the WHC as soon as she heard about it, but all the positions had already been filled. Even though she had just turned fifty and her health was beginning to fail, Inglis was determined to do something. She had dedicated the last thirty years to earning her medical qualifications and building a highly reputable career as a doctor. After being turned down by the RAMC, Inglis decided to establish her own organisation, a hospital unit entirely staffed by women. Inglis was a supporter of women's suffrage, yet unlike Garrett Anderson and Murray, she preferred the more moderate strategy of the National Union of Women's Suffrage Societies (NUWSS). Inglis held positions in both the Edinburgh National Society for Women's Suffrage, and the Scottish Federation of Women's Suffrage committees (which came under the NUWSS). With the Scottish Federation's support, Inglis founded the Scottish Women's Hospital (SWH). Inglis wanted a name that would attract wide (financial) support so she proposed the use of 'British' rather than 'Scottish', but was overruled. However she managed to veto the use of 'suffrage' in the title.[34] Rather than putting together a unit within a matter of weeks as the WHC had done, Inglis and the other members of the NUWSS network envisaged what would become a much larger organisation and spent most of September and October fundraising. At first only the Belgians accepted the SWH's offer of a hospital, but the German advance prevented this from happening. In November, the SWH once again offered itself to Britain's allies. With the WHC in the process of setting up its second hospital in France, the French accepted the SWH on 7 November, and was followed by Serbia a day later.[35]

Dr Alice Hutchinson, who had gone to Bulgaria with Stobart, went to France as an envoy for the SWH to make preparations. Yet on arrival in Calais, she was aghast at the prevalence of typhus amongst the soldiers, so she chose to establish the first SWH unit in Calais and provide as much medical assistance as possible. At the end of November, Inglis herself travelled to France, looking for a suitable building for the SWH hospital, and found the old abbey at Royaumont, at Asnières in the Oise valley, just north of Paris. After a month of preparations and several French military inspections, the new hospital at Royaumont received its first patients in January 1915 and remained open until the end of 1918.

The first SWH unit to go to Serbia arrived in January 1915 and established itself in the town of Kragujevac. Serbia was experiencing a large-scale typhus epidemic and in response to the crisis the SWH sent several more units over the next six months. Inglis herself travelled out to Serbia and arrived there in May. There were several other organisations already in Serbia. One was the 'Berry Unit', run by a married couple, Dr James Berry and Dr F. May Dickinson Berry, which oversaw the Anglo-Serbian Hospital in Vrnjacka Banja. Another group was the Serbian Relief Fund (SRF), which employed both female and male doctors and had already deployed its first hospital in Skopje in mid-November. In April another SRF hospital was established, this time in Kragujevac, under the administration of Mrs Stobart, who had decided to leave the Western Front for Serbia.

Over the course of the war, the SWH would send units to Salonika in Greece, Corsica and Russia. Despite the reservations of the RAMC, the women proved that they were capable of working in a war zone, of undertaking surgical work and enduring the long hours.

As the war continued, Britain faced a severe shortage of doctors. With the advent of conscription, the gradual expansion of wartime roles for women and the inevitability that suffrage would be granted, in 1916 the RAMC finally conceded that it would employ female doctors. However, rather than being conscripted like men, the women were invited to volunteer and were employed as civilians on short-term contracts. They were not given a uniform, nor were they given a rank, and they were sent to hospitals far away from the front in Salonika, Malta, Egypt and India.[36] In wanting to work with the military, female doctors had to contend with an additional factor in their quest for professional equality – rank. In all-women hospitals such as the WHC and the SWH, rank was less important because their female staff established their own hierarchy, which they and their patients generally respected. But for women working alongside male doctors with officer rank, the lack of status was a distinct disadvantage. They would always be viewed as inferior to the male doctors and treated as such. Uniforms were important because they were a symbol of respect and authority and showed that the person was actively engaged in war work. In 1916, Louisa Garrett Anderson campaigned for the women employed by the RAMC to be awarded equivalent rank to the RAMC doctors, but she was ignored.[37] There was a general concern that if the RAMC awarded rank to medical women this would set a precedent for the rest of the armed forces.[38] What the British military authorities failed to acknowledge, however, was that it was their professional qualifications that entitled the women to a rank, which was an argument that wouldn't necessarily extend to the rest of the armed forces. In 1917, the Women's Army Auxiliary Corps (see Chapter Eight for further explanation) was formed and employed women doctors. Although they weren't given ranks, they did have uniforms and wore the RAMC badge. Eventually the RAMC permitted the women that it contracted to wear the same uniform and the RAMC badge too, but it was not willing to allow them to wear the RAMC uniform.

The decision as to whether or not to award women doctors a rank varied from army to army. Sometimes it simply depended on the disposition of the army officers. The Canadian Army granted its military nurses the relative rank of lieutenant, which entitled them to the same pay and benefits attributed to the rank. Although the nurses did not have any military command, and were not allowed to use the title but were addressed as 'nursing sister'[39], it did place them firmly in the hierarchy of the Canadian military medical system.

The Canadian Army Medical Corps (CAMC) did not permit female doctors to work for it as doctors. However, Dr Frances Windsor managed to enlist as an officer for overseas service with the CAMC. In October 1916, Windsor left Calgary, Canada to take up her new post in London. One version of events is that she persuaded a member of the Canadian Federal Parliament, R.B. Bennett, to help her secure an appointment. It is said that he was deeply in love with the twenty-seven-year-old and happy to help. The ambiguity of her Christian name meant that from the forms the CAMC was expecting a man and was deeply surprised that Windsor was a woman.[40] With the paperwork in order the CAMC accepted Windsor, awarding her the rank of lieutenant and referring to her as a nursing sister, suggesting she was restricted to nursing. Within a short period of time the CAMC orchestrated her transfer to the RAMC, which was by then employing women. She worked as an anaesthetist in London's military hospitals, including the WHC's hospital at Endell Street. In June 1917 she married and soon after became pregnant. The RAMC did not know how to deal with a pregnant officer as there were not any regulations to cover this situation. In the end, Windsor (married name Leacock) was discharged 'on the grounds of "ill health"'.[41]

Another Canadian, Dr Irma LeVasseur, decided to volunteer rather than enlist. In April 1915 she joined a voluntary unit, along with four male doctors, which went to Serbia. On arrival they realised the extent to which disease was rife and the doctors decided to separate and work independently in order to help more people. LeVasseur worked in Kragujevac.

Dr Caroline Twigge Matthews, who was British, also decided to volunteer. In her career Matthews had been very proactive. Following the Messina earthquake of 1908 she went to Italy and worked with the Italian Red Cross through the subsequent crisis. During the Balkan War of 1912–13 she had worked as a correspondent for the illustrated newspaper *The Sphere* and for the Montenegro army in which she held the rank of surgeon and was awarded a medal. This time, in 1915, she volunteered through the Serbian Red Cross to work with a Serbian army field unit. Financially independent and paying for all her own equipment, Matthews was readily accepted, and she looked forward to working in first aid posts on the frontline. Only when she arrived in May 1915, she was disappointed to discover that she had been assigned to a hospital in Skopje, away from the front.

With the large numbers of soldiers from Australia and New Zealand being sent to Europe, Agnes Bennett decided in early 1915 that she wanted to volunteer overseas. She found that the New Zealand army was not interested in enlisting a forty-two-year-old woman. Friends in Europe recommended that she apply to the French Red Cross, and she was accepted. As she made plans to leave, Bennett received multiple requests from friends and acquaintances to find out news of their relatives and how the New Zealand forces were faring. Her journey took her via the Suez Canal where troops of the Australian and New Zealand Army Corps (ANZAC)[42] were encamped along the banks. The men were as eager for news from home as the passengers were for news from the front. By now the Gallipoli Campaign had begun, which would claim the lives of nearly 13,000 ANZAC soldiers by the time the area was evacuated in January 1916. Concerned by the rumours of the high casualty rates, Bennett stopped her journey at Port Said and then went on to Cairo to obtain more reliable information. In her search she came across the New Zealand director of medical services, Colonel Matthew Holmes, who immediately offered her work. The medical services were unable to cope and they needed more doctors. According to her biography, the next day, Bennett took an oath of allegiance and was awarded the rank and pay of captain.[43] The assignation of rank was possibly an impulsive act by Holmes in a time of great need, but for Bennett it was not of primary importance. Instead she simply wanted to provide medical care where it was needed.

In 1916, following the evacuation of Gallipoli, Bennett left the New Zealand army and went to Britain. Here she met Elsie Inglis who, on her return from Serbia, was planning a new Scottish Women's Hospital unit to send out to Salonika on the Macedonian front. She eagerly recruited Bennett as its leader.

Meanwhile, two British women, Nina Hollings and Helena Gleichen, neither of whom were doctors at the beginning of the war, took it upon themselves to train in Paris. Initially they had worked together as ambulance drivers and translators for a hospital in Compiègne, France, from February to May 1915. With a severe shortage of radiology units operating near the front, one of the hospital surgeons recommended that the women train as radiologists in Paris, which took six months. Hollings and Gleichen then raised the funds to buy their own equipment and cars before offering a unit to the French. Although they were accepted, Gleichen said the situation turned into a farce as the French tried to confiscate the equipment for their own use. Appalled at their duplicity, the two women went instead to the Italian front. Now affiliated with the joint committee of the Red Cross and St John Ambulance, the women remained in Italy for the next two years. They were attached to the Italian army, wore khaki uniforms (the blue Red Cross uniform was considered too conspicuous near the front) and both were given the rank of major so that they could hold their own in the military hospitals and first aid posts that they worked in. This is not to say that they did not have confrontations with soldiers from different regiments who were unfamiliar with their work as radiologists and accused them of being spies.

In contrast to British women doctors, Flora Murray says that French women doctors found themselves in a less favourable position. Many took on subordinate posts in hospitals as dressers, orderlies and nurses[44] and Murray felt that they had ultimately failed to assert themselves. Compared to Britain, there were fewer qualified women medics in France and even in peacetime they had faced a greater struggle than their British counterparts to secure employment on a par with men. The campaign for women's suffrage in France was not as strong nor as advanced as the British campaign, and Murray found that they didn't share the same drive and ambition as she did. Murray and Louisa Garrett Anderson met with a group of French women doctors in Paris who complained that without surgical experience, all-women hospitals like those in Britain, or a representative council, they simply did not have the same opportunities. At the start of the war they had applied to military hospitals, but their offers had been quickly dismissed. Both Murray and Garrett Anderson declared, however, that it was up to the women to create their own opportunities as they themselves had done.[45] There was one French woman who was prepared to take on the challenge and she was Dr Nicole Girard Mangin.

Before the war, Dr Nicole Mangin had married André Girard, but after the birth of their son, the couple had divorced and their son was brought up by his father. Mangin chose to return to medicine, working in hospitals where she specialised in tuberculosis and contagious diseases. Her choice to retain her ex-husband's surname led to a administrative error in August 1914 that would set her on course to becoming the first French woman doctor to attain a military rank. Like other French women medics, Mangin registered for duty, but when a clerk misread her name, Girard Mangin, as Gerard Mangin, she was officially mobilised on 2 August 1914.

At first Mangin was posted to a hospital in Paris before being sent to a hospital situated in a former health spa in Bourbonne-les-Bains, over 180 miles to the south-east of the capital. When she arrived, the chief medical officer, a captain, was horrified that he had been sent a woman and was embarrassed that she was a member of his staff. Numerous times the captain wrote to his superiors demanding that she was removed, but each time he was refused. Her paperwork was in order (if somewhat ambiguous) and she had been officially enrolled. The army had a shortage of doctors and as far as they were concerned Mangin should be allowed to continue her duties if she wished. The hospital had to provide Mangin with accommodation, a wage and a tobacco ration, although she didn't smoke. Despite the hostile reception she received, Mangin was prepared to stick it out. At that time the French army still wore its traditional blue coat and red trousers, but quickly the French realised how visible they were on the battlefield and in 1915 replaced it with the 'horizon blue' uniform. Mangin was not provided with a uniform so she put one together herself which looked very similar to the uniform of the British women doctors rather than the French: a flat cap and a long green tunic with large flat pockets.

The spa at Bourbonne-les-Bains was large, but it was not suitably furnished or ready to be used as a hospital. Therefore, in order to keep busy, and because she was practically minded, Mangin set about adapting the building. After obtaining the approval of her superiors, she organised several wards with the help of her nurses ready to receive patients. She acquired a baker's oven, which was used to sterilise the surgical instruments, and she prepared splints in advance. Her proactivity paid off, as only a week after arriving, Mangin was asked to go and meet a train which was expected to have a number of civilian refugees needing treatment. Instead, Mangin found a hospital train full of seriously wounded soldiers. She did her best to make arrangements to remove the most serious cases (those who were unlikely to survive a further train journey) and to take them to her hospital. The men had been evacuated from nearby conflicts in Vosges and Lorraine.

In the autumn of 1914, Mangin requested a transfer to a hospital in Reims, the town where both her father and her brother were living. Knowing that the town was under bombardment, she thought she could do more valuable work there. She exchanged posts with a colleague and found herself in charge of a hospital train. Warned by others that it was a great responsibility, she worked extremely hard. Pleased with her performance, her new chief medical officer gave her the official grade of 'Auxiliary Doctor of the Army Health Service', but in terms of money and status she was only equivalent to a frontline nurse.

At the start of the winter of 1914–15, the commander of the Health Service decided that Mangin would be better off in Verdun, a region that the French army anticipated would be fairly quiet. Verdun was a fortified town surrounded by nineteen forts, fourteen of which had been reinforced by concrete.[46] A friend gave Mangin, in her new role, a female puppy which she called 'Dun' (an abbreviation of Verdun), which accompanied her everywhere. A single woman on her own at the front, Mangin was grateful for Dun who would go with her as she did her hospital rounds on her own at night. Dun became Mangin's faithful companion, protecting her from any unwanted attention.

Indeed, for 1915, Verdun was relatively quiet compared to the rest of the Western Front. Mangin worked in a number of different hospitals in the Verdun area before settling into work at a typhoid hospital (Glorieux No.13) where she remained for a year. She was working in the same hospital the following year in February 1916 when the German army launched a surprise assault on Verdun.

The defences of Verdun had been seriously neglected and it lacked any substantial heavy artillery. Concerns had been raised in the French army as late as December 1915 that the fortifications should be reinforced, but work did not begin until the end of the following January. The Germans had planned their assault for early February, but delayed it by nine days due to a heavy blizzard. These nine days were invaluable to the French as they worked on their defences, but ultimately they were heavily outnumbered with two divisions against Germany's nine divisions.[47] The Germans made rapid progress and the French were seriously worried about losing Verdun.

Mangin was given orders to evacuate current patients to make way for the incoming wounded. However it was a long, laborious process as the hospital only had one ambulance which it had to share with another hospital a little distance away which housed patients with contagious diseases. Despite the risk of infection, they spent the week working day and night to deliver the patients to the woods where they waited to be placed on board a hospital train. Compared to the Germans who had access to extensive rail networks behind their frontlines to remove wounded and bring in fresh troops, at Verdun the French only had one narrow gauge rail and one main road.[48] During the course of the week it began to snow, making the conditions for the evacuation of the patients via the forest even worse.

Back in the hospital the medical staff had to work despite heavy bombardment. When they lost their electricity they had to rely on candles and paraffin lights. The speed of German advance meant that inevitably Mangin's hospital was given full evacuation orders. However Mangin did not want to abandon the worst patients, fearing for them should the Germans overrun the hospital. She successfully appealed to the chief medical officer to be allowed to remain with the worst patients who could not risk being moved. It was an extremely brave decision as the Germans were expected to arrive at any moment. However, when the conditions at the hospital became intolerable, Mangin was ordered to evacuate and her superiors would not take no for an answer. The patients were to be taken to another hospital further from the line of fire. Given the proximity of the fighting, the evacuation was extremely risky. At one point a shell hit the windscreen of the ambulance and Mangin was superficially wounded by the shattering glass, but she and the medical staff continued until all the patients had been moved.

Arriving at the new hospital, Mangin was asked to see Inspector-General Mignon immediately and to give him a full report of all events in Verdun. This time Mangin, with nearly two years' experience in the army, was more assertive and used the opportunity to demand that from now on she should be treated as an officer. Her request was escalated to senior officers, and five months later (October 1916) she was given a decree confirming her officer status as a Doctor Major, 2nd Class, and she was to be awarded back-pay retrospectively. Her pay was the equivalent to that of a lieutenant and she remained working in hospitals at the Verdun front throughout 1916. Money was of secondary importance to her; instead status was her principal concern. She knew that she deserved to have been given a rank and to be on equal footing with her male colleagues.

The battle of Verdun continued until mid-December 1916. Ultimately it was a French victory as France managed to hold on to Verdun and retake most of the territory it had lost, but the losses were great on both sides. The Germans had a total of 81,600 casualties and the French 89,000.

Mangin continued to work in hospitals near the front as well as to drive ambulances. More than once she ventured into no-man's-land to retrieve wounded men. On one occasion recounted in her diary, she came across a group of soldiers hiding in the trenches who were incredulous at her audacity brazenly to go over the top. She later transferred to work at the Edith Cavell hospital in Paris.[49] As with Britain, France experienced a great shortage of qualified doctors and began allowing women to take up posts further behind the lines to release male doctors to the front. It wasn't until 1918 that France officially awarded the rank of assistant surgeon, second-class, to women doctors employed in its military hospitals.[50]

Although the United States did not join the Allies until 1917, the nation actively supported many fundraising projects for the European War, ranging from the provision of ambulance vehicles to supporting voluntary medical units and providing many volunteers. The philanthropic support given by countries from around the globe during the war was of vital importance. In addition to providing resources for the military, they supported voluntary groups which did a great deal to alleviate the suffering of civilians caught up in the conflict. In Serbia, for example, the Scottish Women's Hospital treated the local population where it was based as well as soldiers. The story of Ruth Farnam, an American, illustrates how much Serbia recognised and appreciated this support.

Like Drs LeVasseur and Matthews, Farnam was determined to go out to Serbia to help during its crisis. She was friends with Mabel Grouitch, the American wife of a Serbian minister, who was instrumental in co-ordi-nating the Serbian Relief Fund. In August 1913 Farnam had gone out to Belgrade with Grouitch during the Second Balkan War and worked as a hospital administrator. Early in 1915, Farnam applied to join the Serbian Relief Fund, but despite her experience of Serbia during wartime, she was rejected for lack of official qualifications, for she was neither a doctor nor a trained nurse. Instead, Farnam travelled out with another American friend, Princess Alexis Karageorgevitch, whose husband was the cousin of the Serbian King, Peter I. Working with the royal couple, Farnam once more acted as a hospital administrator co-ordinating valuable medical supplies.

At the end of the summer, as the epidemic receded, Farnam returned to England to secure more supplies. But that autumn, the Central powers invaded Serbia, gaining control of most of the country. Unable to return to Serbia, Farnam travelled home to the USA and raised funds for a new 'American' unit of the Scottish Women's Hospital in partnership with the Serbian Relief Committee of America.

In the autumn of 1916, Farnam returned to Eastern Europe to conduct a review for the committee, and met with Dr Agnes Bennett who was now working with the American unit after Inglis had recruited her earlier in the year. In October, after Farnam had completed her work and prepared to leave, she was invited by the chief of the Serbian army's medical service, Colonel Dr Sondermayer, to travel with him to the front. Climbing up to an observation post, the officers accompanying Farnam invited her to give the signal for the Serbians to recommence firing on the Bulgarians. Farnam recalls that the honour filled her with emotion and that as she gave the signal 'in the name of American Womanhood', the Serbian sol-diers shouted 'Givela Amerika!'[51]

Farnam's account, which was written in 1918 during the last year of the war, did much to promote the friendship between the USA and Serbia, and to encourage more fundraising. In recognition of Farnam's stirling work, but also perhaps to enable her further to expand her fundraising capabilities, the officers made Farnam a member of the First Cavalry Regiment of the Royal Serbian Army as she stood on the battlefield. 'I was no longer a woman helper. I was now a soldier, and, as I write this, – the only American woman soldier in this great war.'

Back in the USA, Farnam received material from her Serbian friends which she had made up into a uniform and wore during her fundraising tours.

While in Serbia, Farnam had come across another American volunteer, Dr Rosalie Slaughter Morton. By now, Morton had moved from Washington DC and was running a practice in New York. During a trip to Canada in 1915 she was so impressed by the level of war work being undertaken there that throughout the following winter she regularly donated to different relief funds. It was during this time that Morton heard about the invasion of Serbia and how the army was forced to retreat over the mountains and was now stationed in Salonika on the Macedonian front. When two of Morton's friends, both male doctors, returned from a relief mission to Serbia, they told her all about the situation there, which only hardened Morton's resolve to go to Serbia herself. The medical head of the American Red Cross, Colonel Kain, was surprised by Morton's request to be sent to 'fever-ridden Serbia', but in the spring of 1916 he assigned her to escort medical supplies to the Serbian army.

Having crossed the Atlantic, Morton spent time in England waiting for the shipment to be prepared. She visited the Women's Hospital Corps at work in Endell Street and met with other women doctors and medical staff, looking at how their hospitals were run. Once she reached the Serbian front she visited the different SWH units to see how these all-women organisations worked, and then she took up a temporary position at a field hospital in Sedes, Macedonia. Here there was a least one other woman doctor, a laboratory expert from Poland. In the autumn, Morton was obliged to return to New York to look after her practice, but she fully intended to return.

During the winter of 1916–17 it looked more and more likely that America would join the war and Morton became involved in plans to mobilise the female doctors of the USA. Using all the knowledge she had gained from her observations of the military hospitals, the SWH and the SRF, she helped to organise the Women's Army General Hospital No. 1 to treat the wounded repatriated to the USA. Regardless of whether or not the USA joined the war, Morton was keen to set up a hospital unit which she herself could take to Europe. The USA declared war on the Central powers in April 1917 and Morton still hoped to return to Europe. However, she sacrificed her aspirations in order to oversee a large-scale scheme with the USA's Medical Women's National Association, to establish a series of women's units called the American Women's Hospitals (AWH) which served in both the USA and overseas. Morton's knowledge and understanding was fundamental to the scheme being successful. A small voluntary AWH group went out to France in August 1917 under Dr Esther Pohl Lovejoy, but it wasn't until the following year that they sent out their first hospital unit. Raising funds to finance the AWH took longer than expected but they received over 1,000 requests from women doctors wishing to join. In March 1918 the AWH became affiliated with the American Red Cross and sent out its first unit to the French village of Neufmoutiers, 25 miles outside of Paris in June 1918.[52] More units followed, treating both civilian and military patients beyond the Armistice in November and on into 1919.

At the same time, America's women doctors campaigned to be accepted into the USA military. The most recent legislation (1916) relating to the expansion of the USA's army medical corps stipulated the qualifications required from a civilian commissioned into the corps. However the wording was ambiguous, referring to the individual as a 'civilian' with no reference to gender. Furthermore, when war was declared, registration forms were sent to all qualified doctors on the assumption that they were all male. All of the women who completed their forms were as a consequence rejected, resulting in them petitioning the US war office. This culminated in a judicial ruling in August 1917 stating that at the time the legislation was made, 'civilian' was intended to mean 'male', as all army doctors were at that time men, and that women were not allowed to serve.[53]

For a group of four women doctors from Portland, Oregon, the definition of 'civilian' crossed over in the debate for women's suffrage. Oregon had awarded the vote to women in 1912 and now the women turned their attention to the military. In the spring of 1918 they drove to an officer training facility in Vancouver, Washington state. Armed with all the required paperwork and qualifications they demanded to be admitted, but they were refused.[54]

Before the end of the war, the USA did employ women on contract, but they held no rank and were given the same allowances as a 1st Lieutenant. At least fifty-six women did work as contract surgeons, prepared to accept their lower status, believing that it was more important to undertake the work whatever the conditions. The others, who felt contract work was a poor move professionally, continued to protest and instead joined voluntary organisations.[55]

Alongside the AWH was the Women's Overseas Hospitals (WOH) established by the National American Women's Suffrage Association in 1917. In February 1918 the WOH sent their first unit to France. They had expected to take charge of a refugee centre, but the German advance meant a change of plans and instead they were sent to a military hospital in northern France, near Senlis, close to the frontline. The medical officer in charge was unhappy that he had been sent women and apparently refused to give them any orders. As a result they spent the first thirty-six hours finding work for themselves cleaning and bandaging wounds and administering injections. Begrudgingly, the medical officer had to acknowledge their training and began to allow them to do surgical work: with the influx of patients he couldn't afford not to. The WOH sent out more units which treated refugees and soldiers who were recovering from gas attacks and did a large amount of work helping the people of Lorraine (on the French-German border) as they returned after the war to rebuild their lives.

Since the mid-1800s women doctors had achieved a great deal; being accepted at university, being allowed to practise medicine and establishing their own schools, hospitals and practices as well as taking up teaching positions. In 1914 no one could have predicted that the war would last nearly four and a half years and that there would be such a great loss of life, so the women campaigning to enlist at the beginning were opportunistic. Certainly the women's movement incorporated many of the women who had fought hard for a career in medicine and wanted equality. Those that wouldn't take no for an answer, such as the Women's Hospital Corps, the Scottish Women's Hospital and individuals like Draga Liocic and Nicole Mangin, provided ample evidence that women were perfectly capable. However it took most countries until 1916 to realise, or to admit that they could benefit from women doctors. Yet even then there were restrictions. Russia, which was one of the first countries to employ women in military hospitals, paid them significantly less than their male peers. In general women were restricted to hospitals in the rear or at home, away from the fighting and immediate danger. Once they were able to work alongside men, women demanded to be given official status, a comparative rank to the male officers, which, if awarded, was done begrudgingly.

When Elizabeth Garrett Anderson had bid farewell to the Women's Hospital Corps in 1914 she had hoped that the experiences of the women and the obstacles they would face would advance them professionally. Universities, particularly those in France, responded to the need for doctors by providing more places for women, but those that graduated at the end of the war with little or no surgical experience found themselves competing for employment against war veterans. Once the war was over, some universities chose no longer to admit women, but to return to their pre-war days. The First World War had provided a challenge, which the women rose to, surpassing expectations, but the fight for professional equality was by no means over.

Notes

1 Murray, Flora, *Women as Army Surgeons – Being the History of the Women's Hospital Corps in Paris, Wimereux and Endell Street, September 1914 – October 1919*, p.4.

2 Mary Anne Elston in, *Careers of Professional Women*, ed. Rosalie Silverstone and Audrey Ward, p.106.

3 Dyhouse, Carol, *Students: A Gendered History*, p.61.

4 Jensen, Kimberly, 'Volunteers, Auxiliaries and Women's Mobiization: The First World War and Beyond (1914-1939)' in Hacker, Barton C. and Vining, Margaret (eds), *A Companion to Women's Military History*.

5 Slaughter Morton, Rosalie, *A Woman Surgeon – The Life and Work of Rosalie Slaughter Morton*.

6 Clark, Linda L., *Women and Achievement in Nineteenth-Century Europe*, p.224.

7 Elston, M.A., 'Anderson, Elizabeth Garrett (1836–1917)', in *Oxford Dictionary of National Biography*.

8 Slaughter Morton, Rosalie 'A woman surgeon - the life and work of Rosalie Slaughter Morton'

9 Manson C. and Manson C., *Doctor Agnes Bennett*.

10 As quoted in Leneman, Leah, *Elsie Inglis*, p.34.

11 Harrison, Mark, *The Medical War*, p.4.

12 Ibid., p.5.

13 For more details on the role of the medics in the army see Harrison.

14 Pantelic, Ivana, 'Liocic (Liotchich-Milosevic), Draga (1855-1926)' in *A Biographical Dictionary of Women's Movements and Feminisms*.

15 Hutton, Marcelline, *Russian and West European Women, 1860–1939: Dreams, Struggles, and Nightmares*, p.88.

16 Hutton, Marcelline 'Women in Russian Society from the Tsar to Yeltsin', p 64, in Rule, Wilma and Noonan, Norma C. (eds), *Russian Women in Politics and Society*.

17 Whitehead, Ian R., *Doctors in the Great War*, p.108.

18 Elsa Winokurow in *Women Physicians of the World – Autobiographies of Medical Pioneers* ed. McGregor Hellstedt, Leone, p.13.

19 Ibid., p.15.

20 Jensen, Kimberly 'Volunteers, Auxiliaries and Women's Mobilization: The First World War and Beyond (1914-1939), p.192, in Hacker, Barton C. and Vining, Margaret (eds), *A Companion to Women's Military History*.

21 Daughter of Elizabeth Garrett Anderson.

22 Murray, Flora, *Women as Army Surgeons*, pp.3–4.

23 Ibid., p.5.

24 Ibid., pp.10–1.

25 Cicely Hamilton, who was a member of the Scottish Women's Hospital (formed by Doctor Elsie Inglis), wrote an article for the NUWSS journal 'The Common Cause' in which she reported that Elizabeth Garrett Anderson had said the same about the SWH. Garrett Anderson recognised the great opportunity that these all-women medical organisations had to demonstrate their skills and to prove that they were equally competent as their male peers. 'The Common Cause', journal of the NUWSS, 1914-1919, 24 December 1914, p.622, in the London Collection of documents, Scottish Women's Hospital Collection, Imperial War Museum as cited in Crofton, Eileen, *The Women of Royaumont: a Scottish Women's Hospital on the Western Front*.

26 Louisa Garrett Anderson to Elizabeth Garrett Anderson 17 September 1914: London Metropolitan University, The Women's Library, document 7LGA/2/1/06.

27 Murray, Flora, *Women as Army Surgeons*, p.39.

28 Leneman, Leah, 'Medical Women in the First World War – Ranking Nowhere' in British Medical Journal Vol. 307 no.6919 (18–25 December 1993), pp.1592–4.

29 Murray, Flora, *Women as Army Surgeons*, pp.85–6.
30 Finzi, Kate John, *Eighteen Months in the War Zone – The Record of a Woman's Work on the Western Front*, p.47.
31 Ibid., p.41.
32 Murray, Flora, *Women as Army Surgeons*, p.160.
33 Leneman, Leah, 'Medical Women in the First World War: Ranking Nowhere' in British Medical Journal Vol. 307 no.6919 (18–25 December 1993), pp.1592–4
34 Leneman, Leah, *In the Service of Life*, pp.2–4.
35 Ibid., pp.2–5.
36 Whitehead, Ian, *Doctors in the Great War*, p.109.
37 Murray, Flora, *Women as Army Surgeons*.
38 Whitehead, Ian, *Doctors in the Great War*.
39 Jensen, Kimberly, 'Volunteers, Auxiliaries and Women's Mobiilzation: The First World War and beyond (1914 - 1939)' in Hacker, Barton C. and Vining, Margaret (eds), *A Companion to Women's Military History*.
40 Hacker, Carlotta, *Indomitable Lady Doctors*.
41 Ibid., p.185.
42 The Australian and New Zealand Corps (ANZAC) was established in November 1914. The intention was to bring together the Australian and New Zealand troops, but the corps also contained British officers and men from the British Indian Army.
43 Manson C. and Manson C., *Doctor Agnes Bennett*.
44 Darrow, Margaret, *French Women and the First World War*.
45 Murray, Flora, *Women as Army Surgeons*, pp.69–72.
46 Martin, William, *Verdun 1916*.
47 Willmott, H.P., *World War 1*, p.138.
48 Ibid., pp.138–9.
49 Schneider, Jean-Jacques, *Nicole Mangin: Une Lorraine au Coeur de la Grande Guerre – L'unique femme médecin de l'armée française (1914–1918)*.
50 Jensen, Kimberly, 'Volunteers, Auxiliaries, and Women's Mobilization: The First World War and Beyond (1914-1939)' in *A Companion to Women's Military History* ed. Barton C. Hacker and Margaret Vining, p.191.
51 Farnam, Ruth, *Nation at Bay: What an American Woman Saw and Did in Suffering Serbia*, p.192.
52 Pohl Lovejoy, Esther, *Certain Samaritans*.
53 Bellafaire, Judith and Herrera Graf, Mercedes, *Women Doctors in War*, p.33.
54 Jensen, Kimberly, *Mobilising Minerva – American Women in the First World War*, pp.89–90.
55 Bellafaire, Judith and Herrera Graf, Mercedes, *Women Doctors in War*, p.35.

5

Wartime Resistance and Espionage

Although in the eyes of our enemies she was a spy, surely all right-minded people will consider that those who work in their *own* country and for their *own* people against a common enemy ought to be known by a more honourable name.

Princess Marie de Croy referring to Gabrielle Petit[1]

As Europe's armies settled into a protracted trench war, the role of the intelligence services became more important. They had the potential to break the stalemate and change the course of the war.[2] Officers in the trenches were ever fearful of spies amongst them, as seen by the way in which the British officers readily accused members of the FANY and Dorothy Lawrence of being spies and how Italian soldiers challenged Helena Gleichen's movements to and from the front with medical supplies. As the war progressed there were fewer and fewer civilians near the frontline because they had either abandoned their homes or had been evacuated. Therefore women working in and around the front seemed even more out of place and suspect. Yet it was the spies within the occupied civilian communities that proved to be of a greater concern to the different intelligence organisations.[3] Here, individuals had more freedom and the opportunity to take on a range of guises. In the civilian world, any information that was gathered could be carried away from the front, away from the concentration of soldiers and over the border to neutral or friendly countries. Therefore, different countries established intelligence bureaux in neutral countries such as Holland and Spain. Spy novels such as Conrad's *The Secret Agent* (1907) or *Under Western Eyes* (1911) had become extremely popular in the years leading up to the conflict. Although fictionalised accounts of male spies, they featured women living lives of skulduggery with the exotic Natalie Haldin or the murderous Mrs Verloc and her conniving husband. Amidst this world of fiction, the idea grew of a *femme fatale*, a woman who would use her feminine charms to seduce the enemy in order to obtain information. This was in part a reaction to the women's movement and the rise of the 'New Woman'. It reflected society's fears that such assertive, strong-willed and independent women were 'sexually voracious and decadent' and did not 'recognise the boundaries of appropriate behaviour'.[4] In his memoirs, Henry Landau, an officer in wartime British military intelligence had to clarify that:

> The beautiful female spy is not an essential to every Secret Service coup – she rarely figured in our wartime services … nor is drugging or rifling of safes and strong-boxes a common practice. Physical violence is an exception, and so also is the carrying of firearms or any other weapons, even as a means of defence.[5]

In reality, the majority of female spies were ordinary people. It was a basic rule that undercover agents dressed inconspicuously so that they could blend in and pass unnoticed.[6] A great number of women involved in espionage were either unable to tell their story or chose to return to a life of anonymity. 'The spies who were caught and shot and whose cases attracted the greatest publicity were not always the greatest spies.'[7]It is important to differentiate resistance from espionage. Resistance against the occupying forces developed in response to an enemy that was greatly disliked and also perceived as having committed many crimes against people and their property. As well as patriotic duty, resistance developed from an obligation to protect life. Acts of resistance ranged from providing escape routes for soldiers caught in enemy-occupied territory to circulating underground newspapers and war propaganda. There were many resistance networks operating in German-occupied France and Belgium, with some individuals working for more than one group. It is a common misunderstanding that the British nurse Edith Cavell was tried and executed by the Germans for espionage. In fact, she was not a spy, and was charged with treason for aiding Allied soldiers. Of course, resistance and espionage were not mutually exclusive and sometimes went hand in hand. Acts of espionage ranged from collating information on the movement of troops and military supplies to sabotage. The Germans responded by enforcing more laws, strengthening the frontiers between Belgium and neutral Holland and developing their counter-espionage service. By 1916, following a number of high profile arrests and trials of civilians by the Germans, the situation became more difficult for the Allies' intelligence bureaux and their remaining agents to operate. As a consequence, the Allied networks that operated in the latter half of the war were more structured and organised.

Occupied Belgium and France

The invasion of Belgium happened so quickly that its civilians had little warning that the enemy was about to arrive and precious little time to decide what to do. Did they stay and protect their property or did they take their families and flee for their lives? Belgium and its people were proud, and had refused to permit German troops to march through the country to invade France's borders. From the moment Germany invaded Belgium it became the aggressor and Belgium the victim. There are many accounts from this period that the invading army was brutal: treating civilians badly, desecrating churches, appropriating food supplies, destroying anything they could not consume, and stealing valuables. For those living in the occupied zone, it was as if their own homes had become a prison. The local German commandant issued directives, curfews were enforced and movement between towns and cities was restricted as the occupiers endeavoured to control the civilian population.

Resistance groups began to develop in response to the occupation, along with a general dislike of the Germans, but in some cases it took time for these to connect and form an effective network. As the Allies retreated, wounded men were left behind, and in the chaos others became separated from their regiments. Upon discovery of an allied soldier who was stranded behind enemy lines, the individual Belgian faced a moral dilemma: should one turn over for imprisonment an ally, a man who had fought for one's freedom and who might need medical care, or ought one to conceal him, thereby risking being imprisoned, or worse, shot.

One of the most documented of the early resistance networks began in August 1914 at the de Croy family home, Bellignies, which was situated on the French side of the Belgian border near the town of Bavay[8]. Approximately 14 miles to the north-east was the Belgian town of Mons where, on 23–24 August, the British Expeditionary Force tried and failed to hold the line against the German advance. Only a few days before, the locals had turned out onto the streets to cheer the Allied soldiers as they marched heroically to battle. The de Croys, Princess Marie and her brother Prince Reginald[9], had entertained some of the British officers at their home, never imagining that the German army would reach Bellignies. On 24 August, the de Croys heard reports that there were casualties from Mons lying by the roadsides and at nearby farms, so the prince and his chauffeur went to look for the wounded and bring them back to Bellignies, where his sister could treat them. The princess had trained as a nurse and the family had offered its house as a Red Cross hospital should it be needed.

Later that day the British returned, but this time in full retreat. Defeated and heavily outnumbered, they had no alternative. The de Croys managed to evacuate most of their patients, sending them to the hospital at Bavay or finding retreating groups who would take them, but the next day when the first German officers arrived, they still had several patients in their care. Fearing that anyone found with firearms would be shot, the princess had disposed of her patients' weapons in an old cistern. She was horrified that when several German officers entered the house at Bellignies, they forced the patients out of bed to ascertain whether or not the men were faking their injuries. Satisfied, they allowed the wounded men to return to their beds.

In the weeks that followed, the de Croys made regular visits to the hospital at Bavay, which housed both British and French patients who were now prisoners of war. They acted as translators because they both spoke English, and the prince took the opportunity to find out more about the current military situation. Following the occupation, the community had become cut off. They did not know which accounts of the war were true and which ones were just rumour and propaganda. The de Croys were surprised when, in the hospital, they discovered one of the officers they had treated on the day of the retreat, a Captain Preston. They had hoped that he had been evacuated, and were dismayed to find out otherwise. The prince discreetly offered Preston a place to hide once he was fit enough to escape. On 7 October, Preston managed to get away in the middle of the night and the de Croys concealed him behind a false wall in an old tower within the house at Bellignies. The next challenge the de Croys faced was how to get Preston out of the occupied zone.

At the end of September, the de Croys came into contact with a pair of French women who would play a significant part in their escape network. One day Louise Thuliez and her friend Henriette Moriame arrived at Bellignies, wishing to talk with the prince. Thuliez had been staying with Moriame in the nearby village of St Waast La Vallée when the Germans arrived. Together they had set up a makeshift hospital at Moriame's home and 'collected' a small group of soldiers. They had hung a Red Cross banner outside the house to make it look official, but they worried that it was only a matter of time before their patients were transferred to Germany. They had managed to delay this so far by offering to pay for all their patients' food and medical care. Unsure of what to do next, they hoped that the prince, a well-respected man with good social connections, would be able to help, which he did. He arranged for the women to hide the men in a property concealed in the nearby Mormal Forest, and for the mayor to announce publicly that the men had escaped after the women were unable to stop them. Thuliez and Moriame then began going on long walks around the countryside, looking for more soldiers and making contacts in the different parishes (in her diary, the princess referred to Thuliez and Moriame as the 'Girl Guides').[10] Thuliez's brother had trained as a priest, and she used her family connections with the church to build up a large network of helpers.[11]

The men were safe in the Mormal Forest for the time being, but the question of how to get them out of the country remained. There were rumours that the town of Lille was still in French hands, but there was no guarantee. At the beginning of the occupation, the de Croÿs' local postmaster had managed to walk the 50 miles to Lille, passing through the lines to collect a large amount of mail that had been accumulating. He returned, distributing the letters to the delight of all, and bringing news of the Allies' success at the Battle of Marne (5–12 September) in which they prevented the Germans from reaching Paris. However, as the postmaster set out a second time to take the local post to Lille, he was arrested by the Germans for carrying information and imprisoned.[12] Shortly afterwards, a priest was shot for delivering letters he'd collected from Dunkirk.[13]

As the 'Girl Guides' went on their rounds, they hoped to find someone who knew a way out. Instead, they discovered a large group of about forty soldiers who had made a camp in the forest near Englefontaine. The men were happy in their camp, supplied by helpers from the local village. Most of the villagers knew the men were in the forest, so only one small indiscretion on their part could lead the Germans straight to them. The men themselves could also be reckless, leaving marks on trees so that they could remember how to reach the camp, and trying to blow up a nearby railway line. They only achieved minimal damage, but Thuliez knew that acts of sabotage would raise suspicion.[14]

At the end of October and into November, the Germans began to search the forests systematically. The men had decided to build a new dug-out a short distance from their camp. They were away working on it when a German patrol stumbled onto the camp. The patrol waited for the men to return and fire was exchanged, but the men managed to get away. About thirty of them managed to regroup at the dug-out, and, on hearing of the episode, Captain Preston asked Thuliez to take him to the forest. He wanted to have a conference with Lieutenant Bushell, the one officer in the group. The men agreed that if the situation became too risky, Preston would order them to abandon the forest and make their way to Bellignies. As Thuliez guided Preston away from the forest, she says that he asked her to take charge of the situation and do the right thing. He appointed her a 'captain'. For Thuliez this was an honour and she took her responsibility to the men very seriously. The Girl Guides spread the rumour that the men had left of their own accord, but less than two weeks later, the searches had got too close for comfort and their helpers from the nearby village became too nervous to bring supplies to the men. The time had come to leave. The men destroyed the evidence of their new camp and anything that might have incriminated those who had helped them. Thuliez describes their journey to Bellignies:

> To avoid giving the alarm in the occupied villages through which we had to go, the men put their socks over their boots, slung their rifles on their backs and their rugs and coats around them, and with what remained of the provisions made up into hasty bundles, they set out upon their march in the dark forest. It was eleven o'clock at night.
>
> We had divided the men into two groups. Mlle Moriame led the way with the first and I followed at a short distance with Lieutenant Bushell and the second group. It was not without some trembling that we accomplished the journey ... We had to cross three occupied villages and for some time we followed the high road, which was furrowed with German motorists and patrols.[15]

Bushell stayed in the house with Preston, while the remaining men stayed in the attic of the porter's lodge. Preston and the de Croys were concerned; it was getting colder, they were running low on food and they did not know how they would keep the men concealed for long. It was decided that if a route out of Belgium was not discovered soon, the men would have to surrender themselves, but that Bushell and Preston as officers would remain in hiding in the Bellignies tower.[16] Thuliez was devastated by the idea, and she and Moriame searched relentlessly for a way out, or for someone who could help, but to no avail.

Before handing themselves in, the soldiers had to be smartened up. The small resistance group went to great trouble to make their uniforms complete so as to avoid any suspicion that they were spies or incriminate anyone who may have given them clothes to keep warm. They all agreed that, when questioned, they would deny that anyone had helped them. So with heavy hearts, the Girl Guides escorted the men to Bavay so that they could turn themselves in at the Red Cross Hospital. Thuliez says that she tried to persuade them to escape, saying that she would help them, but the men would not disobey their orders. A few days later, when it began to snow, she accepted that they had been right and that they could not have gone on living in the forest. The men were imprisoned for the remainder of the war.[17]

Bushell and Preston remained living with the de Croys until December, when a family friend, the French Countess Jeanne de Belleville, brought them some important news. She had a son who was near military age and she had been keen to get him to Holland. Her investigations had led her to a priest, the Abbé de Longueville, who was prepared to guide her son across the frontier to Holland. The mission was a success, and so arrangements were made immediately for de Longueville to take the two officers next. The princess used an old camera to take photos of the men and the prince obtained false papers from a Belgian friend working in the *Bureau de la Population*. When his German superintendent left for a meal break, he agreed to acquire the necessary forms and stamps for the prince.[18]

Once they had the documents, the next step was for the men to travel to Mons from where they could take the tram to Brussels. The men were dressed in civilian clothes and according to their passports were 'hair-dressers' assistants'. Neither of them could speak French, so they had to be careful not to talk. Arriving early for the tram, Thuliez and Moriame, who had taken the men to Mons, took them to have lunch in a hotel, only to find that it was full of Germans. Thuliez said, in later years, that Bushell would often recall 'the dreadful moment in the cloak-room, after lunch when a German officer passed him the towel on which to dry his hands.'[19]

The chief risk that the men faced on the tram journey was the routine inspection of all papers at Enghien. Rather than test their fake papers, the group waited for the inspectors to board the tram, and then stepped off onto the pavement, getting back on once the inspectors had moved on to a carriage further down the line. Reaching Brussels they were met by the Countess de Belleville who took them to a safe house until de Longueville was ready to take them the next stage. Once more, de Longueville succeeded in getting his charges to Holland and both men were able to return to active service.[20] Now the group had an effective escape route, they could conduct more soldiers to safety.

During the winter the prince obtained permission to go to Holland. His main excuse was that he needed to withdraw money, because the smaller branches in the occupied zone were closed and the main banks in Brussels only had small cash reserves. But he also wanted information, to find out how the war was really going. He travelled to England, to London, and brought with him lists of the wounded from the local hospitals and the names of those they had helped to bury. As with the lists that Grace Ashley-Smith had brought back from Antwerp, this information was of great importance to the War Office, allowing them to account for soldiers missing in action.

On his return to Belgium, the prince received many requests from people wanting news of their sons, brothers and fathers who were presumed to be somewhere in the occupied territories. In particular, one woman asked the prince to trace her husband, Colonel Boger. The last thing she had heard was that he had been looked after by a British nurse in Brussels.[21] On his return to Belgium, the prince investigated and discovered that the British woman was called Edith Cavell. In her late forties, Cavell is described as having been 'very tall and distinguished'[22] and a most strict teacher. In 1907 she had been invited by the Belgian surgeon Dr Depage to become the matron of a new nursing school, which she had established in the Belgian capital. When Boger had been wounded in battle, he had been left for dead. Yet he had managed to get to a nearby convent where he received treatment. Then, with local help, he and an NCO, Sergeant Meachin, had made their way to Brussels. On arrival, their guide was unable to find them a safe house so began to make discreet enquiries. The guide spoke with Madame Depage, wife of Dr Depage, who immediately recommended that they go to the school and ask for Cavell. After treating the men for their injuries, which had been exacerbated by their journey, Cavell helped them find lodgings and secure a guide to reach Holland.[23] Travelling separately, Boger was arrested and imprisoned, but Meachin succeeded in getting across.

From November 1914 through to July 1915, Cavell assisted men brought to her by the different escape networks[24], and through Cavell, the de Croys and the Girl Guides were able to find another way of getting men to Holland.

The Collapse of the de Croy-Cavell Network

The de Croy-Cavell network broke down in the summer of 1915, but by the spring of that year its members were already concerned that their operations had been discovered. The princess went to Brussels to meet Cavell in person, to discuss what to do, but Cavell reprimanded her for visiting, saying that the nursing school was being watched. The princess suggested they suspend all activities, but when she also mentioned that Thuliez had a group of thirty men in the Cambrai area, Cavell refused to stop, saying that the men needed them. However the Germans had now reinforced the Dutch-Belgian border with electric wires and increased their patrols.[25] It was getting more and more difficult to find a way through. The prince continued to travel to Holland and on to London, but now the German authorities in Belgium were suspicious of him. It did not help that those who made it across later wrote postcards to Cavell expressing their gratitude. Also a British newspaper published the account of several men who had escaped through Belgium after being concealed in a château in

northern France. The prince immediately contacted the War Office telling them to censor the newspaper and prevent any similar stories from
being published. But the damage was done, and both the postcards and
the newspaper were used as evidence against the members of the de Croy-
Cavell network at their trials.[26]

After a certain time spent watching their suspects, the German police
sent agents in undercover. The network had built up its contacts using
friends and family, relying on small communities where everyone knew
everyone else and you knew who could be trusted. Therefore the Germans
posed as allied soldiers, the only part of the chain that wasn't known to its
members. Arriving at both Bellignies and the nursing school in Brussels,
the agent would speak without a hint of a German accent and request
help to get to the frontier. De Croy says that, knowing they were being
watched, she was on the alert and would not be taken in. Cavell was
equally cautious. However, one of the nurses at the school, Jacqueline van
Til, said that earlier in the year, one of the men housed at the school had
disappeared from the group *en route* to Antwerp, and there were genuine
concerns that he had been a spy.[27]

At the end of July, the German counter-espionage organisation made
its move. It began by arresting a number of the guides employed by the
network in quick succession. Next they arrested the Belgian architect
Monsieur Baucq, an accomplice operating in Brussels, along with Louise
Thuliez. Baucq and Thuliez had first met in April 1915, and he was an
enthusiastic distributor of copies of *La Libre Belgique*.[28] Thuliez had
arrived late in the evening at the Baucq family home to help prepare the
papers for distribution the following day when the German police burst
into the house. The police found ample evidence of Thuliez's involvement
in the escape network in her handbag: a coded notebook and a receipt
for the lodging of men in a safe house.[29] A few days later, on 4 August,
the police raided the nursing school, and the following day they arrested
Cavell and one of her nurses, Elisabeth Wilkins. Next the princess was
arrested, but the prince evaded capture and eventually reached Holland.

Sister Wilkins was soon released. Cavell had been careful to keep her
nurses a safe distance from her resistance work and ensured there was
nothing that would incriminate them. The German police now had thirty-
five men and women imprisoned in connection with the escape network.
Over the next eight weeks the prisoners were interviewed. The police
repeatedly asked the princess where the prince was hiding and placed
Cavell in solitary confinement.

The trial of the prisoners and their sentences would go on to make
international headlines. Cavell had been interrogated in French, and this

was then translated and recorded in German. Cavell's biographer Diana Souhami explains that Cavell's answers and her statement were deliberately mistranslated. For example, while Cavell had treated badly wounded men and helped them so that they could reach safety, her statement says that the men were only lightly wounded if at all, and that Cavell's agenda was to help them rejoin their armies so they could return to fighting. In the absence of the prince, the German police claimed that Cavell, as an English woman, was the principal co-ordinator of the network. The trial started on Thursday 7 October and each of the prisoners was dealt with at speed, with only ten minutes of questioning each. On Monday 11 October the prisoners were informed of their sentences. Cavell, Thuliez, the Countess of Belleville, Baucq and a man called Severin were condemned to death, and the rest were sentenced to hard labour or acquitted. Both Cavell and Baucq were to be executed at 7 a.m. the following morning on Tuesday 12 October. The Marquis de Villalobar, the Spanish minister and the American legation tried to intervene, but it was too little too late. Cavell accepted her judgement and was executed by firing squad. The British responded with outrage, declaring that they would not have executed any of their female prisoners. The propaganda mill went into overdrive, Cavell became a saintly martyr and the British government ensured that the story was circulated around the globe. The three other death sentences were reduced to long-term imprisonment, and the Countess de Belleville and Thuliez were sent to Siegburg prison in Germany along with the Princess de Croy. The German Kaiser tried to distance himself from the whole affair, saying that no more women would be shot, but he, or his officers, did not keep his word.[30] Nor was Cavell the first woman to have been executed: four months previously, on 6 June 1915, the Germans had executed a Belgian widow called Louise Derache. The twenty-seven-year-old was in the habit of going to the market in Maastricht, Holland, once a week, posing as a butter merchant. She would collect and bring back false passports concealed in the false bottom of one of her panniers.[31]

Espionage

Meanwhile, as those in the occupied zone tried to establish links with the outside world, their allies were looking for a way in. On arrival in Britain, all refugees were interviewed by the British authorities. This was to ensure that they were genuine refugees (not spies) and to gather information from them about the occupied zone which might be useful. At the same time the British were looking for potential recruits, individuals who would be willing to return to the occupied areas and spy on their behalf. This was how they came across Louise de Bettignies from the French town of Lille, which had come under German control in late October after heavy bombardment. De Bettignies had managed to escape and get to Folkestone on the English coast. De Bettignies impressed the British by the way she presented herself and the detailed account she gave of events. She was also fluent in French, German, Italian and English.[32] The British were keen to employ her, but de Bettignies was hesitant. First she wanted to go to free France to find her family, from whom she had been separated. Whilst in France, she was also invited by the French to join their secret service. Having found her family safe, de Bettignies made her decision. She chose the British over the French because they were able to provide their agents with more money than their allies. As the de Croÿ-Cavell group discovered, running a network was an expensive business.

Aged thirty-four, de Bettignies was an intelligent, well-educated woman who had studied at Oxford University. She was worldly, having travelled in Europe, spending time in both Italy and Austria. Yet after the war, her biographer Antoine Rédier presented her as an innocent young girl, barely out of her teens. In his words she was 'animated and lively' with a 'combination of youthful vivacity … light-hearted and gay.'[33] He explained that she was from a devout Catholic family and that she had nearly become a nun, seeking advice from her priest before choosing a life of espionage. This is an example of the fictionalisation of women's war stories, the need to make them into martyrs fighting for their country, with God on their side, while at the same time demonizing the enemy. Rédier justifies de Bettignies' role as a spy by presenting her as a victim of war, presumably making her more acceptable to those reading his book. When describing the women guiding men to the frontier he says, 'though heroines of the war, [they] were frail creatures enough, and had the intuitive yearning of their sex for protection in danger.'[34] In fact de Bettignies was anything but a weak girl; she was a strong, determined woman who proved to be a very capable spy, receiving praise and commendations from her British employers.[35]

The British gave de Bettignies training which included learning to use codes, making up invisible inks, and basic military knowledge. In February 1915 she returned to France under the code name Alice Dubois.[36] Shortly afterwards she recruited Leonie Vanhoutte from Roubaix on the outskirts of Lille as her second-in-command, giving her the alias of Charlotte.[37]

De Bettignies obviously had a degree of charisma and must have been a reasonable judge of character, for she managed to build up a large network of contacts and informants. Her mission was to compile information on the movements of the German army. Reports ranged from the number of carriages in a train convoy to the number of troops and names of regiments being sent to the front, anything that could forewarn the Allies of a new offensive being planned or a change in strategy. In the same way that Dorothy Lawrence succeeded in getting to the front by only asking accomplices to help her with one stage of her plan, using her alias, de Bettignies limited what each person knew about the extent of the network and the details of the other members involved. That way, if someone was arrested it would limit the damage and the number of subsequent arrests so that the network could continue to operate. De Bettignies would collate most of the reports herself, meeting her informants at local markets and writing up their observations in the early hours of the morning. She wrote on thin sheets of rice paper in tiny handwriting that required a magnifying glass to read. She then travelled to Holland and on to England to deliver the reports in person in London. She did this between fifteen and twenty times.[38] In the summer of 1915, the collapse of the de Croy-Cavell network caused de Bettignies some concern as she shared a number of the guides and members who had been arrested, but her network continued to function until the autumn. In October 1915, both de Bettignies and Vanhoutte together with others from their network were arrested. Rédier suggests that de Bettignies had become too confident and had started to take unnecessary risks. Both de Bettignies and Vanhoutte were sentenced to imprisonment and encarcerated in Siegburg Prison in Germany.

Another woman recruited by British intelligence was a Belgian called Gabrielle Petit. She grew up in the town of Tournai and later moved to Brussels. At the start of the war she was engaged to a young Belgian soldier who took part in the defence of Liège where he was wounded. Together, Petit and her fiancé made the bold decision to travel to Holland so that he could rejoin the army. On arrival in Holland they were interviewed at the British military headquarters and, as with de Bettignies, Petit was enlisted as a spy. She proudly declared that while her fiancé was away fighting at the front, she too could fight for victory behind the lines. She returned to Tournai where she had grown up and in addition to passing on military information she helped distribute the allied publication *La Libre Belgique* which both Baucq and Thuliez had circulated.[39] On 20 January 1916, Gabriele Petit's luck ran out and she was arrested and taken to the same prison where Cavell had been held the previous summer, St Gilles in Brussels. Allegedly the judge asked Petit what she would do if the Kaiser sanctioned her release. She defiantly replied that she would continue in her work. As a consequence, the judge sentenced her to death, despite the Kaiser's assurances that this would not happen following Cavell's execution. While the executions that followed that of Cavell did not command

the same international outcry, all accounts of Petit's death include a powerful demonstration of unwavering patriotism. On 1 April 1916 when
she faced the firing squad, Petit shouted out, 'You will see how a Belgian
woman will die!'[40]

Another woman who was executed for the same cause made an equally
strong pro-Belgian statement. Elise Grandprez who lived in the Ardennes
region of Belgium worked for British intelligence alongside her two brothers and her sister. In January 1917, Grandprez, one of her brothers, and
a family friend, were arrested and all given the death penalty. Apparently
at her execution Grandprez got hold of a red, black and yellow drape, the
colours of the Belgian flag, which she held onto after being blindfolded
and called out, 'Long live Belgium!'.[41]

Prison

The women who escaped the death penalty were sentenced to imprisonment or hard labour. De Bettignies, the Princess de Croy, Louise Thuliez
and the Countess de Belleville were all sent to Siegburg Prison which was
situated about 9 miles north-east of Bonn in the Rhine Valley in Germany.
The prison had two separate wings, one for men and one for women. It
is estimated that in the last few years of the war 'at least three hundred
women political prisoners moved through' the prison.[42]

On arrival at the prison, the women were processed, their papers
checked and their identities confirmed, and then they were taken to the
bath-house to be stripped, washed and given their prison uniforms. Those
who were sentenced to hard labour wore a brown blouse and skirt; the
others wore grey. With this they wore stockings and a neckerchief which
were both blue and white striped, a white apron and sandals. From 1917,
due to a clothing shortage, the women were allowed to wear their own
clothes. As one can imagine, the prison was a truly depressing place. The
cells measured 12 by 8ft and were 9ft high. The bed consisted of a narrow
wooden plank with only basic bedding. During the winter the cells were
not heated; instead the women were supplied with extra blankets and
woollen underwear in order to try and keep warm.[43]

Woken at 7 a.m. every morning, the prisoners' daily meals consisted of
black bread and coffee for breakfast, a vegetable soup (that generally had
bugs floating in it) for lunch, more black bread and coffee in the afternoon and then a bowl of thin gruel in the evening. The oil lamps in the
prison were only lit for a short period each day, meaning that during the
winter, the prisoners spent many hours in their cells sitting in darkness.

The women were given needlework, clothes making and menial tasks. When Louise de Bettignies discovered that the women were expected to help assemble munitions for use against their own men, ever defiant, she led a boycott. As punishment she was placed in solitary confinement, in wintertime, without extra clothing for warmth. She contracted pneumonia, from which her health never fully recovered.

The hospital doctor failed to provide proper treatment for the women. Quick to dismiss their ailments, they called him Dr 'Sortez' as he always demanded they 'get out' of his office. Towards the end of 1917, de Bettignies discovered that she had a growth, a large tumour. Although the prison doctor was not an expert in her condition, he undertook to operate on it at Siegburg in April 1918, but this was not a success. Over the next five months, de Bettignies's health worsened and she was then transferred to a hospital in Cologne where she died on 17 September 1918.[44]

Mata Hari

The name most famously associated with female espionage in the First World War is undoubtedly that of the Dutch dancer, Mata Hari. An international celebrity since arriving on the scene in 1905, her dances were overtly sexual, a spectacle of revealing costumes and nudity, which, at the beginning of her career, attracted large audiences, high fees and an extremely long list of male lovers. As a consequence her war story captured the public imagination and her story has been retold and re-imagined many times over. She was believed to be a true *femme fatale*, when in reality she was a victim of circumstance.

Her real name was Margaretha Zelle and she was born on 7 August 1876. During her early childhood her father was devoted to her, spoiling her with many gifts and showing off to their neighbours. She relished the attention, but when her father filed for bankruptcy in 1889 and left his family, Zelle felt completely abandoned. Six years later, aged eighteen, she married a Dutch officer called Rudolf Macleod who was over twenty years her senior. They moved to the Dutch East Indies and had two children, but their relationship began to sour. Macleod was jealous of the attention his young attractive wife received and disapproved of her frivolous expenditure, while he was a hard drinker and Zelle claimed he became physically abusive. Things deteriorated further when their son died in 1899, and in 1902 they legally separated, divorcing four years later. Their daughter remained with her father and Zelle embarked on the next chapter of her life. Zelle's early childhood contributed to creating a woman who loved being the centre of attention, wanted men to love her, and was determined to be restored to a luxurious lifestyle. The separation from her husband was a catalyst for change.[45]

Zelle went to Paris where she joined a circus troop and was encouraged to dance. She was a tall and attractive woman and throughout her career men referred to her striking beauty. Unlike the typical Dutch woman who generally had blonde or light brown hair and fair skin, Zelle had very dark hair and tanned skin which made her appear 'foreign', and when she had been in the Dutch East Indies, many had thought she was Indian. Her dance routines incorporated elements she had seen in the East Indies and her dark looks reinforced the image of an exotic dancer. She adopted the stage name of Mata Hari in 1905 and her career took off. She was paid a large amount for her performances, but at the same time she began to spend more and more on the lavish lifestyle she felt she deserved. Travelling across Europe to perform her dances, Mata Hari collected lovers in different cities who would bestow gifts and money upon her, which in turn supported her expensive needs. She did not see anything wrong with having multiple lovers and receiving money from men, however immoral it was in the eyes of society. After the first five or six years, Mata Hari's career was no longer as lucrative as it had been, because there were now other younger dancers with similar routines competing against her. In times of difficulty, she looked more and more to her lovers for financial support to an extent that was tantamount to prostitution. Generally Mata Hari's lovers were officers or senior politicians: she was attracted to men of high rank and wealth.

When the war started, Mata Hari was in Berlin, in the middle of a series of performances and enjoying the attentions of her German lovers. Although a Dutch citizen (and therefore neutral), she was a resident of France and she was keen to return home to secure her property. With France and Germany at war, overnight Mata Hari had become an enemy. The bank and her agent denied her access to her money and she had great difficulty trying to leave Germany. She was abandoned by her lovers, who did not want to be tainted by association. With the help of a fellow Dutchman who paid for her travel to Amsterdam, Mata Hari eventually made it to Holland, but not before all her belongings were confiscated.

Mata Hari then took up residence in the Hague, where she remained for most of 1915. In the autumn of that year, she was approached by Karl Kroemer, a German consul based in Amsterdam. He attempted to recruit her as a German spy and gave her 20,000 francs, which was a very large sum of money at the time. When interviewed later on, Mata Hari said that she accepted the money as compensation for everything she had lost in

Germany the previous year. She had no intention to spy, but treated it as a gift from a lover. During the winter of 1915–16, Mata Hari decided to leave the Hague and look for work, travelling to Paris, Spain and Portugal. When the boat she was travelling on stopped at Folkestone, the British interviewed Mata Hari several times. They were suspicious of this woman independently travelling through Europe. Mata Hari's accounts were sometimes contradictory and the admission that she had a lover (or two) meant that they labelled her as an immoral and untrustworthy woman. She was allowed to resume her travels, but was placed under watch, and the British forwarded their concerns to Paris. They declared that if she were to return to England she would be arrested, but Mata Hari was unaware of all this.

In the summer of 1916, Mata Hari was back in Paris and it was at this point that she met Georges Ladoux, head of French military intelligence. Subsequent accounts of their meeting differ, but there are several theories. The first theory is that Ladoux knew the British suspected Hari of being a German spy and was keen to find evidence to incriminate her and further his career, so he invited her to spy for France to gain her trust. Furthermore, Ladoux may have been a double agent himself and saw in Mata Hari an opportunity to create a scapegoat. Alternatively an incompetent Ladoux recruited her only to discover that she was a suspected enemy agent, and went to great efforts to cover his tracks and incriminate her, so as to look like he suspected her all along. Either way, there is little evidence that Mata Hari was actually a German agent.

According to Mata Hari, Ladoux agreed to pay her 1 million francs if she brought him some useful intelligence. Needing money, Mata Hari agreed to work for Ladoux, and in November 1916 she left for Holland. Yet when the boat stopped on the English coast she was arrested, not for being Mata Hari, but because they thought she was a woman called Clara Benedix, a German spy. There is not much information on Benedix except in relation to Mata Hari's story. The British had issued a warrant for Benedix's arrest. To confirm Mata Hari's identity the British contacted Ladoux, only for him to distance himself from her, claiming she was a known German agent and he had employed her in order to obtain evidence about her. On this basis the British refused her passage to Holland and instead she returned to Spain.

Unable to proceed to Holland and follow Ladoux's orders, Mata Hari decided to find a German officer in Madrid whom she could tap for information and who could earn her money. She chose a German intelligence officer called Kalle. She returned to Paris in January 1917 and tried to meet with Ladoux to collect the money, although she had not found out a great deal of information for him. However Ladoux was evasive and when they met he was dismissive of the information she had supplied. The French arrested Mata Hari in February and she was placed in solitary confinement in Paris's St Lazare Prison. The conditions were dire, far removed from the luxury she so loved, and over the following months, the harsh conditions, the affects on her health and the hardline interrogations broke Mata Hari's spirit. There was no evidence of any specific information that Mata Hari was supposed to have supplied to the Germans and it wasn't until April that Ladoux produced a series of telegrams sent by Kalle in Madrid which had been intercepted by the French. It is suspected that, keen to secure her conviction, Ladoux doctored the telegrams. Along with Mata Hari's admission that she had taken money from Kroemer, the telegrams were deemed sufficient grounds to incriminate her, and her trial was held in July 1917.

In her hour of need, Mata Hari was once again abandoned by her lovers, who did not want to be accused of espionage themselves. Only one testified on her behalf, Henri de Marguerie, but Mata Hari was condemned to death. Her lifestyle meant that she was viewed as an immoral woman, and a seductress, the worst type of woman, unlike Cavell who was transformed into a martyr, Louise de Bettignies who was reinvented as a good young Christian girl, or Gabrielle Petit and Elise Grandprez who were driven by patriotic duty. Mata Hari's arrest took place in 1917, a year in which the French army was suffering particularly low morale, men were mutinying and the Allies were coping with the loss of their ally Russia, which withdrew from the war following the Russian revolution and the abdication of the Tsar. Hari's arrest and the charges brought against her became symbolic in raising French morale against the Germans. She was denied an appeal and the Dutch were unable to reduce her sentence to imprisonment. She was executed on Monday 15 October 1917. Shortly afterwards, Ladoux was arrested for being a double agent. Because of his senior position and the fragility of French morale it was kept out of the public eye and Ladoux was not acquitted until May 1919.[46]

Marthe Richer

The same summer that Ladoux met Mata Hari, he also enlisted another female agent, Marthe Richer, whose story bears many similarities to that of Mata Hari. According to historian Margaret Darrow, 'Mata Hari's status as a best-seller after the war encouraged a few French women to audition for the part of her French equivalent' and one of the most successful claimants was Richer.[47]

After founding the Patriotic Union of Aviatrices at the beginning of the war, Marthe Richer had become a widow when her husband had died at Verdun in 1916. In June 1916, Ladoux says he received several messages relating to Richer. The first was from a young pilot: 'Beware of Madame Marthe Richard. She is a remarkably intelligent woman. She has been trying to get access to our training camps, and we have not succeeded in discovering what she wants to do there. She speaks German and might very possibly turn out to be a German agent.'[48]

The other was from a French aviation official:

I wish to recommend to you little Madame Richard. I have known her long, because she is the wife of a good friend of mine, now driving a truck at the front. She is very intelligent, but especially she is the most astonishingly high-spirited. After moving heaven and earth and doing everything imaginable to organise a free corps of women aviators, and then to secure permission to fly her own machines, she has just applied to me for permission to enlist in a man's clothes. And yet she is very much of a woman!

I think you could make use of her in your services. She speaks German fluently.[49]

Intrigued, Ladoux ordered a report on Richer, part of which he published in his biography, but he omitted the rest saying the information was classified. Twenty-seven-year-old Richer, née Belenfeld, had been born in the Alsace-Lorraine region when it was under German control, hence her fluency in the language. What Ladoux's informant did not say, or Ladoux chose not to print, was that the young Marthe Richer had been a prostitute in Nancy where she had apparently contracted a venereal disease before moving to Paris. Here, like Mata Hari, she reinvented herself. She came under the protection of Henri Richer who encouraged her to learn to fly and in 1907 became her husband.[50]

Through her marriage, Richer had succeeded in leaving behind her life of poverty to enter the upper social classes of Paris society and became an aviatrix celebrated for her daring and her near death experiences. In August 1913 she was involved in a flying accident and was widely reported to have died.[51] Ladoux invited Richer to his office and questioned her about her determination to join the French Air Force. Richer explained that she had become 'bored' waiting at home for her husband to return, and now that he had been killed she was determined that 'the Germans shall pay.'[52] The discussion then moved on to whether Richer would be prepared to become a French spy. Ladoux was sure that she could use her flawless German to persuade officers to talk. In her biography, Richer says Ladoux suggested she could also use her sex to her advantage:

> 'It will be difficult,' he replied. 'But then you have youth and intelligence – two great assets that will not fail to cajole our enemies.'
>
>   A sly smile lit up his rather alert face as he said these words. An acute psychologist, he tacitly demanded that I should use all my womanly wiles to succeed as a spy.[53]

Like Mata Hari, Richer went to Spain where she too acquired a German lover, this time a naval officer. According to her, she was forced into becoming a double agent in order to protect her true identity as a spy for France, rather than a disillusioned French woman wishing to escape the horrors of war.[54] After the war, Ladoux wrote a successful book about Mata Hari followed by an account of Richer. In the latter he makes his position clear. He describes Marthe Richer as a 'highly pedigreed French race-horse' whose cause was France, while Mata Hari was 'a Dutch half-breed' whose cause was German, 'where she had been adulated and treated like a queen, so that, whether from gratitude or arrogance, she had made of it her adoptive country.'[55] Yet after the war, when Richer established herself in a new career as a fiction writer, she was accused of fabricating her war story and the details of both hers and Ladoux's accounts are highly questionable.

Marthe Cnockaert

Marthe McKenna (née Cnockaert) was engaged by the British during the First World War and survived to write her memoirs in the 1930s. In a fast-paced account she skims over what she refers to as 'the normal routine of transmitting unimportant information, the arrival and departure of troops, the destinations of German regiments, and the like' for fear of sounding 'tedious'[56] and focuses on a series of missions that she was charged with. Perhaps having learned a lesson from the treatment of Mata Hari, and now being a respectable married woman, Cnockaert is careful when referring to the advances from or any flirtations with German soldiers. Each encounter is conveniently interrupted if it goes too far, or she runs away. On one occasion Cnockaert hopes to get information from a lecherous officer about activities at the local aerodrome and admits that she flirted with him and allowed him to kiss her. But when he tries to rape her she is rescued just in time by another officer, a pilot, who then invites her to dinner. When he becomes drunk he too tries to kiss her, and as he tries to grab her, Cnockaert manages to push him off and lock him in his room.

When the Germans arrived in her home village of Westrozebeke in West Flanders (about 10 miles north-east of Ypres), Cnockaert was part way through her medical degree at Ghent University. She took a nursing position at the hospital in the nearby town of Roulers and shortly afterwards she was approached by Lucelle Deldonck, an old family friend. Deldonck revealed that she worked for British intelligence and recruited Cnockaert, giving her the code name 'Laura'. The first mission Cnockaert recalls was organising a bombing raid on the local station when the ordnance train was in situ, but she had to find out when the next train was due. As a nurse she regularly escorted patients to the station and was aware that the German officer in charge there was sweet on her. When he offered her a cigarette she readily agreed, but said that she only smoked indoors, so he took her into his office where he served her tea. While they talked '[as] though by accident, I felt his podgy little hand close over mine. I did not move. I felt that he was becoming "malleable."'[57] Agreeing to go on a date with the officer, she looked over his shoulder as he consulted his diary and spied the date and time of the next ordnance train. In her account, this flirtation was deemed acceptable, because should the mission be successful (and it was) the officer would not survive to keep their date. But the idea that in the autumn of 1914, Cnockaert was able to instruct an aerial bombing raid, seems highly unlikely. The British air force established in 1912 consisted of two branches, the Royal Flying Corps (RFC) for military aviation and the Royal Naval Air Service (RNAS) for maritime aviation. The British were far behind the rest of Europe when it came to military aviation and had yet to prove their worth in wartime. The machines were expensive, fragile and prone to mechanical failure: even crossing the Channel to reach France was full of risk. Initially the RFC was tasked with aerial reconnaissance, and its pilots had to get to grips with maps of foreign territory and navigate through inclement weather. It wasn't until March 1915 that the RFC began to experiment properly with aerial bombing, when it was first asked to bomb a specific target.[58] Meanwhile the RNAS focused on maritime reconnaissance, but it did introduce bombs earlier on in the war, primarily targeting coastal areas and zeppelin shipyards.

While Cnockaert's account may have been heavily fictionalised, she was an active agent (Winston Churchill wrote the foreword for her memoirs). Her story highlights the conflict between the traditional life-giving role attributed to women and the militarised life-taker. As a nurse, Cnockaert found herself in a difficult situation, informing the British of bombing targets, such as locations where large numbers of troops were concentrated, and then having to deal with the aftermath, treating the wounded at the hospital. She is very clear that she carried out her nursing duties to the highest standard, regardless of her role as a spy or the nationality of her patients. Early on in the war, there was a shortage of doctors serving at the advanced dressing stations on the frontline. Cnockaert volunteered to go until the relief arrived. The chief medical officer declared it impossible because she was a woman, but Cnockaert argued that the situation was urgent and as they had no other choice they agreed to send her to the front. She was horrified by everything she saw and the apparent complacency of the medical staff who had seen so many terrible things:

> A sickening stench of blood, disinfectant and stale perspiration greeted my nostrils. Two central hurricane lamps hanging low over a rough kitchen table, wet with ominous stains, lit a large dugout with boarded walls. Four corpses covered with overcoats lay stretched in a far corner, and opposite sat three medical orderlies laughing and smoking.[59]

When a patient called for more morphine the officer told Cnockaert that there was none, and that instead he had filled the empty morphine bottle with water, hoping the placebo effect would calm his patients. Once the next wave of patients arrived, Cnockaert was thrown into work with no time to rest. Later she returned in an ambulance, taking casualties to the hospital in Roulers, when they became caught in a heavy bombardment. A shell exploded in front of the ambulance, smashing the windscreen and overturning the vehicle. Fortunately Cnockaert's injuries were minor, but one of her patients did not survive. Help arrived and they made it back to the hospital. Cnockaert was later awarded an Iron Cross in recognition of her medical work.

When her family relocated to Roulers to run a cafe, Cnockaert found herself in a position where she could overhear careless talk and befriend their German customers, only for a German officer, referred to as 'Otto', to try and recruit her as a German spy. Cnockaert did not know how to say no.

> ... I felt like screaming, like beating myself against the wall with agonised suspense. I was in a terrible quandary; against my will I had become a spy for friend and foe. But I must bring forward some information for the Germans which would not hurt my friends of the Allies, but which nevertheless seem of value to Otto.[60]

The Women's Sick and Wounded Convoy Corps, a pre-war organisation formed by Mabel St Clair Stobart training in England *c*. 1912. (Library of Congress, LC-B2-3197-15)

Mabel St Clair Stobart (left) with a fellow member of the Women's Sick and Wounded Convoy Corps whilst at a training camp in England *c*. 1912. (Library of Congress, LC-B2-1412-10)

Two women members of the St John's Ambulance Brigade Voluntary Aid Detachment. The woman on the left is wearing the nursing uniform and the woman on the right wears the general service uniform. (Australian War Memorial Collection, H07533, public domain)

First Aid Nursing Yeomanry uniform. (Australian War Memorial Collection, H07528, public domain)

A group of First Aid Nursing Yeomanry ambulance drivers attached to the Belgian Army at Calais on 8 May 1918. (© IWM (Q 3257))

Elsie Knocker (Baroness de T'Serclaes) and Mairi Chisholm outside their first aid post in Pervyse, Belgium with their tin hats and wearing their nurses' wimples. (27 April 1917 *The Illustrated War News*, public domain)

Knocker and Chisholm driving their Wolseley ambulance in Pervyse. (1916 *The War Illustrated*, public domain)

Knocker and Chisholm talking with two men of the Royal Garrison Artillery amongst the ruins of Pervyse, *c.* 1917. (Australian War Memorial Collection, H08761, public domain)

Marie Marvingt in her Deperdussin in April 1912. During the war Marvingt disguised herself as a male soldier in the French infantry and flew in several bombing missions. (Courtesy of Rosalie Maggio)

Dr Elsie Inglis photographed shortly after her return from Serbia in 1916, wearing her Scottish Women's Hospital uniform. (Eva Shaw McLaren)

Dr Nicole Girard Mangin in her uniform with her dog 'Dun'. (Public domain)

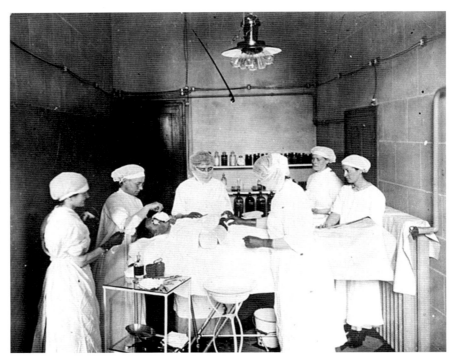

Members of the Scottish Women's Hospital unit performing an operation at their hospital in Royaumount Abbey, France. (Australian War Memorial Collection, H18905, public domain)

Ambulance drivers of the Scottish Women's Hospital talking on the street, probably in Troyes, France 1915. (Australian War Memorial Collection, P01352.004, public domain)

Olive King, driver with the Scottish Women's Hospital with her Alda ambulance, Troyes, France 1915. (Australian War Memorial Collection, P01352.002, public domain)

A studio portrait of Olive King, taken *c.* 1928, wearing the uniform of an ambulance driver in the Serbian army. King joined the Serbian army in July 1916 when she left the Scottish Women's Hospital. She was awarded a number of medals for her service, including the Serbian Order of St Sava, 3rd Class, worn at her neck. (Australian War Memorial Collection, P01352.003, public domain)

The first contingent of the Women's Overseas Hospitals. (US National Archives, 165–WW–(600A)10)

Sergeant Major Flora Sandes. Sandes first went to Serbia as a nurse but joined the army during the great retreat through Albania and Montenegro in the winter of 1915 and rose to the rank of sergeant major. (Library of Congress, LC-B2-3197-15)

Edith Cavell, *c.* 1912. Cavell ran a nursing school and hospital in Brussels. During the early occupation of Belgium she provided shelter and medical care for men attempting to escape the occupied zone. Her arrest and execution by the occupying German forces in 1915 caused international outrage. (Library of Congress, LC-B2-3652-1)

Mata Hari in her dance costume, 1910. Margaretha Zelle MacLeod adopted the stage name 'Mata Hari' and became famous in the decade before the war for her exotic dances and erotic performances. During the war she was accused of being a double agent, acting for both the French and the Germans. (Public domain)

Maria Bochkareva enlisted as a female soldier in the Twenty-fifth Reserve Battalion and undertook a fighting role on the frontline from 1915 to 1917. She then returned to the trenches as the commander of an all-female combat unit, the 'Women's Battalion of Death' in the summer of 1917. (Library of Congress, LC-B2-4599-14)

One of the Russian women's battalions from Petrograd relaxing outside their tents, c. 1917. (Library of Congress, LOT 8882)

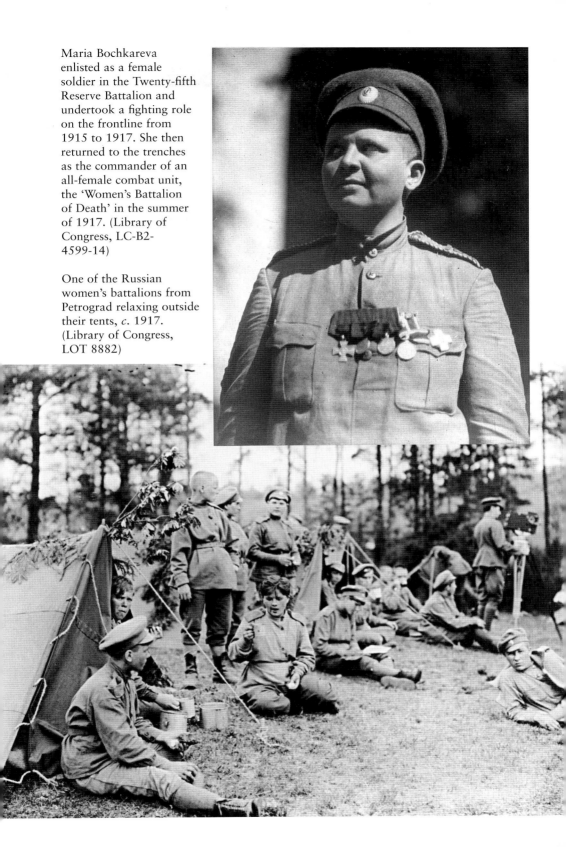

Emmeline Pankhurst standing next to Maria Bochkareva and women of the Battalion of Death during her visit to Russia in the summer of 1917. (Dorr)

Group photograph of members of the Women's Army Auxiliary Corps (WAAC) which was formed in Britain in 1917. (Australian War Memorial Collection, A03567, public domain)

A member of the Women's Royal Naval Service (WRNS) instructs new male recruits how to use gas masks, Britain, *c.* 1918. (Australian War Memorial Collection, H08274, public domain)

Members of the Women's Army Auxiliary Corps employed as air mechanics, working on the fuselage of an Avro 504 aircraft. (© IWM (Q 72637))

Members of the Women's Army Auxiliary Corps and soldiers on the edge of a crater in Abbeville, France, caused by an enemy bombing raid which took place 22 May 1918. (© IWM (Q 7890))

The ruins of a British Red Cross hospital in Étaples, France after a heavy bombing raid during which both patients and hospital staff were killed. (Australian War Memorial Collection, H09726, public domain)

Women's Signalling Corps for the US Army aka the 'Hello Girls' in France in 1918. (US National Archives, 28-0782a)

Dame Katharine Furse leading the Women's Royal Naval Service in the Victory March passing Westminster Abbey, 19 July 1919. All sections of the women war workers were represented in the march. (Australian War Memorial Collection, D00823, public domain)

Grace MacPherson, a young Canadian who decided to travel to Europe so that she could undertake war work close to the action. She worked as a Voluntary Aid Detachment ambulance driver behind the lines in the French hospital town of Étaples, which was subjected to devastating aerial bombing raids in the latter stages of the war. (Australian War Memorial Collection, H07037, public domain)

A group photo of San Francisco Yeomen (F) attached to the Naval Reserve, June 1918. (US National Archives, 165–WW–598B(7))

Cnockaert came up with an idea to play for time. One way in which the Allies had tried to communicate with those in the occupied zone was with carrier pigeons. In response the Germans ordered a cull of pigeons and that anyone found rearing pigeons, let alone using them, would face imprisonment at the very least. Allied planes would drop baskets of pigeons tied to a small parachute enabling them to smoothly float to the ground. If a pigeon was found with a message tied to it, the message was immediately taken away for analysis in case it incriminated the sender or recipient. Sometimes the Germans returned pigeons with messages in an effort to pass on false information or find out who in the area was using them.[61] Cnockaert was reminded of this when she saw a German soldier shooting at a pigeon, and so she immediately made up a fake message with a combination of numbers that could be a code. She smeared it with raw meat to stain it red and then presented it to Otto, saying that she had retrieved it from a dead pigeon. However Otto soon returned saying that no one could break the code and it may be a decoy. Despairing, Cnockaert shared her predicament with another agent who evidently passed the information further up the network as several days later Otto was conveniently found murdered and Cnockaert was safe once more.

Cnockaert's final mission in October 1916 was a plan that she and a fellow agent, Alphonse, had concocted to destroy an ammunition dump in Roulers. Alphonse had discovered that the old sewers ran from under the town through which they could reach the dump. They successfully identified the section of the sewer under the dump and managed to plant the dynamite, which they set off using a long fuse, allowing them time to return underground and conceal the entrance to the sewers. Afterwards, Cnockaert realised that she had lost her gold watch which was engraved with her initials. She was concerned that she had lost it during the mission, but she couldn't be sure. Then a short while later, she saw a notice proclaiming that a soldier had been caught stealing and a list of various items to be reclaimed by their owners, including Cnockaert's watch. Wanting it back for sentimental reasons, Cnockaert went to collect it, only to realise that it was a trap. The Germans had discovered the entrance to the sewers and when they traced their route back towards the hospital they discovered the watch. The Germans immediately searched the Cnockaert family home and found two messages that she had been preparing to send that day, signed 'L' for Laura. Unknown to Cnockaert, the Germans had intercepted some of her previous messages signed 'L', and with this evidence Cnockaert was imprisoned. However she refused to talk, preferring to starve herself to death.

At one point a Belgian woman was allowed into Cnockaert's cell to look after her in her deteriorating state. She tried to befriend Cnockaert and encouraged her to confide in her. But Cnockaert was wise to this ploy. It was increasingly common practice when trying to break a prisoner to use what was called a 'stool pigeon'. Typically when a new prisoner arrived, the police would persuade a fellow prisoner (maybe with threats or the offer of a reduced sentence) to befriend them, to earn their trust and trick them into revealing information.[62] In this case Cnockaert claimed the Belgian woman was the policeman's mistress and she refused to tell her anything.

Cnockaert was sentenced to death, despite the strong testimonies given in her favour by the German doctors with whom she had worked at the Roulers hospital. After an appeal, her sentence was reduced to life imprisonment, on account of Cnockaert having been awarded the Iron Cross. Cnockaert remained in prison in Ghent until the end of the war. Towards the end of her account, Cnockaert says that after the war her husband suggested that she go to the War Office to claim back the money she had gifted to others and the costs incurred during her time as a spy. Her request was dismissed as she had already been formally discharged. Instead of highlighting another sacrifice she had made for the war, this incident strongly suggests that the couple hoped to earn a significant amount from the publication of Cnockaert's memoirs and that they were embellished accordingly.[63]

Fraulein Doktor

Relatively little is known about the women working for the Central powers as spies. Germany's most famous female spy was called 'Fraulein Doktor', but factual details of her work and her true identity remain a mystery. Fraulein Doktor was said to be a woman determined to work in military intelligence who succeeded in securing a junior position sorting through post, reading letters and summarising her findings in written reports in Belgium. She then progressed to the German Espionage Bureau in Antwerp where she helped to train agents who worked across Europe. The nickname 'Doktor' was attributed to her academic qualifications: either she was a medical doctor or she had obtained a doctorate in another subject. She is most often identified as either Anna-Marie Lesser[64] or Elsbeth Schragmüller. Both of them had a skill with languages and were thought to be good-looking, something both women used to their advantage.[65]

After the war there were many fantastical tales associated with Fraulein Doktor. In a 1969 film of the same name, she was portrayed as a beautiful morphine addict who assumed fake identities and travelled across Britain and France, sleeping with anyone in order to get information. In addition (in this fictional film) she orchestrated the assassination of British Field Marshal Kitchener.

Antoine Rédier (de Bettignies' biographer) identified her as Anna-Marie Lesser, whom he said was power-crazed and enjoyed terrifying senior German officials by implying that, as she worked in intelligence, she knew all their secrets. Rédier had the fanciful notion that Lesser was an expert on Belgium and for many years she had been instrumental in finalising the details of the Schlieffen plan, identifying and remedying any holes in its planned execution. He also said that she owed her appointment in military intelligence to a German general who was her lover.[66]

The alternative candidate, Elsbeth Schragmüller, had graduated from the University of Freiburg with a doctorate in political science. One of the few German women to pursue a doctorate at that time, she was said to be a perfectionist, determined to succeed. At the start of the war, she worked distributing rations, but, needing a more demanding role, she wanted to be sent closer to the front.[67] Lesser died in the 1930s and Schragmüller died in 1940, allowing for more speculation and fictionalised accounts to emerge of their alter-ego, Fraulein Doktor.

The White Lady

Throughout 1916, with the increased fortifications along the Dutch-Belgian border, it was more and more difficult for the Allied intelligence services to set up new networks to replace those that had collapsed. At the same time they were having problems getting information in and out via the networks that were still operational. Henry Landau arrived in Holland in May 1916, tasked by British Intelligence to reorganise the train watching service and re-establish communication with north-eastern France. It wasn't an easy task and several of the networks he helped to establish collapsed. Then, in the winter of 1916–17, a Belgian man by the name of St Lambert arrived in Holland and Landau's luck changed for the better.

St Lambert was one of three Belgian men who had taken it upon themselves to set up an extensive new espionage network. They wanted the official support of an Allied government and the financial support that came with it. Landau was on the verge of saying yes when St Lambert explained that all members of his network, the White Lady, were soldiers and that they used a military structure. He wanted Landau to have all members officially enlisted in the British Army before they began working for the network. This was a problem, because Landau knew that the War Office would not agree to enlisting foreign subjects in the army. Furthermore, they would never agree to enlisting the female members. If Landau was not prepared to agree, St Lambert would take his offer elsewhere. Landau could not afford to lose such a great opportunity and although he had no authority to do so, he agreed. He pretended to refer the matter to his senior officers and claimed he had their approval. He agreed to confirm everything in a letter which St Lambert could take back to other founders of the organisation. It was decided that the best way to enlist the members was for them to swear an oath of allegiance and then, after the war, Landau would ensure they were officially recognised.

Unlike earlier organisations, Landau ensured that the wording of the oath of allegiance prevented the member becoming involved in tasks outside of collating information, such as distributing written material and guiding men across the frontier. He believed that it was these activities that invariably led to the agents being caught. The militarisation meant there was a clear hierarchy and strong sense of purpose. For the members unable to leave the occupied zone, it took away the feeling of shame that they were not fighting at the front or working in the auxiliary and support services.[68]

A highly effective organisation, the White Lady recruited men and women of all ages and social classes. Significantly, in case the senior members were arrested, they had created 'a shadow executive body comprised entirely of women' ready to step in and take charge of the whole organisation.[69] At the end of the war it took a large amount of campaigning for the British to accept the militarisation of the members of the White Lady. Landau appealed on their behalf to explain that the women and the men had faced the same risks and were entitled to the same level of recognition. The male members refused to accept anything from the British Government unless their women did too, and with great reluctance the British conceded.[70]

The Middle East

As well as looking for women who could blend into the crowd, or women prepared to charm and seduce the enemy, intelligence bureaux also sought women with academic credentials, an expertise or a knowledge that they had built up through years of experience that would now prove useful. Away from the Western Front, British military intelligence was working hard to establish itself in the Middle East. The most famous story from this part of the war is that of T.E. Lawrence, otherwise known as Lawrence of Arabia. Working alongside him in Cairo was a British woman called Gertrude Bell, whose extensive knowledge of the Middle East and whose social connections led to her appointment as political officer. Bell was an Oxford academic who had travelled widely, throughout the Ottoman Empire (including Jerusalem and the Syrian Desert) as well as Romania, Germany and Persia (modern-day Iran). Her uncle was a British minister in the Foreign Office and through him she socialised with diplomats and politicians, readily discussing political issues. In addition she learnt both Persian and Arabic and published works on archaeology and her travels. Interestingly Bell was an anti-suffragist, believing that the militancy of the Suffragettes undermined everything that women had so far achieved in education, but that in general women were not yet sufficiently educated to cast informed votes.

Bell first met Lawrence in 1911 and had a number of male friends, all of whom would work in military intelligence in the Middle East. At first, when the war started, Bell worked for the Red Cross, tracing the missing and wounded. In October 1915, David Hogarth, whose sister was her great friend from university, invited Bell to join him in Cairo where he was setting up a branch of British intelligence. Bell arrived the following month and initially worked on documenting the different tribes in Arabia, but quickly graduated to policy development. There was a conflict between the Indian government, which oversaw affairs in Arabia, and the Cairo headquarters, which believed Arabia should come under Egyptian jurisdiction. In response to this, Bell campaigned strongly to set up an Arab bureau in Basra, which she achieved in May 1916. She was now made part of the Indian Expeditionary Force and official correspondent to Cairo. Previously Bell had not had an official appointment, and while she believed being a political officer reduced her freedom (holding her accountable to those senior to her), she relished the opportunity. In April 1917 she moved to Baghdad where she remained until the end of the war before going on to advise on the peace treaty negotiations and question of leadership in the Middle East.[71]

By supporting the British during the war, the tribes of the Middle East hoped to gain some form of reward, maybe the chance to assert their authority, acquire new territory or gain independence. Similarly, the First World War provided several European countries with the opportunity to fight for their independence. As the Balkan Wars had seen the demise of the Ottoman Turk Empire, now both Poland and Italy seized their chance.

Poland

Joseph Pilsudski was a military commander in Austrian Poland who became a major political figure in the early twentieth century and helped achieve Poland's independence in 1918. Up until then, Poland had been divided between Austria and Russia who were now at war with one another. In 1914 Pilsudski took up command of a series of military units called legions, which were officially under Austrian command, the members bound by an oath of allegiance. However on several occasions Pilsudski disobeyed direct orders from Austria, setting his sights on reclaiming Russian Poland. In a bid to reduce Austria's power, Pilsudski entered negotiations with Germany. In exchange for their support, Pilsudski was prepared 'to offer them the use of the excellent secret service of the legions, run, for the most part by women.'[72] The women reported on the movements of the Russian army. In his own words, written in 1918, Pilsudski said:

> Great work was done by Belina [commander of a Cavalry Legion] and my Intelligence Service (consisting almost exclusively of women) in enabling me to obtain information from the enemy. ... The women fulfilled their duty with ... great self-sacrifice. They jolted alone in carts over every road, covering considerably greater areas than the cavalry, even getting as far as Warsaw, Piotrkow, and Demblin.[73]

Italy

When Italy joined the war in May 1915 on the side of the Allies, Luisa Zeni saw it as a chance to secure the independence of north Italy from Austria. She was an Italian Irredentist, which meant she believed in the unification of all areas occupied by Italian-speaking people. In the northern section of modern-day Italy, a number of these areas that she wanted to liberate were under the Austro-Hungarian Empire. Much writing on Italian history refers to the First World War as the 'Fourth War of Independence'.

Zeni was from Arco, a town in Trentino that considered itself Italian, but belonged to the Austrian Empire. As with many other women, eighteen-year-old Zeni joined the Red Cross, training in Milan. It was here that she met with other Irredentists, fuelling her patriotic zeal.[74] Before Italy had declared war and when it was still officially part of Austria, she was recruited as a spy by an Italian colonel called Tullio Marchetti. On 22 May 1915, Zeni crossed the front into Austria by posing as an Austrian woman with the name Joesephine Muller. Only two days later the shelling between the two sides began. On occasion Zeni was stopped by Austrian patrols and her fake papers were checked, but she managed to make it to Innsbruck. Here she found lodging in a central hotel, the Union Hotel, which was full of Austrian officers and soldiers, and therefore a place that offered a lot of useful information. However it was not a suitable place for a young single woman and she put herself at great risk.[75] She operated from the end of May through to 9 August 1915, posing as a mute nurse in hospitals and other buildings, sending all her observations back to Italy. At the end of July in Innsbruck, her arrest seemed inevitable. She thought that if she ran away, she would only incriminate herself, so she remained. However it looked highly likely that she would be charged and possibly executed, so on 6 August she managed to board a train full of Italian refugees bound for Switzerland. As she passed through the border, she dressed as a man from Tirol who merely wanted to return to his home. Once she was back in Milan, she was debriefed by Colonel Marchetti, but then she resigned her post.[76]

In almost all the geographical areas touched by the war, women participated in both resistance and espionage roles. Whether these women were driven by a need for justice, a sense of patriotism, political activism or a desire for money or fame, the social and sexual mores of the time affected the way in which their contributions were recorded for posterity. Shaped by a judgemental attitude towards female morality, many of the women were remembered either as innocent saints or untrustworthy whores. The very ability of women to blend into civilian life, to pass unnoticed as members of the resistance or as part of an espionage network while doing genuine humanitarian work as nurses, makes their contribution to the war incalculable. The best spies remained anonymous or undiscovered and we may never know the full extent of women's contribution to this aspect of the war.

Notes

1   Croy, Princess Marie de, *War Memories*, p.304.
2   Nicolai, Walter, *The German Secret Service*, p.85.
3   Landau, Henry, *Spreading the Spy Net: The Story of a British Spy Director*, p.161.
4   Proctor, Tammy, *Female Intelligence: Women and Espionage in the First World War*, p.125.
5   Landau, Henry, *Spreading the Spy Net*, p.160.
6   Nicolai, Walter, *The German Secret Service*, p.151.
7   Landau, Henry, *Spreading the Spy Net*, p.160.
8   Although the family home was technically in France, the de Croys were an old Belgian family and over the centuries the border between France and Belgium had moved back and forth.

9 Their brother Leopold had joined the Belgian Army.
10 Croy, Princess Marie de, *War Memories*, p.75.
11 Thuliez, Louise, *Condemned to death*.
12 Croy, Princess Marie de, *War Memories*, pp.60–2.
13 Ibid., p.63.
14 Thuliez, Louise, Condemned to Death, p.18.
15 Ibid., pp.27–8.
16 Croy, Princess Marie de, *War Memories*, p.88.
17 Thuliez, Louise, *Condemned to Death*.
18 Croy, Princess Marie de, *War Memories*, p.100.
19 Thuliez, Louise, *Condemned to Death*, p.35.
20 Ibid., pp.35–6.
21 Souhami, Diana, *Edith Cavell*, p.191.
22 Van Til, Jacqueline, *With Edith Cavell in Belgium*, p.9.
23 Souhami, Diana, *Edith Cavell*.
24 Ibid., p.194.
25 Croy, Princess Marie de, *War Memories*, pp.127–8.
26 Ibid., p.133.
27 Van Til, Jacqueline, *With Edith Cavell*, p.87.
28 Thuliez, Louise, *Condemned to Death*, p.88.
29 Souhami, Diana, *Edith Cavell*.
30 Ibid..
31 Van Rokeghem, Suzanne; Aubenas, Jacqueline and Vercheval-Vervoort, Jeanne, *Des Femmes dans L'histoire: En Belgique, Depuis 1800*, p.101.
32 Proctor, Tammy, *Female Intelligence: Women and Espionage in the First World War*, p.116.
33 Rédier, Antoine, *The Story of Louise de Bettignies*, p.5.
34 Ibid., p.31.
35 Proctor, Tammy, *Female Intelligence*, p.116.
36 Ibid., p.116.
37 Vanhoutte later married Rédier and contributed heavily to his biography of de Bettignies.
38 Proctor, Tammy, *Female Intelligence*, p.116.
39 Van Rokeghem, Suzanne; Aubenas, Jacqueline and Vercheval-Vervoort, Jeanne, *Des Femmes dans L'histoire: En Belgique, Depuis 1800*, p.100.
40 Ibid.
41 Ibid., p.102.
42 Proctor, Tammy, *Female Intelligence*, p.93.
43 Landau, Henry, *Spreading the Spy Net*.
44 Thuliez, Louise, *Condemned to Death*.
45 Shipman, Pat, *The Femme Fatale: Love, Lies and the Unknown Life of Mata Hari*.
46 Ibid.
47 Darrow, Margaret, *French Women and the First World War*, p.292.
48 Ladoux, Georges, as printed in *Marthe Richard – The Skylark*, p.35.
49 Ibid., pp.35–6.
50 Miles, Rosalind and Cross, Robin, *Warrior Women: 3000 Years of Courage and Heroism*.
51 Ladoux, Georges, *Marthe Richard – The Skylark*, p.37.
52 Ibid., p.42 and p.49.

53 Richer, Marthe and Griffin, Gerald (trans.), *I Spied for France*, p.48.
54 Proctor, Tammy, *Female Intelligence*, p.131.
55 Ladoux, Georges, *Marthe Richard – The Skylark*, p.40.
56 McKenna, Marthe, *I was a spy!*, p.71.
57 Ibid., p.52.
58 Norris, Geoffrey, *The Royal Flying Corps – A History*.
59 McKenna, Marthe, *I was a spy!*, p.63.
60 Ibid., p.160.
61 Thuliez, Louise, *Condemned to Death*, p.66–7.
62 Landau, Henry, *Spreading the Spy Net*, p.135.
63 McKenna, Marthe, *I was a spy!*
64 There are several variations on Lesser's first name, including Anna, Anna-Marie, and Marie.
65 Proctor, Tammy, *Female Intelligence*, pp.133–4.
66 Rédier, Antoine, *Louise de Bettignies*.
67 Marianne Walle in *Les Espionnes dans la Grande Guerre*.
68 Landau, Henry, *Spreading the Spy Net*.
69 Proctor, Tammy, *Female Intelligence*, p.77.
70 Ibid., p.91.
71 Goodman, Susan, *Gertrude Bell*, part of the Berg Women's Series edited by Miriam Kochan, 1985.
72 Landau, Rom and Dunlop, Geoffrey (trans.), *Pilsudski Hero of Poland*, p.105.
73 Pilsudski, Joseph and Gillie, D.R. (trans. and ed.), J*oeseph Pilsudski – The Memories of a Polish Revolutionary and Soldier*, p.192.
74 Scardino Belzer, Allison, *Women and the Great War – Femininity Under Fire in Italy*.
75 Charbonnier, Alain, *History, Facts, Anecdotes and Legends – Women Secret Agents who Acted in the Risorgiemnto*.
76 Scardino Belzer, Allison, *Women and the Great War – Femininity Under Fire in Italy*.

6

Flora Sandes

> Looking back, I seem to have just naturally drifted by successive stages from a nurse into a soldier.
>
> Flora Sandes

Born in 1876, Flora Sandes was the daughter of a clergyman who had hoped that a stint at a Swiss finishing school would transform her into an ideal wife for a gentleman. Yet from a young age Sandes showed a passion for adventure, enjoying family camping trips, horse riding, hunting and driving cars.[1] As a child she prayed that she could be a boy before realising 'that if you have the misfortune to be born a woman it is better to make the best of a bad job, and not try to be a bad imitation of a man.'[2] Like many women during the First World War, Flora Sandes joined a voluntary medical organisation and worked behind the frontlines as a nurse. She was sent to Serbia, a country which she grew to love and a nation whose people she respected and felt a deep loyalty for. As part of a large voluntary medical community she worked in Serbia during its darkest hours. Then when Serbia was invaded in the autumn of 1915 and the medical staff were offered the choice of either staying or joining the general retreat, Sandes chose instead to join the Serbian army. This is the background to how she made the transition from nurse to soldier. Serbia is a mountainous country which in 1914 was covered by large forested areas. There were many orchards, principally plum trees, from which the fruit was distilled to make *Rakiya*, the national spirit. A predominantly agricultural nation, Serbia had only recently gained its independence from the crumbling Turkish Empire. Emerging from centuries of occupation, Serbia seemed positively 'medieval'[3]. For instance it had yet to adopt 'modern methods of farming.'[4] The population would travel between towns to sell their wares at local markets, although nearly all the towns in Serbia were closer in size to what we would now think of as small villages, and the distances between them were relatively great. The condition of the roads, even in the cities, was poor, as Dr Caroline Matthews recalled of her 1915 visit to Serbia's second largest city Nish:

> An English carriage would have soon been knocked to pieces on the roads at Nish. The public vehicle which plied for hire was a type of small springless Victoria generally drawn by a pair of weedy horses. To venture on a drive was to enter adventure in itself. At every step the carriage might plunge into great uneven holes, filled with mud and slush – unless the sun's rays had baked it into clay. The cobblestones were large and woefully uneven – it was not a town for dainty shoes, high heels, and bewitching little feet. The small, narrow-shaped bullock carts were eminently fitted as carriers of farm produce or merchandise under such conditions.[5]

During the First World War, these same bullock-drawn carts were used to evacuate the sick and wounded from the front, and to transport them to hospitals and railway stations. Bumping and jostling the casualties who were already in pain, the journeys sometimes took days and field dressings remained unchanged until arrival at a hospital. It was far from ideal, but there were very few cars in Serbia and the roads were not really suitable for them. Olive Aldridge recalls that when they needed a car all one did was:

> ... stand in the middle of the village street, hold up a spread-out hand and command a conveyance to halt as a policeman does at home to stop the traffic. A conveyance might not come for several days, but we had to be ready to start at any moment ...[6]

Serbia did have a railway though, which ran the length of the kingdom, connecting the capital city of Belgrade with the southern provinces and on into Greece and the coast. Following the assassination of Archduke Ferdinand and its subsequent declaration of war, the Austro-Hungarian Empire prepared to invade Serbia. Serbia's army was worn out from the recent Balkan Wars (October 1912–May 1913 and June–August 1913), and the country's medical infrastructure was unlikely to cope with a high volume of new casualties. A landlocked country, Serbia shared its northern border with the Austro-Hungarian Empire; to the north-east was Romania, to the east was Bulgaria, to the south Greece, and to the west Montenegro and Albania. Beyond the Empire was Germany, and on the other side of Bulgaria was Austria–Hungary's other ally, Turkey. The great fear was that Serbia would be crushed by its enemies.

On 12 August 1914, Austria–Hungary began its invasion, yet despite being under-resourced and outnumbered, within two weeks the Serbian army had succeeded in pushing the Austro-Hungarians back over the border. In early September the Austro-Hungarians mounted a second invasion, but were once more driven back, although they did manage to establish a series of footholds along the Bosnian border.[7] Austria–Hungary was in fact waging war on two fronts, which significantly compromised its military strategy. Russia had come to Serbia's support and began to mobilise against Austria-Hungary. On 1 August Germany declared war on Russia. After suffering several defeats, the Russians began to make progress, crossing over their common border into the Galicia region of northern Austria–Hungary. On 11 September the Russians forced the Austro-Hungarians to order a general retreat from the area. Needing to make a stand and halt the Russian advance, the Austro-Hungarians diverted men from the Serbian front. They found they were unable simultaneously to hold back the Russians and launch a successful invasion of Serbia. The Austro-Hungarians maintained their offensive along the Serbian front, but until they could gain the upper hand over the Russians, the main area of fighting was concentrated in the north-west region of Serbia. Serbia's other allies were preoccupied with events on the Western Front, and with the situation in Serbia deemed to be relatively stable they left the Serbian army to fend for itself militarily. However Serbia's friends and allies did provide substantial and much-needed medical support.

In August 1914 an American woman arrived in England desperately seeking help for Serbia, which was her adopted homeland. This was Mabel Grouitch, the forty-one-year-old wife of Slavko Grouitch, a Serbian foreign minister. During the Balkan Wars she had worked in the country's hospitals and witnessed first-hand the horrors of war. This time she was determined to reach out to other countries and organise medical aid for Serbia at the earliest opportunity.

Recruiting a medical team that would be ready to leave within a fortnight had proven to be more difficult than Grouitch had anticipated. She conducted numerous interviews before she found herself sitting across from an Englishwoman of a similar age, who was fuelled with equal drive and ambition. Her name was Flora Sandes and she had been a member of the First Aid Nursing Yeomanry in its formative years before joining Mabel Stobart's organisation, the Women's Sick and Wounded Convoy Corps. On learning that Britain was at war she immediately applied for voluntary aid detachment training but was turned down. She had heard that Grouitch was looking for nurses and was excited by the opportunity of immediate war work and of going overseas. Sandes convinced Grouitch that with her basic medical training, a fluency in both French and German, combined with her practical nature, she was worthy of a place within the unit. On 12 August 1914, the same day that Austria–Hungary invaded Serbia, Grouitch led her team of eight women (not all of whom were qualified nurses) on a two-week journey by land and sea to Eastern Europe.

Grouitch's party arrived in the Greek port of Salonika and from there they travelled by train up through the states of Macedonia and Kosovo, both of which had recently become part of the Serbian Kingdom.[8] They continued northwards to the town of Kragujevac in central Serbia where they began work at a large military hospital. During the journey Sandes had become firm friends with a fellow nurse, the American Emily Simmonds, but she got on less well with the others. On first impressions Sandes had seemed respectable, but on closer inspection her hair was too short and her behaviour (a fondness for alcohol and smoking) proved she was not at all ladylike.[9]

After the women were settled in at the hospital in Kragujevac, Grouitch continued her international campaign on behalf of Serbia, and more voluntary medical units followed. In Britain Grouitch helped to establish the Serbian Relief Fund (SRF), which sent its first unit to Skopje (central Macedonia) in November. The administrator in charge of the unit was Lady Paget, whose husband Sir Ralph Paget had been until recently the British minister in Serbia. During his time there, Lady Paget had worked alongside Grouitch in the Belgrade Army Hospital in 1912.[10] Like his wife, Sir Ralph had also returned to Serbia, this time as the commissioner for the British relief units. As with many of the voluntary medical units which operated behind the Western Front and elsewhere during the war, the first challenge was to transform the designated building into a clean and functioning hospital. Lady Paget's unit took over a series of buildings about a mile outside of the main town, which were already being used by the Serbians as a hospital with 330 beds. Immediately Paget instructed that the entire hospital needed a thorough cleaning and all but twenty of the patients were transferred to neighbouring hospitals while this was done. The unit scrubbed every inch of the place with turpentine to try and eradicate vermin. The rooms were heated by wood-burning stoves and lit by oil lamps. The operating theatre did have electric lighting, but this was not always reliable. As the water supply was sometimes cut off they had to depend on a large water tank as a reserve.[11] Despite the relatively primitive conditions, within a week Paget's unit officially opened its hospital to new patients.

Over the course of the winter, more medical units began arriving in Serbia, including three American Red Cross hospitals in Belgrade.

Another medical organisation that played a significant role in Serbia was the Scottish Women's Hospital (SWH). When Dr Elsie Inglis of Edinburgh had formed the SWH, she had offered units to Britain's allies and both France and Serbia had gratefully accepted. While the SWH was organising its French hospital at Royaumont outside Paris (which of course was entirely staffed by women), the SWH despatched its first unit to Serbia and it arrived in January 1915. Under the leadership of Dr Eleanor Soltau, the unit, like Grouitch's first group of women, went to Kragujevac. Although there was currently little fighting along the Serbian front, the women found that the hospitals were struggling to cope with the sick and wounded that they did receive. Like Paget's unit, the hospital that they took over was filthy and in urgent need of sanitisation. In comparison to British hospital standards there were too many beds in the overcrowded wards. The long journey from the front and the understaffing of the hospitals meant that many of the patients' wounds were suffering from neglect.[12]

By November, the First Reserve military hospital where Emily Simmonds and Flora Sandes had been posted had nearly run out of all medical supplies. As this point, as both Simmonds and Sandes were nearing the end of the initial three-month contract, they made the decision that it would be more effective if they returned to their home countries, raised funds and bought new medical supplies themselves. Both women had developed a strong empathy with the Serbians and were keen to return to Serbia as soon as they could. They had become established members of a highly valuable medical community, which continued to expand.

In December, a married couple of doctors, James Berry and F. May Dickinson Berry, attended one of Grouitch's lectures in London. Grouitch persuaded them to raise funds themselves, calling on friends and family, and to establish a hospital of their own. Both the Berrys worked at the Royal Free Hospital in London, but at that time it was not taking military casualties and May Dickinson Berry felt that, owing to the negative stance of the War Office on women doctors, Serbia offered both of them much more rewarding work. With additional funding from the SRF, the Berrys arrived in the Serbian spa resort of Vrnjacka Banja in mid-January 1915. Despite the hospital's official name of the 'Anglo-Serbian Unit', it was often referred to as the 'Berry Mission' or the 'Berry Unit'. *En route* to Vrnjacka Banja they stopped at Skopje to meet with Lady Paget, to exchange news and learn more about the challenges that they would face.

During their visit, Lady Paget warned the Berrys of a new threat on the horizon. She shared with them her fears that the number of typhus cases was increasing at a worrying rate. Later in her report to the SRF Committee she recalled that:

Although typhus had appeared sporadically in Serbia as early as November and December, it was not until the second half of January that the epidemic began to assume serious proportions. It was about the time that the first cases were recognised in Skopje, and by the first week in February there were over four hundred cases in the town. There was, at that date, no organisation for isolating the cases, and consequently it was spreading through the hospitals and barracks of Skopje like wildfire.[13]

Expecting to be treating war wounds, the Berrys found that Serbia was in fact on the cusp of a nation-wide typhus epidemic. Typhus is a bacteriological infection spread principally by human lice. The epidemic was ultimately to claim over 150,000 lives, although over 50 per cent of those who were infected did eventually recover. It also claimed a substantial number of victims among those nursing infected patients. In February the British units working in Serbia held a medical conference in Nish. All the organisations faced the same problems across the country. The hospitals were understaffed and the wards were overcrowded. The lack of disinfectants, the shortage of clean linen and clothes and the limited means of effectively washing material meant it was impossible to maintain the highest levels of sanitation required. Within the crowded wards and amongst the dirt, the lice that transmitted typhus thrived. The refugees fleeing northern Serbia were forced to share cramped rooms and sleep on floors without any clean changes of clothes, helping to spread the disease further. More pressure was placed on the medical system by the number of Austrian POWs transferred to Serbia's hospitals: it is estimated there were 75,000 such POWS in Serbia.[14]

The result of the conference was a series of letters to the Serbian Relief Fund and the British Red Cross committees in Britain explaining the full extent of the situation. This helped generate more donations and volunteers, but in the meantime those in Serbia had to make do with what little resources and personnel they had. Vrnjacka Banja was a former spa town and both the Berry Unit and the neighbouring Red Cross hospital tried to disinfect all patients in the bath house when they arrived in the town. To begin with patients' hair was cut short, but when nits were discovered the patients were shaved from head to toe. If they were already infected, provided all the lice and eggs were removed, the patients wouldn't infect anyone else. The plan was a good one, but some patients did slip through the net and were taken directly to other hospitals in the area.

Despite taking precautions, many of the medical staff of the different hospitals became ill with typhus. Simmonds and Sandes returned to Serbia in February 1915 during the middle of the crisis. This time they settled in the village of Valjevo where there was a great shortage of both doctors and nurses, because most were ill or had died. The disease took its toll on the Serbian population, as soldiers, civilians and the country's medical staff were all affected. Working in the Fourth Reserve hospital the two women had to assume more and more responsibility. The hospital was designed for 250 patients, but there were over 800 men there, the majority of whom were sick rather than wounded. The two doctors had both contracted typhus and one had died shortly before the women arrived. Simmonds had been a surgical nurse and was therefore more experienced than Sandes, and began performing small operations with Sandes' assistance. After a while, Sandes herself began operating, on cases with frostbite and gangrene requiring the amputation of toes and fingers. In March both women contracted typhus, but they recovered and in due course continued with their work.[15]

In February, members of Paget's unit, including Lady Paget herself, became ill. Fortunately, in March, another SRF unit arrived in Skopje to relieve them, led by Lady Wimborne. The SRF continued to send out further medical staff to support their existing units at a time when they were being stretched extremely thin. At the same time Dr Soltau, whose unit was looking after three separate hospitals, wrote to Elsie Inglis, urgently requesting help. When Inglis received Soltau's telegram, Dr Alice Hutchinson had just set off to Serbia with a second SWH unit. However when they stopped over in Malta, they were commandeered by the British and would not arrive in Serbia until early June. So Inglis decided that she herself would travel out with a reserve team to support Soltau in Kragujevac. With her she brought the suffragist Evelina Haverfield, founder of the Women's Emergency Corps (of which Elsie Knocker and Mairi Chisholm had been members in early 1914) as a probationary hospital administrator. They reached Kragujevac in mid-May.

The third SRF unit to be sent out was led by the one and only Mabel St Clair Stobart, founder of both the Women's Sick and Wounded Convoy Corps, which had gone to the Balkans in 1912, and the Women's Imperial Service League, which had gone to Belgium in 1914. Following the hasty evacuation from Antwerp she had taken charge of a hospital in Cherbourg, but with the consolidation of medical services in other northern French cities such as Boulogne and with growing fears over the vulnerability of the channel crossing from Cherbourg to submarine attack, the number of patients kept falling. Looking for a more active role, Stobart left and returned to England. Having read about the typhus epidemic she now set her sights on Serbia and volunteered to lead a new SRF unit. Believing that women physicians had proven themselves capable of running such an operation, she condescended to employ male orderlies rather than insisting on an all-female group.[16] Instead of taking over a building, her SRF unit planned to set up a tent hospital. The intention was that the tents would be easier to keep clean and sanitise than run-down, vermin infested buildings. True to form, as the same woman who had gone to the trouble of hiring a carriage in occupied Brussels in order to give the German commanding officer the impression he was dealing with a woman of high status and importance, Stobart set out to impress the Serbians. After a brief stop at Skopje to meet Sir Ralph Paget, and to hear that Lady Paget was recovering, Stobart and her unit travelled north to Nish. There she left her unit to their own devices and was met with a grand welcoming committee of government personnel including Slavko Grouitch, the British vice-consul and the president of the Serbian Red Cross.[17] Stobart's group then headed north to Kragujevac, but she recalls not everyone was happy with the decision:

> There was disappointment amongst members of our unit, when they learned that we were to establish our hospital at Kragujevatz [sic]. They would have preferred Belgrade, as being nearer to the supposed front. Fronts, however, are moveable, and as Kragujevatz was the military headquarters, we were, I knew, much more likely to get the work we wanted, if we were immediately under the official army eye.[18]

Although Stobart says that she went to Serbia in response to the typhus epidemic, it is likely that in truth she too was disappointed with Kragujevac. Stobart was forever trying to get near the military action and in due course would lead an SRF detachment towards the front. But until then she focused on making a success of her new hospital.

During the summer of 1915, as the epidemic receded, some of the medical staff took the opportunity to go home, either because their contracts had come to an end, or simply for a well-deserved rest. Yet the Serbian military were concerned should Austria–Hungary launch a large-scale offensive whilst the country was at its most vulnerable and weak. The Serbian Red Cross and the Serbian army medical services met with the leaders of the different medical units and implored them to stay, as they would surely be needed. Elsie Inglis wrote to the SWH committee and requested that they send out two more units.[19] While the summer months seemed relatively quiet compared to the previous winter there was a growing number of aerial bombing raids. In Kragujevac, Serbia's military headquarters were subjected to many raids, and on one occasion a bomb fell on Stobart's camp. Fortunately no one was hurt as the bomb failed to detonate. Another time the planes were targeting a nearby wireless station and shrapnel cut through several of the tents, but again no one was hurt.

Whilst in Serbia, Stobart set up a series of dispensaries in the villages surrounding Kragujevac. Olive Aldridge served as a housekeeper at one based in Vitanovac. She describes how the Serbians steadfastly held on to the hope that the Allies would soon arrive to help them, to support their tired army and fight off the Austro-Hungarians. The villagers would decorate the stations anticipating their arrival only to be disappointed. The British were divided over their military strategy: one side, the 'Easterners', argued for more forces on the Eastern Front and the 'Westerners' argued in favour of the Western Front. They were also preoccupied by the disastrous Gallipoli campaign. France was willing, but lacked sufficient numbers to offer substantial support. Serbia's allies also faced a serious logistical problem. As Serbia was landlocked, the main access to Serbia was to land at Salonika and travel north, but Salonika was in Greece and Greece was neutral. To land a significant allied force in Salonika would compromise Greece, which itself was divided on the issue. The government was pro-British and wanted to join the Allies, but the king was not and overruled the government. Russia was also unable to reach Serbia as Austria–Hungary and neutral Romania stood in the way. Meanwhile both the Allies and the Central powers tried to persuade Serbia's other neighbour, Bulgaria, to join their side in the conflict.[20]

In June, Flora Sandes and Emily Simmonds both left Valjevo. They hoped to find work with a military ambulance but they were turned down. They were then accepted by a field hospital but the following month, as there was little work to do, both women decided to go home for a much needed rest.[21]

Meanwhile, the Central powers had successfully driven the Russians out of the Galicia region of north-east Austria–Hungary and were chasing them through Poland. By the middle of September, Russia had lost possession of its Polish provinces and now, with the balance of power in their favour, the Austro-Hungarians and the Germans prepared to invade Serbia. They had to act fast before the harsh winter made the mountains impassable. On 7 October Austria–Hungary and Germany crossed Serbia's northern rivers, the Sava and the Danube, and within two days they arrived in the Serbian capital Belgrade. The Serbians were outnumbered nearly two to one.[22] On 14 October, Bulgaria entered the war on the side of the Central powers. Following its defeat against Serbia during the second Balkan war, Bulgaria watched with jealousy as Serbia incorporated Macedonia into its kingdom. The Allies had failed to persuade Serbia to surrender the region in return for Bulgaria's support, while Germany said

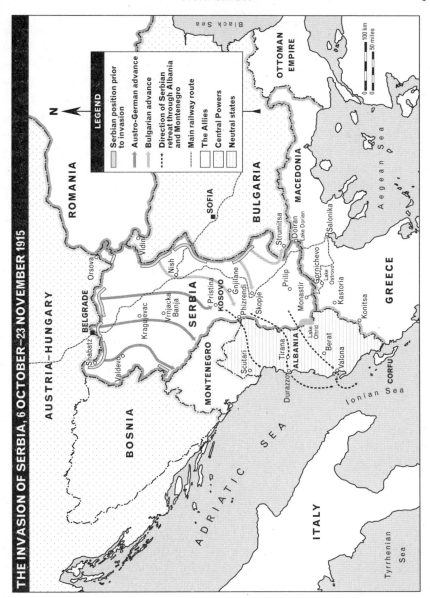

THE INVASION OF SERBIA, 6 OCTOBER–23 NOVEMBER 1915

LEGEND

Serbian position prior to invasion

Austro-German advance

Bulgarian advance

Direction of Serbian retreat through Albania and Montenegro

Main railway route

The Allies

Central Powers

Neutral states

that if Bulgaria took it, they could keep it. So, a week after the loss of Belgrade, Bulgaria attacked from the east with the intention of cutting the north/south Serbian railway in half, cutting off Serbia's army in the north from its reserves and possible allied support in the south.

With the invasion, the medical units found themselves one by one under orders to evacuate. Suddenly they were on the frontline. When Dr Caroline Matthews arrived in Serbia in May 1915, like Sandes and Simmonds she had hoped to work with a military ambulance. She even adopted a military style uniform and wore breeches, but instead was sent to work in a hospital. In the autumn, with Austria–Hungary preparing to strike, she tried once more to be assigned to an ambulance, but instead she was sent to a military hospital in Uzsitsi, in the north-west of Serbia close to the border with Bosnia, part of the Austro-Hungarian Empire. On 15 October the hospital was ordered to Montenegro, but Matthews said she could not live with herself if she left her patients to the mercy of the enemy, and chose to stay. The majority of the staff went; only the orderlies stayed. Suddenly Matthews felt very alone, the only British person left in Serbia, for she was sure that the other units would all evacuate. She says that those around her changed. They no longer wanted to associate themselves with her, in case they were punished by the Germans and the Austro-Hungarians. Waiting for the enemy was an anxious time, but finally at the end of October the first patrol arrived. Matthews retreated to her office where she retrieved her pistol, which she had brought with her to Serbia for protection. Concealing it, she went back out on to the ward to meet the Austrian soldiers. The officer, looking Matthews up and down and taking in her uniform, saluted her. He then asked whether she was the English officer in charge of the hospital, to which Matthews replied she was. The fact that the only English 'officer' was a woman had obviously surprised him, but he showed Matthews due respect. Others, in particular the doctors who were later stationed at the hospital, were not so kind to Matthews, but for the next three months she continued to work at the hospital.

At about the same time that Matthews was posted to Uzsitsi, Mabel Stobart put her next plan into motion. In Kragujevac, the Serbian military headquarters, Stobart successfully offered the army a complete flying ambulance made up of members of her SRF hospital. Stobart even had a number of cars at her disposal, which had been sent out for the dispensaries to use. Using their hospital tents they could set up camp quickly and evacuate with equal speed. Stobart was of course appointed to command the unit, holding the equivalent rank of major, of which she was very proud. Attached to the Schumadia division of the Serbian army, the flying hospital shadowed their every move. Barely spending more than one or two days in any one place, the unit became very efficient at pitching their tents and then packing them away. Patients arrived in dribs and drabs and were quickly moved on. Progress between camps was slow as the cars had to weave in and out of the marching troops and the luggage carts. In central Serbia, the unit seemed to move around in circles as the division tried to hold off the advance. Once they had taken Belgrade, the Central powers marched on Kragujevac and at one point the unit was only 6 miles away from the fighting and it could hear the deafening thunder of the artillery. Stobart only hoped that her hospital that she had left behind had been evacuated in time. Ultimately, the Serbian army made the decision to retreat before the Bulgarians cut them off from the south.

Meanwhile, back in England, when she learned of the invasion, Flora Sandes immediately set out to return to Serbia. She travelled on the same boat as the SWH's 'Girton and Newnham' unit which had previously been in France. On board she met Dr Isabel Emslie who described Sandes as 'A tall handsome woman with short grey hair and a faultless khaki coat'.[23] Arriving in Salonika on 3 November 1915, the Girton and Newnham Unit travelled 50 miles up the line to the town of Ghevgeli near the Serbian-Greek border where they established their hospital. Sandes at first wanted to return to the hospital in Valjevo, but on learning that the town was now occupied, she then decided to make for Nish and find work with the Serbian Red Cross. Yet these plans also fell through when she learned it would require a ten day journey, with little food, through dangerous countryside, and that the army was commandeering all the horses. Finally, Sandes found a doctor and a small group of nurses who were in a similar situation, unable to reach their hospitals, and so together they travelled to Monastir by train. Once there she persuaded the English Consul to help her get to Prilip, a town 25 miles away, where she found work in a Serbian military hospital. With the enemy advancing all the time it was likely that the hospital in Prilip would be evacuated and Sandes would be sent back to Salonika, which she did not want. With the help of the hospital director she secured an attachment to the ambulance of the Second Regiment (the ambulance was a mobile medical unit that travelled with the regiment). Many of the hospital staff tried to persuade her to stay with them, warning her that it would be a hard life in the army, but Sandes had made up her mind.

Arriving at the ambulance late at night, the soldiers were unsure of where Sandes should sleep and decided to give her a tent. Sandes described her new surroundings:

The ambulance itself consisted of one largish tent, where the patients lie on their clothes on very muddy straw, until they can be removed to the base hospital by bullock wagon. This is done as often as transport permits. There were a few cases of dressings, drugs etc, in the tent, and a small table for writing at. There were about twenty patients in at one time, some of them sick and some wounded. About a dozen little tents, similar to mine, for the soldiers and ambulance men, and two or three wagons completed the outfit.[24]

The two regiments which the ambulance supported were engaged in the nearby battle of Babuna. The Serbians were trying to hold the Babuna Pass to prevent the Bulgarians advancing to Monastir. The English consul offered Sandes one more chance to return to Salonika, but once more Sandes refused. She recognised that as an Englishwoman she represented the eternal hope that Serbia's allies would come to its aid and that her staying was important for morale. The ambulance men also tried to persuade her to leave, but were happy she chose to stay and provided her with a wagon to transport her belongings and to sleep on, which was marginally warmer than the tent. Sandes was not the only woman in the ambulance. There was also a young Serbian woman whom Sandes called 'Kid'. Living amongst the men, Kid wore a solider-like uniform and demonstrated she was a hard worker. As they spoke together in German, Kid gave Sandes plenty of advice on living life with the ambulance. Sandes adopted a uniform as well, wearing breeches which were much more practical.

The ambulance had to be ready to evacuate and move on at short notice. Sandes was advised to sleep in her clothes and keep her boots on. The regiment knew that it could be ordered to retreat at any time and one rainy evening shortly after Sandes' arrival they received instructions to leave. Impressively, the ambulance was ready to go just half an hour after receiving the order. Sandes and Kid climbed into Sandes' wagon and joined the ambulance convoy. Peering out into the pitch-black night, Sandes had no idea of their destination or how long they would be travelling for. Not knowing where the enemy were, Sandes' worst fear as she and Kid were thrown around in their wagon was discovering too late that the Bulgarians had encircled them. Fortunately they made it safely to the next stopping point, somewhere between Monastir and Prilip. Kid used the opportunity to go to Monastir on an errand, but she didn't come back and Sandes did not know exactly what became of her.

Sandes went to great efforts to ingratiate herself with the men, to do her fair share of the work, to join in with conversations around the fire and to learn Serbian, the rest of the time relying on German. The ladies of Grouitch's unit (apart from Simmonds) had disapproved of her tendency to drink, but the soldiers did not. She was more than happy to share a drink and exchange cigarettes with the men. Sandes quickly grew attached to them, appreciating their genuine concern for her, always ensuring she was comfortable and close enough to the fire. After the winter snow began to fall, the men would sleep four in a tent to keep warm and were terrified of waking up to find Sandes alone, frozen to death in her wagon, but Sandes assured them she was an experienced camper and would be fine. She also admired the soldiers' faith that

Britain would come to their aid and their rejoicing when they received new English rifles.

Sandes certainly had a privileged position amongst the ambulance. The commandant insisted that she use his spare horse, rather than ride in the wagon each time the ambulance moved. He also ordered a sentry to guard her while she slept. Furthermore, when the British consul had first taken Sandes to Prilip he had left her with a Serbian orderly called Joe to look after her. Joe joined the ambulance with Sandes and continued to work as her orderly. When it was quiet, Sandes would ride out with the commandant and inspect the Serbian lines. Some evenings she would have supper with him as an officer would have done and he would explain the current military situation to her. The Serbian army was tired, outnumbered and did not have any large artillery to support it. The Bulgarians did, and their men were in better health with good supply lines. All available men were at the front attempting to slow the progress of the Bulgarians, whose strategy was to march around the Serbian line. Stretched thinly, there were no reserves to support the Serbians and they were retreating in progressive stages. From the ambulance, Sandes could hear the rifle fire in the background and Bulgarians shouting 'Hourrah, Hourrah!' as they took the Serbian trenches. At one point the fighting got so close that shells flew over their heads. Soon the next order to retreat came and Sandes watched as the soldiers retreated across the snow in the twilight, lit by the flashes of the nearby guns. As they went, they sang a forlorn and dismal song and Sandes found the whole sight extremely depressing. In her autobiography, Sandes makes the very subtle transition from describing the Serbians as an onlooker to referring to the trenches as 'our trenches'.

Sandes admits in her autobiography that what she had envisaged in her head and the reality of war were quite different:

> The firing had ceased, as it usually does at night, and at last, about nine o'clock, the Commandant appeared and the horses were brought out, and instead of the wild cinema gallop I had pictured we had one of the slowest, coldest rides you can imagine. There was a piercing blizzard blowing across the snowy waste, blinding our eyes and filling our ears with snow; our hands were numbed, and our feet so cold and wet we could hardly feel the stirrups. We proceeded in dead silence, no one feeling disposed to talk, and slowly threaded our way through crowds of soldiers tramping along, with bent heads, as silently as phantoms, the sound of their feet muffled by the snow.

The decision was made to progress to Monastir and then make for the Albanian mountains because the Bulgarian advance from the east had cut off their route south to Greece. The lack of roads through the mountains meant they had to leave the ambulance – it was no longer practical – so the members of the ambulance fell in with the rest of the regiment. Sandes ceremoniously removed her Red Cross arm band and the commandant, Colonel Militch, then removed the brass number '2' of the Second Regiment from his own epaulettes and fixed it to Sandes' shoulder straps. She was now the regiment's latest recruit. When they reached Monastir, Militch took her to meet with the commandant of the division, Colonel Vasitch, who officially made her a private in the Second Regiment. Yet Sandes did not pick up a gun and become an ordinary soldier straight away.

Private Sandes then rejoined the men as they set off towards Albania. Progress was slow as those, like Sandes, who were on horseback picked their way through the crowds of walking men. Every hour they stopped and made fires to warm their frozen feet, and regular halts were called to allow those at the back to catch up. Sandes describes passing by animal corpses, frozen where they had fallen, but not before they had been stripped of their hides and their flesh. Rations were scarce and any additional food was too valuable to waste. The snow gave way to black mud and along the worst roads it reached the knees of the horses.

Sandes took the opportunity to go and see the First Battalion take up position defending the retreating forces. She accompanied its commander Captain Stoyadinovitch, who could speak only Serbian. Scaling a hill they took refuge behind the wall of one of the few remaining buildings and watched as the Serbians defended a series of natural trenches. When the shelling became intense the group had to move, narrowly missing a direct hit from a shell:

> We had to cross a piece of open ground, which we did in single file, to reach this wood, and before we got to it we got a whole fusillade of bullets whistling round our ears.[25]

After descending back down through the forest they came across Serbian artillery. The officer in charge showed Sandes how the guns were fired and then allowed her to take up position in one of the gun teams. Later she had a pleasant evening sitting round the fire with the men of the Fourth Company, and decided to pitch her tent alongside the battalion that night, rather than alongside the officers. However, Sandes was brought back down to earth the next morning, when they had to fall in at 3 a.m. in the rain.

The following day, Sandes was offered the choice of staying with the transport of the Fourth Company or climbing 1,790m to the top of Mount Chukus. Of course Sandes chose the climb. It was hard sweaty work, despite the cold winter, for there was no clear path and they had to scramble and pull themselves up the steepest sections. They took regular halts so those at the back could keep up and so that they all stayed together. In total it took about thirteen hours to reach a plateau where they set up their tents for the night. The next day they saw the Bulgarians positioned higher up from them. Sandes and the Serbians took cover behind many of the large rock formations. Sandes was armed with a revolver (such as an officer would carry) and she was lent a rifle. This is the first point in Sandes' memoirs that she mentions having a gun. The Bulgarians were clearly the enemy, but throughout her memoirs, when she is instructed on how to fire artillery or whenever she uses a gun, she never describes hitting, wounding or killing anyone. The implication is always that she was shooting to keep the enemy in place and defending her fellow soldiers, but never actually killing anyone. This resonates with the public attitudes of the time, that a woman was a life-giver, and the idea of a woman taking life, even in war, was abhorrent. Sandes' adventures made her a wartime hero, but when she wrote her memoirs she wisely avoided the issue. Up on Mount Chukus, Sandes said that the Fourth Company fired at the enemy and that the enemy fired back until it got dark and they stopped. She makes no mention of either side hitting its targets. That evening, Sandes was officially enrolled in the Fourth Company by its commander Lieutenant Jovitch, with the promise that she may make corporal.

In the morning, waking up covered in frost, the company resumed its positions from the day before, crouched in the snow behind the rocks, and recommenced the exchange of fire. Food ran short and the company was ordered to return back down the mountain in the moonlight to re-join the regiment. Sandes had settled into her army life very quickly and the men accepted her. When she and Lieutenant Jovitch visited an Albanian village, the population asked the lieutenant whether Sandes was a woman or soldier, to which Jovitch replied that whilst she was an English woman, she was also a Serbian soldier. This simply confused them.

Exhausted, the retreat continued. Those whose horses had died on the way were forced to walk: to stop ran the risk of dying by the roadside. Finally, at the end of December 1915, the Fourth Company reached Durazzo on the Albanian coast. It was being shelled by the Austrians from the sea, so they camped 10 miles away, where they remained for about a month. Due to the Austrian submarines and aerial bombings it was difficult to get supplies to Durazzo. Yet with the help of some British officers that Sandes met in the main town, she procured some food and returned to the camp a hero. On New Year's Day 1916 Sandes was made a corporal. The regiment had a formal ceremony in which all the new recruits, who like Sandes had joined the army during its retreat, were officially sworn into the Serbian army. The regiment then moved to Corfu, some sailing from Durazzo and the remainder marching to the port of Valona. Sandes went from Durazzo where she and other members of the regiment boarded a series of long flat barges and were towed out to an Italian steamer. As the barge that Sandes was on drew level with the steamer, a plane appeared and dropped its bombs either side of them, creating large jets of water rising up into the air. The barge was an easy target and the Italian captain, wanting to avoid being sunk, forced them to return to the shore and wait for another steamer.

After a few weeks in Corfu, Sandes got leave to go and work with the Serbian Relief Fund unit, which was now based there, treating those who'd survived the retreat. Many were suffering the effects of near starvation and exposure and some, having made it through the mountains, died once they reached safety. Having learnt a great deal of Serbian, Sandes also acted as an interpreter. There were British soldiers in Corfu, and Sandes was anxious about how they would receive her. At first she said they were suspicious of her, thinking that she was a camp follower, but that they came to accept her.

At Easter the regiment sailed to Salonika where the Serbians were given new British khaki uniforms. Here they celebrated the regimental Slava Day and Sandes was promoted to sergeant. Sandes then took leave to return home to Britain for a couple of months.

The hospital units that had chosen to stay in Serbia during the invasion rather than retreat faced an uncertain future. As medical workers, they hoped that they would be protected from harm under the Geneva Convention. Dr Caroline Matthews continued working for several months as a doctor, although she was transferred to a civilian hospital. Then one evening, early in the new year, Matthews was alone in her room when she says several soldiers barged in and ordered her to get dressed and collect her things. They took her outside into the snow and instructed her to get into a bullock cart. Apparently Matthews was charged with espionage, but she believed it was merely an excuse to remove her. She was taken to prison in Belgrade, where she says she met an acquaintance who was a Canadian woman who wore breeches and had her hair cut short, although she does not say exactly who this was. Matthews was then transferred to Hungary where she was imprisoned with Dr Alice Hutchinson, whom she knew, and over thirty other members of the SWH. Hutchinson said that

they had been there for about three months. The women were then permitted to travel to Britain via neutral Switzerland.[26]

Inglis and her remaining team were in Krusevac when the Germans
arrived, but they then joined the town's Czar Lazar hospital where
Dr Holloway's sister SWH unit was based. Here they maintained an
extremely overcrowded prisoner of war camp, doing their best in adverse
conditions. The Germans asked Inglis to sign an attestation as to the good
behaviour of the Germans towards the women, but Inglis refused. When
she returned to England, she learned that a month before this seemingly
odd request Edith Cavell had been executed in Belgium. Following the
international outcry at her death a signed attestation from Inglis would
have been valuable propaganda for the Germans.

Some members took the opportunity to be repatriated in December, but
a small group, including Inglis and Evenlina Haverfield, remained until
they were forced to return home in February.[27] Inglis immediately set to
work raising funds for more SWH units. Agnes Bennett arrived in Serbia
in August with the American unit, while Inglis took a new unit to Russia.

As mentioned, the Girton and Newnham SWH Unit had sailed to
Salonika with Flora Sandes in November 1915. Previously they had run
a hospital in Troyes, France, but Dr Inglis had requested that they come
to Serbia. The Girton and Newnham unit travelled a short distance over
the Serbian border to the town of Ghevgeli. But within a week of arriving
there, they received refugees from the town of Monastir, which was being
evacuated. Then, on 4 December, they were ordered to leave Ghevgeli.
Fortunately the lower section of the railway was still running, but it was
greatly overcrowded.[28] Within the unit there were three drivers and one of
them was an Australian woman called Olive Kelso King. She had been visiting family in England when war broke out, and she became fixed on the
idea of driving ambulances. She had a great deal of driving experience back
in Australia, and undertook a St John Ambulance first aid course, as well
as persuading a local garage to give her lessons in mechanics. A wealthy
woman, she tried buying an ambulance, but finding that the government
had taken them all, she bought an Alda lorry and converted it, proudly
dubbing it 'Ella the Elephant'.[29] She spent a brief period in Belgium as
a driver for the independent organisation Allies Field Ambulance Corps
before joining the SWH in May.

She continued to drive Ella and had the vehicle brought out to Serbia.
However poor the roads were, the vehicles were still valuable assets, which
made it all the more difficult for the drivers to evacuate from Ghevgeli, as
precedence for space on the trains was of course given to people:

By midnight, the whole staff had got away, with the exception of us three chauffeurs with their cars. There was no room for us, and we were left to trust to luck. There was no road, or it would have been an easy job. There was one rough track, going round by Doiran ... Thirteen French ambulances had tried to find their way to Salonika by this route, but were ambushed by the Bulgars, their cars taken and the men all killed or taken prisoners. We three girls were luckier. We were desperate as none of us could face the thought of burning our cars or remaining to be taken prisoners and forced to work for the Bulgars. The last train came in, we were standing by the station and to our joy saw there were three empty trucks.[30]

When the unit arrived back in Salonika they were forced to spend the night in a tent by the station that was generally used for the wounded waiting for evacuation. The trestles that they had to use for beds were bloodstained and covered in lice. With huge numbers of people of all nationalities arriving in Salonika, all available accommodation had been taken, yet somehow, the unit's administrator, Mrs Katherine Harley, managed to find waste ground within the city that was close to the sea and where they could pitch their hospital tents.[31] When Flora Sandes arrived back in Salonika in April 1916 after three months in Corfu, she met up with Emslie, who proudly wrote in her diary:

Flora Sandes ... arrived here today from Corfu ... she had got her wish without much difficulty, for I remember on the Mossoul she told me that she had always wished to be a soldier and fight ... she got caught in the retreat, however, shouldered a gun and was made a soldier ... she looks well and in good spirits.[32]

The following month, the administrator Harley decided to leave the Girton and Newnham Unit and return to England, where she planned to organise a new transport unit that she would bring out to the Macedonian front. Following the retreat through Serbia, the Allied forces congregated in Salonika facing onto a new battle line across Greece's borders with Albania, Macedonia (part of the Serbian Kingdom) and Bulgaria.

In July, King also decided to leave the SWH unit, although she was going to join the Serbian army as a driver. She needed a change and explained in a letter home that in the army:

I'd get much more and far better work with that than with any S.W.H. Column ... I've written to Mrs Harley, and will tell her when she comes,

that I'll be in her Column if she's counting on me, but refuse to be under
any but army discipline, or any orders but Sondermayer's [the commander of the Serbian medical services]. I've had enough of women's
discipline, or rather lack of it, & I don't want any more.[33]

As the Serbian army had lost most of its transport during the retreat, it
was grateful for volunteers such as King and Harley's new unit who could
provide their own cars. King was soon joined by two other members of the
SWH, Miss Percival and Miss Allen, and the three of them shared a flat.

Meanwhile, Sandes returned to Eastern Europe to rejoin the 2nd
Regiment in the middle of August 1916. The Romanians had now joined
the Allies and the French had taken command of the Allied forces on
the Macedonia front and were preparing for a new offensive against the
Bulgarians. Sandes summarised life in the army as they forged their way
back into Serbia:

> Scorching days followed by freezing nights, when we lay on the bare
> mountainside in clothes soaked with perspiration, and shivered, with no
> covering but our overcoats. Incessant fighting, weariness indescribable,
> but hand-in-hand with romance, adventure and comradeship, which
> more than made up for everything. Days and weeks went by during
> which one never took one's boots off; always on the alert, contesting
> every inch of the way; steadily driving the Bulgars from the positions on
> one mountain-top after another.[34]

Returning to Serbia, Sandes and her fellow soldiers had to travel light and
be ready to move off at a moment's notice. Sandes chose to arm herself
with a revolver and a carbine rather than a rifle. The carbine was lighter
and easier for Sandes to carry and to use. In addition to her cartridge belt
she carried a square of light canvas which proved very versatile. She could
either use it as a groundsheet, wrap it around herself at night, or along
with three other pieces create a bivouac to share. Later on, as Sandes
recalls climbing a muddy hill, she admits that unlike the others she did not
carry a pack on her back.[35] Wearing a khaki uniform of British issue, she
also wore an iron helmet which she found hot and quickly grew to hate.

When Sandes first joined the army and chose to retreat along with the
men through the Albanian mountains she was a focus for raising morale,
representing Serbia's ally Britain. Now she felt that she had become a
sort of mascot and was accepted as 'one of the men'. She would eat and
drink with them and continued to improve her Serbian. As was common
amongst Serbians, they called her 'Brother'.[36] When her company was in

reserve, she chose to mess with the officers, enjoying the variety it offered. Sandes explained that the soldiers did not always have full grasp of the regiment's movements or of the Serbian army in general. Instead their world was focused on daily life in their platoon and the company of which it was part. Loyally following orders, they dreamed of driving out the Bulgarians and reclaiming their home country. Sandes became fully immersed into army life.

Now advancing, rather than retreating, Sandes once more found that the reality of war was nothing like what she had imagined. Rather than brave 'hand-to-hand fighting with the bayonet' in which Sandes and her company saved the day in the final hour, Sandes spent much of her time sitting in muddy 'funk-holes' in the pouring rain, without firing a shot.[37] In the absence of trenches or natural defences, funk-holes were simply holes about 3ft deep and wide enough for two people,[38] which were dug to provide the soldiers with cover. Sometimes they had to sit for many hours with little to do but try and sleep, waiting for the next order to advance. When there was no cover at all, the soldiers lay flat on the ground, their noses pressed into the earth and their arms round their heads. It was not easy to advance through the mountainous areas. The ground was steep, covered with rocks and boulders, making it difficult to march in formation. During the day it was boiling hot, but at night it was freezing cold. When their positions were shelled by the Bulgarians, the noise would be deafening as rocks splintered and explosions echoed through the area. But Sandes declared, 'the louder the racket the more soundly I slept.'[39]

Despite snatching sleep whenever possible, Sandes suffered from fatigue, which was further exacerbated by the perpetual rain and long waits between meals. On one occasion, after a steep climb, exhausted and footsore, Sandes had to run across open ground to reach cover, but however hard she tried she could not pick up her feet and run. Her company sprinted away in front of her crossing the line of fire, but Sandes could not keep up and slowed to a walk. Bullets zipped past her, yet amazingly she was not hit and managed to reach the others who had thrown themselves flat on the ground. Many of the men watched Sandes do this, which instantly earned her a reputation for bravery that she said was completely undeserved. Yet the men were superstitious and they thought that Sandes had a charmed life.

Shortly afterwards, Sandes once again avoided death following a case of mistaken identity, reaffirming her status as untouchable. The French had supplied most of the Serbians with new, blue French uniforms, but along with a number of others in her regiment, Sandes retained her British khaki that she had acquired in Corfu. However the Bulgarians also wore khaki. In the midst of a counter-attack by the Bulgarians, Sandes found herself running towards a ravine after one of the Serbian captains to take cover. A Serbian sergeant, who did not know Sandes, thought on first sight that a Bulgarian soldier was chasing a captain as part of a brazen assault. Determined that he could hit this audacious Bulgarian, the sergeant fired at her three times before Sandes reached safety. The Sergeant could not believe he had missed, as he had a reputation as an excellent marksman. To determine that it wasn't his gun at fault he picked out and fired at a white stone near where Sandes had been, hitting it perfectly. Later, on learning of his mistake, he guiltily apologised to Sandes, saying that indeed she must be blessed. However, Sandes's luck was not to last much longer.

November brought with it much colder weather and it soon began to snow high up in the mountains where Sandes and her company were. It was about this time that Sandes wrote in a letter home that she expected that she would soon be promoted to sergeant-major.[40] Sandes was planning to spend ten days' leave with the English hospital in the town of Ostrovo, when the company was ordered to the front. Colonel Militch, to whom she always spoke in German (their common language), told Sandes that they were only going to be in reserve and that she should still go to Ostrovo as she was unlikely to miss anything. However, not realising how much Sandes had progressed with her Serbian, he then turned to his staff and said in Serbian, 'You know we are going right into the thick of it, and it's such a pity for her to get killed. I'd like to keep her out of it.'[41] Hearing this, Sandes replied in Serbian, thanking the colonel for his kind consideration, but insisting that she would prefer to stay with the men and go to the front.

Sandes and her regiment were to take part in an assault on Hill 1212, which, if successful, would reopen the Serbian army's route to Monastir. Sandes' memory of the days leading up to the attack are patchy. She remembers that on the evening of 15 November the remnants of the regiment, numbering approximately 500, were sent in as reinforcements. Hill 1212 overlooked Monastir, and the Bulgarians were in control of the summit. Climbing up towards the enemy position in the evening, Sandes' company, who were to be battalion reserve, halted and set up camp behind a large series of rocks. Laying out their groundsheets on the snow, Sandes and the soldiers tried to sleep, with only their overcoats for cover. It was freezing cold. Then, in the early hours of dawn, Sandes awoke to rifle fire followed by the ominous cry of the Bulgarians, 'Hourra! hourra!'. Immediately the corps sprang to attention with fixed bayonets. The Bulgarians were in the process of chasing the Serbian battalion, which had been higher up, back down the hill through the morning mist towards Sandes' company. The officers were trying to get all the Serbian forces to turn and face the Bulgarians:

> A moment's hesitation, a 'now or never' sort of feeling, and we scrambled to our feet and raced forward, and I forgot everything else except the immediate business in hand. As we flung ourselves on our faces again a group of Bulgars emerged out of the mist, not ten paces above us, and, dodging behind the rocks, welcomed us with a volley of bombs. They were almost on top of us, and it was actually our close quarters that saved us, for they threw the bombs over and behind us instead of into our faces.
>
> I immediately had a feeling as though a house had fallen bodily on the top of me with a crash. Everything went dark, but I was not unconscious for I acutely realised that our platoon was falling back. ... I could see nothing, and it was exactly as though I had gone suddenly blind.[42]

Sandes felt the tail of an overcoat brush over her face and immediately grabbed hold of it, desperate not to let go. The lieutenant wearing the coat was bemused when he felt the pull, and every single one of his buttons burst off his coat. Looking round to see what had snagged his coat he saw Sandes lying on the ground. The lieutenant was a small man and unable to carry Sandes, so he dragged her by the arm, unaware that he had chosen her injured side. Then he found a sergeant-major and the two men bundled Sandes into a tent, and for want of a stretcher, dragged her further across the snow covered rocks. Fortunately they were soon found by a team of stretcher-bearers who dressed Sandes' wounds, at the same time reassuring the group that the Serbians had succeeded in halting the Bulgarian advance. The ambulance man was sad that he had to cut open Sandes' new pair of breeches in order to bandage her wounds.

Thankfully Sandes' revolver belt, along with her revolver, had in fact shielded her from the full impact of the bomb-blast. However her right arm was badly broken and she had shrapnel wounds across her back and down her right side. Having started out as a nurse, Sandes now found herself on the receiving end of medical attention. Surely having seen the terrible injuries that had afflicted her patients she would have thought twice about joining the army, but Sandes had been determined to do so. The ambulance men plied her with brandy and cigarettes, for the Serbians believed that giving water to a wounded man would chill him. She was then taken to a dressing station. Sandes recalls that when she let out a wail in front of one of the doctors, rather than sympathise with her, 'he lit a cigarette, thrust it between my lips, and told me to "shut up and remember that I was a soldier"'.[43] Sandes then began the journey to the base hospitals in Salonika.

From Monastir it was approximately a four day journey from the front and through the mountains. For two days, patients would either lie flat in handcarts pulled by soldiers as Sandes was, or they were transported in an oxen cart. There were also teams of mules for those able to ride or cling on. They were then collected by an ambulance car and driven to the station at Vodena, where they were loaded on to cattle trucks and taken southwards down the line to Salonika. Mrs Harley's Women's Transport Unit was by now fully operational and it was in fact one of its ambulances that transported Sandes to the railway station at Vodena. Sandes was relieved to have been transferred from a cart to a car and was deeply impressed by the unit. In Vodena, Sandes spent one evening at the SWH and was then taken in by the new Serbian Relief Fund hospital that had just arrived. Sandes remained there for three days before taking the train to Salonika. It was a slow and uncomfortable journey and although there were several doctors on board, the wounded received little attention. By the time Sandes reached Salonika, the Allies had successfully retaken Monastir.

Meanwhile, when she arrived in Salonika, Sandes was taken to the 41st General Hospital, a British military field hospital for Serbian soldiers. She discovered that they had another woman sergeant who had been wounded, a Serbian peasant called Milunka who was about seventeen years old. Sandes said that because Milunka was a peasant, the men did not treat her with the same respect as they did Sandes.[44] Both women were in fact in the same regiment, but because they were in different battalions they had not met until now. Milunka was a loud and difficult patient and the hospital staff feared that Sandes, another woman soldier, would be equally challenging. During her time in hospital, Sandes was visited by the aide-de-camp of the prince regent, Alexander of Serbia, who awarded her with the Kara George Star. It was an award for non-commissioned officers and automatically promoted Sandes to sergeant-major. According to Sandes, after being wounded five times, Milunka returned to the regiment once more and was also awarded the Kara George Star by Prince Alexander himself. She then went to France where she won both the *Legion d'Honneur* and the *Croix de Guerre*, before returning to Serbia and marrying. Sandes was not ready for her military career to end and she was determined to get better quickly and return to the front. When officers called in to see her, she declared she would be back at the front in a matter of weeks, but in fact it would be six months.

During her convalescence period, Sandes had a series of issues with her gender identity, arising when those around her did not know whether to treat her as a lady or as a sergeant. At the hospital she spent the majority of her time in standard issue pyjamas or 'blues', yet she had managed to acquire a replacement Serbian uniform after her own uniform had been cut to shreds by the ambulance men. At Christmas she was invited to a grand dinner and planned on wearing the uniform, but an old-fashioned colonel thought that if Sandes appeared dressed as a man, it would upset several of the visiting doctors. Wanting to keep the peace, Sandes wore a nurse's uniform instead, complete with a white cap to cover her short hair.

After being discharged in January, Sandes then spent three and a half months recovering in Bizerta where she was invited to a lunch party by a French admiral. The admiral later complained that Sandes as a sergeant had not demonstrated the proper degree of respect to the officers present, yet he had seated her on his right at the table and throughout the meal treated her as a woman. Subsequently she adopted a more military demeanour in front of the admiral, but the reactions of others could be confusing. There was a Serbian commandant who was always contradictory towards Sandes. One time, when they were dining together, he was charming and treated her as a respected guest, only suddenly to criticise her uniform for being dirty and demand that she cut her hair, as it had grown too long. On another occasion Sandes was a regular visitor at an army camp and decided as a ruse to visit dressed as a woman. At first the colonel there did not recognise her, to the great amusement of the others. However, they soon asked her to change back into her uniform, saying that they did not know how to speak to her while she wore a dress. In her uniform, and sporting a strong suntan, Sandes found that many took her for a man until she spoke.

As Sandes at last returned to the front, she became increasingly concerned that the war would be over before she got there. Her old company, the 4th, no longer existed, so she was transferred into the battalion's 1st company instead and was posted to the trenches. Fortunately she found herself amongst many old friends who had also been transferred into the 1st. The Serbians, flanked by the French, British and Italians, had entrenched themselves across southern Macedonia, from Monastir across to Lake Doiran. Life in the trenches was very different from the early advance back through the mountains. Typically the company spent fifteen days on the front before moving back to spend fifteen days in the second line in reserve. The trenches were only wide enough for single file and their depth varied, depending on how rocky the terrain was, and the distance across no-man's-land ranged from 50–500yd.[45] Using communication trenches at dusk they would take up their positions overnight and at dawn they would return to their dug-outs to sleep, leaving a minimum guard in the trenches during the day armed with machine guns. Entrenched on a steep hillside, there was little if any shade during the day, and under the blazing heat there was little activity. The Serbians and Bulgarians would exchange artillery fire in the morning and then again in the afternoon. Water had to be brought up to the trenches and in the early hours of the morning the soldiers were brought tea, but as the kitchen was a fair distance away it was not particularly hot and there was no milk. For Sandes, 'life became regular and monotonous'.[46]

At regular intervals they were to man an outpost – usually three soldiers sitting in a hole in no-man's-land charged with watching vigilantly for any sign of enemy movement. Straining their eyes into the pitch darkness, they had a bell with which to raise the alarm and they were relieved every two hours. Sandes said that it was 'an eerie sort of feeling'[47] to leave the trenches and go into no-man's-land. One night, Sandes was invited to go on a raid. Avoiding the moonlight by keeping in the shadows, the raid party passed through their own barbed-wire defences. Whenever a flare lit the sky they lay flat on the ground, keeping totally still. Getting as close to the Bulgarians as they dared, they launched their bombs into the enemy trenches, hoping that they would hit their target. The explosions were met with screams and shouts followed by rifle fire, during all of which, the Serbian soldiers had to lie still and wait until it was over before returning to their own trenches.

Sandes' wounds began to give her trouble and she was forced to return once again to Salonika to have more shrapnel removed. Sandes then returned home to Britain for two months' convalescence in time for Christmas 1917. Back home she continued to wear her uniform, despite being stared at, only to realise that she had become something of a celebrity.

Once home, Sandes wanted to procure clothing and raise funds for the Serbians, and ended up working with Evelina Haverfield, the former administrator of the Scottish Women's Hospital (SWH). After being repatriated from Serbia, Haverfield had gone out with the SWH to Russia, but following the revolutions of early 1917, she had returned once more to Britain. Together Sandes and Haverfield established their own canteen fund, which provided canteens for the Serbian soldiers. Using her celebrity status, Sandes raised money for the fund through newspaper articles and public speaking. She even had an audience with Queen Alexandra to which she wore her uniform and showed the queen her revolver. Anxious to return to the front once more, Sandes found that her leave had been extended and she was asked to do a further series of lectures in France. In return she would be granted a permit to visit the Western Front. This greatly excited Sandes, but when she arrived, in March 1918, the Germans had just launched a massive new offensive, and, with the anticipation that the Allies would be forced to retreat, Sandes was not allowed to go. The general who refused her permission assured her it was nothing to do with her being a woman.

Leaving Haverfield in charge of the canteen fund, Sandes went back to Serbia, but she continued to be plagued by her injuries, which limited her activity. In September 1918, the Allies began a major offensive to retake Serbia and by 29 September Bulgaria signed an armistice. On 30 October Turkey also accepted an armistice and two days later, on 1 November, the Allies liberated the capital Belgrade. An armistice with Austria–Hungary was signed on 3 November and with Germany on 11 November. Sandes was promoted to second lieutenant and continued to serve in the Serbian army until she was demobilised on 31 October 1922.

Notes

1 Miller, Louise, *A Fine Brother: The Life of Captain Flora Sandes*.
2 Sandes, Flora, *An Autobiography*, p.9.
3 Morrison, Dr Lt-Col, *Experiences in Serbia 1914–1915*.
4 Gordon, Winifred, *A Woman in the Balkans*, p.42.
5 Matthews, Caroline, *Experiences of a Woman Doctor in Serbia*, p.22.
6 Aldridge, Olive, *The Retreat from Serbia*, p.41.
7 The state of Bosnia and Hervegovina was part of the Austro-Hungarian Empire and shared Serbia's north-western border.
8 Prior to the Balkan Wars they had been part of the Ottoman Turk Empire.
9 Miller, Louise, *A Fine Brother*.
10 Krippner, Monica, *The Quality of Mercy: Women at War, Serbia 1915–18*.
11 Paget, Dame, 'With our Serbian Allies', report to the SRF Committee on 16 June 1915.
12 *Leneman, Leah,* In the Service of Life, p.17.
13 Paget, Dame, 'With our Serbian Allies', p.12.
14 Miller, Louise, *A Fine Brother*, p.53.
15 Ibid.
16 Stobart, Mabel St Clair, *The Flaming Sword in Serbia and Elsewhere*.
17 Ibid., p.20.
18 Ibid., p.18.
19 Krippner, Monica, *The Quality of Mercy*, p.91.
20 Jordan, David, *The Balkans, Italy & Africa 1914–1918*, p.49.
21 Miller, Louise, *A Fine Brother*.
22 Jordan, David, *The Balkans, Italy & Africa 1914–1918*, p.49.
23 Emslie Hutton, Isabel, *With a Women's Unit in Serbia, Salonika and Sebastopol*, p.37.
24 Sandes, Flora, *An Englishwoman Sergeant in the Serbian Army*, pp.22–3.
25 Ibid., p.130.
26 Matthews, Caroline, *Experiences of a Woman Doctor in Serbia*.
27 Leneman, Leah, *Elsie Inglis*.
28 Emslie Hutton, Isabel, *With a Women's Unit in Serbia, Salonika and Sebastopol*, p.37.

29 De Vries, Susanna, *The Complete Book of Heroic Australian Women*.
30 Excerpt from a speech given by Olive Kelso King after the war, as printed in King, Hazel, *One Woman at War – Letters of Olive King*, pp.19–20.
31 Emslie Hutton, Isobel, *With a Woman's Unit in Serbia, Salonika and Sebastopol*.
32 Ibid., pp.67–8.
33 King, Hazel, *One Woman at War*, p.32, letter to Olive's father dated 20 July 1916.
34 Sandes, Flora, *The Autobiography of a Woman Soldier*, p.16.
35 Ibid., p.56.
36 Ibid., p.17.
37 Ibid., p.19.
38 Ibid., p.29.
39 Ibid., p.20.
40 Ibid., p.16.
41 Ibid., p.60.
42 Ibid., p.63.
43 Ibid., p.68.
44 Ibid., p.76.
45 Ibid., p.93.
46 Ibid., p.93.
47 Ibid., p.99.

7

Russia

There are peculiarities in all peoples; and one of those of the Russians is the number of females serving in their ranks, many of them as officers. Indeed, I heard that one lady commanded a regiment of Cossacks! This seems to me on a par with a General nursing a baby! But I never was 'a lady's man' so perhaps I better reserve my opinions. All I say is that I am glad the lady referred to was not the Colonel of any regiment under the wings of which I fought; and I should imagine that any 'mere male' brought before a court-martial of Amazons would stand more danger of being spanked than shot.

John Morse, *An Englishman in the Russian Ranks*[1]

It is estimated that between 400–1,000 Russian women served as individuals in their country's army.[2] It was against Imperial Law for women to enlist in the army, so the majority posed as men, avoiding medicals and joining the regiments as they marched by, or slipping into the ranks along the front. Very few actually joined as women, and for those that did, it was at the discretion of the commander to ignore the rules. It is not possible to get an accurate number of female soldiers, as their true sex was generally only discovered when they were injured and received medical treatment. Others remained undiscovered, undocumented or may have died in battle.[3]

As with elsewhere in Europe, Russia was experiencing the women's movement. In addition to those studying medicine, there was a general increase in the number of women attending university in Russia, which was around 40,000 by 1914, second only to the USA at that time.[4] Suffrage groups such as the League for Women's Equality and the Women's Progressive Party had campaigned in the years leading up to the war.[5] When war was declared, these groups provided the platforms for organising women's contribution and support. As in England and France, in 1914 there were women's groups and individuals who tried to establish corps of militant women such as S.P. Iureva in Petrograd (St Petersburg),[6] and the idea was discussed seriously in written literature.[7] However, little came of it in the first three years of the war.

Russia was also on the cusp of major political change. It was ruled by Tsar Nicholas II: the epitome of an absolutist monarch, he and his wife believed that they were divinely appointed to rule. Discontent amongst the Russian people with the way in which the country was governed, and the increasing gulf between the wealthy elite and the peasants, contributed to a political revolution in 1905, which the Tsar only narrowly survived. Tsar Nicholas responded by establishing the Duma, a legislative assembly, in a move towards representative government. However, the Tsar was reluctant to give away his power and continued to pass laws without the Duma's assent. Following its humiliating defeat in the 1905–06 Russo-Japanese war, Russia made efforts to repair its economy and modernise its army and navy. An alliance with France resulted in French investment in Russia's military and the expansion of its railways. Thus Russia was on course to match the other European armies by the end of the 1910s. In anticipation of war in western Europe, Germany watched France's ally nervously. If Germany was to declare war on France, it knew that it would also face the wrath of Russia. For Germany's Schlieffen plan to work, it relied on Russia being slow to mobilise, so that Germany could first concentrate on occupying and neutralising France and then give Russia its full attention. If Germany waited too long, it would have to contend with a much more efficient and powerful Russian army. As it was, in 1914 the Russian army 'contained 114 infantry divisions to Germany's 96, and contained 6,720 mobile guns to the German's 6,004.'[8] Despite its size advantage, the Russian army suffered from poor strategic planning and co-ordination.

The Russian Empire was vast, stretching from Scandinavia in the north-west to China in the east. In the years leading up to the First World War, the treaty that Russia held with France was a bid to create a power balance against its neighbours Germany, Austria–Hungary and the Ottoman Turks. Russia resented the interference of the latter countries in the Balkans. Consequently when war was declared, Russia defended Serbia (which had gained its independence from the Ottoman Turks in 1878[9]), declared war on Austria–Hungary and joined the Allies.

Russia justified its action by advocating freedom for the Slavic nations. The promotion of independence of the Balkan states would in turn damage the empires of Austria–Hungary and the Ottoman Turks, both of which were struggling to exert their authority over the different states under

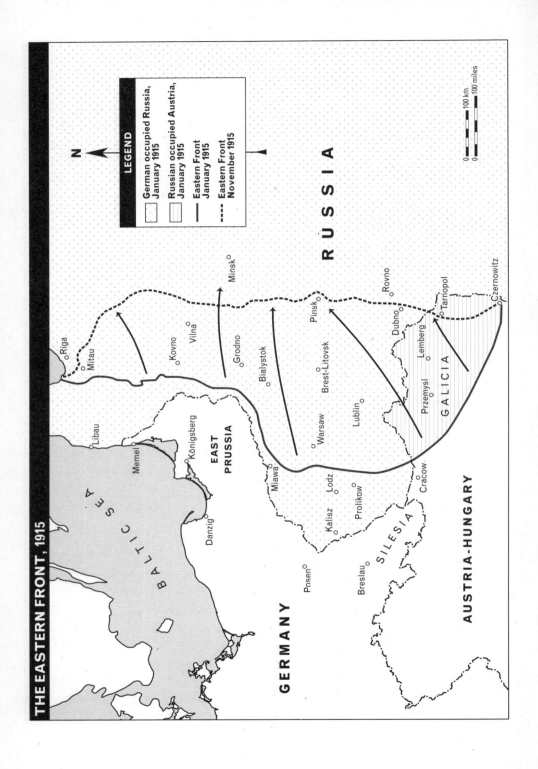

THE EASTERN FRONT, 1915

LEGEND

German occupied Russia,
January 1915

Russian occupied Austria,
January 1915

Eastern Front
January 1915

Eastern Front
November 1915

N

0   100 km
0   100 miles

BALTIC SEA

Riga

Libau

Mitau

Memel

Danzig

Königsberg

EAST
PRUSSIA

Miawa

Posen

Breslau

SILESIA

GERMANY

Kalisz

Lodz

Prolikow

Cracow.

Warsaw

Lublin

Bialystok

Grodno

Vilna

Kovno

Minsk

Brest-Litovsk

Pinsk

Przemysl

Lemberg

GALICIA

Dubno

Rovno

Tarnopol

Czernowitz

AUSTRIA-HUNGARY

RUSSIA

their control. Following Russia's declaration of war on Austria–Hungary, Germany responded by declaring war on Russia.

In what became known as the Eastern Front, the German region of Prussia shared its northern border with Russia, and directly to the south-east of this, Russia bordered the Galicia region of the Austro-Hungarian Empire. Further to the east, beyond the Black Sea in the Caucasus region, Russia bordered the Turkish Empire.

On the Western Front, as we know, the Schlieffen plan did not work as intended and soon the armies became entrenched. Although the Russians mobilised more quickly than Germany anticipated, the German army was better equipped and better trained than the Russians and with a supe-rior transport network it was able to move more quickly to deploy troops along the front. Meanwhile Russia had anticipated that the greatest threat would come from the Austro-Hungarians, choosing to concentrate its forces against them. As a result, during the opening stages of war on the Eastern Front, Russia found its victories in Galicia countered by defeats in Prussia. Turkey did not join the Central powers (Germany and Austria–Hungary) until November of 1914, but Russia nonetheless deployed reinforcements to its southern borders in the Caucasus region. This area included Armenia and Georgia. It was politically contentious and Russia feared Turkish provocation there.

Of the individual women who fought in Russia's army, several wrote their memoirs and this chapter examines three of these. Certainly each of the accounts contains a degree of exaggeration and events are drama-tised, but together they provide valuable insights into the varied lives led by women in the Russian army.

Marina Yurlova

Marina Yurlova did not set out to join the Russian army, but when war was declared she was swept up in the moment and found herself on a train bound for the front. Yurlova was only fourteen years old in 1914. The daughter of Colonel Yurloff of Raevskaya and Ekaterinodar in south-ern Russia, she had grown up in privileged circumstances in the heart of Cossack country.

Despite her comfortable life, Yurlova recalled that as a child she was always eager for adventure. Her father would captivate her with stories of the men and women who worked his land. Desperate to be amongst these exciting and romantic characters, Yurlova begged her father to let her join them in the fields and pretend to be one of them. He agreed, but told her that she would have to be ready at 3 a.m. because work would start early. Excited, Yurlova was determined to stay awake all night, but had to be shaken awake by her father's steward who was tasked to look after her. Catching up with the workers, Yurlova arrived in the fields but over the course of the morning she found it hard work, her hands blistering and her body aching. Resting for lunch, the workers began to sing, which pleased her enormously, only for them to be suddenly interrupted by the local churches ringing their bells in alarm, calling for all to come and hear the news. It was July 1914 and messengers had arrived announcing that Russia was mobilising its army. The Cossacks were dedicated fighters with a fearsome reputation amongst the rest of the Russians. In 1912 there were approximately 4 million of them, with the majority hailing from the Don and Kuban areas of the empire.[10] Traditionally they rode on horse-back and carried sabres.

Immediately everyone set off to the nearest Cossack village, but as they made their way there, Yurlova realised that rather than heading back towards her home at Raevskaya as she would have expected, the group was arriving at the neighbouring town. As they gathered, the crowds began to ready themselves, fetching uniforms while officers shouted commands. Women and children came out to join in the excitement and walked with the men as they travelled the 3 miles to the local railway station. Caught up in the excitement, Yurlova followed. Already men and horses were being loaded on to the freight trucks and soon the train was ready to leave. Yurlova recalls that suddenly it dawned on the women that their men were leaving and that they were to be left behind to fend for themselves. The large crowd began to try and stop the train, demanding that they go too. Finally they were appeased when they were permitted to follow the men to the front on the next train. Enthralled by the animated chatter, Yurlova stuck close to the women and was treated as part of the group. She had become separated from her father's steward, but as she climbed on board the second train, in the rush to find a seat she was sure that she heard someone call her name across the crowd. As the train moved off, travelling south to the Caucasus where Russia bordered Turkey, an exhausted Yurlova fell asleep.

Much later on the journey, Yurlova was shaken awake by a soldier who wanted to know who she was and where she was from. Overwhelmed and not knowing what to say, Yurlova burst into tears. The soldier calmed her down and tried again. Showing her immaturity, Yurlova displayed little concern for the anxiety her disappearance would have caused her parents. Instead her first instinct was that she was not ready to go home yet. Her adventure had only just begun, but she also knew that if the soldier found out who her father was, she would be sent home straight away. So she lied and said that her name was Maria Kolesnikova, that she was motherless and that she was following her father who was on the train that had gone ahead of them. Satisfied, the soldier made a note and left her alone. Yurlova stuck to her story.

The excitement of the journey paled into boredom. At various stages, their carriages were left in sidings, waiting for more carriages to join them or for another engine to take over hauling the train. The women became increasingly anxious that their men would be far away by now. Yurlova lost track of time but watched the changing countryside as they arrived in the south. The land was dry and yellow, unfamiliar and unfriendly. Once they arrived near the border, the women set about finding where their men were camped. Yurlova followed them to a Red Cross camp, which had become a large settlement for soldiers' wives, but after one night they pressed on, looking for their men. They arrived at a series of army camps, but found the soldiers unfriendly. They were not Cossacks and they didn't want the burden of another regiment's women and children. At one camp, Yurlova recalled that the soldiers said they could stay if the soldiers could spend the night with the women of their choice, but an officer intervened and sent the group on once more. The boredom of the train journey had now been replaced by the misery of their circumstances, as the women were forced to sleep by the roadside. The next day they managed to find the Cossack camp, and quickly the women went off to meet their men, leaving Yurlova all alone in the middle of an army camp.

Fortunately a soldier called Kosloff took pity on Yurlova and asked her what she was doing there. Repeating her story, Yurlova said she was called Maria Kolesnikova and that she was looking for her father. Kosloff agreed to help her, and she went to great efforts to stay out of the men's way. But on the third day Kosloff took her to the division headquarters and presented her to his commanding officer who shouted 'Get out! We're not running an orphan asylum!'[11] Undeterred, Kosloff took Yurlova to the army supplies store and demanded that the sergeant there find a uniform for her. Looking at the small skinny girl in a ragged dress and covered in dirt, the sergeant was dismissive, saying Kosloff would be better not bothering with her. However Kosloff got his way, telling Yurlova that even though he and his men knew she was a girl, it would be a lot easier on all of them if she didn't dress like one. Yurlova plaited her hair and tucked it securely under her cap and began her military apprenticeship.

In Kosloff, Yurlova had found a protector, someone who would look after her and show her what to do. He instructed her that if anyone asked, she was to say she belonged to the Reconnoitring Sotnia[12] of the Third Ekaterinodar Regiment, and fixed chevrons to the shoulders of her uniform. On the straps were fixed the name and number of her division.

Over time the subject of finding her father was forgotten. In a bid to get away from under the feet of Kosloff and his men, Yurlova spent time in the stables. She had grown up with horses and knew how to look after and care for them. She quickly proved her worth and those tending the horses were more than happy for her to do their work.

   Throughout her autobiography, Yurlova stresses how childlike she was and says that within the army camp the biggest distinction between her and the soldiers was that she was a child and that they were adults, rather than the difference in gender. Compared to other ethnic groups in Russia, the women in Cossack communities took on more responsibility. The Cossacks valued both self-sufficiency and independence amongst both its men and women. It was also practical because when the men were away fighting, the women had to assume control and assert their authority. In addition 'it was not unknown for groups of women to dress as men and defend their land against attacks from nomads.'[13] The Reconnoitring Hundred were deployed to help maintain the border with Turkey, and camp life consisted of routine training. Yurlova would watch the men drill, studying them closely to learn all their movements. After about two months, Kosloff allowed Yurlova to join them occasionally and eventually permitted her to take part in the regular sabre drill. Yurlova was elated when Kosloff presented her with her very own sabre, but was deeply upset when she discovered it was a ceremonial sword made of tin. She demanded a real sabre, but Kosloff said that she would have one in due course.

   When Russia declared war on Turkey, the Cossack camp was split in two, with half moving up to the front and Yurlova's half remaining in reserve. As the weather became colder, those in the camp were charged with building huts to provide more substantial accommodation. Yurlova lived in a hut with Kosloff and his men, but the enclosed quarters were the source of great embarrassment to the young teenager. As ever, lice were a problem, facilitating the spread of disease amongst the troops. Inside the hut the men would strip off their clothes and de-lice each other. Never having seen a naked man before, Yurlova was horrified and fled the building. Yurlova says that on the first occasion she had stayed outside in the rain until the men went to bed. Returning inside, she tentatively began to undress so that she could dry her clothes, but on hearing one of the men move in his sleep, she quickly jumped into bed in her wet clothes and shivered under the covers. When, a number of weeks later, they moved to the front, she was relieved to leave the confines of the hut, but found that the trenches were just as bad. There was no personal space.

   In the trenches, the men would generally sleep during the day and then go out on patrol at night. Yurlova was finally allowed to go out with them, but says that when the men reassured her that it wouldn't be dangerous she felt disappointed. Yet as they went out into the dark she became nervous, with little idea of where they were. At one point she had to dismount in the dark and hold all the horses while the rest of the party disappeared into the darkness. Later on she was allowed to be a sentry, a responsibility she readily accepted. Waking at 3 a.m. she was told she had to remain vigilant for two hours, but she became increasingly cold and found it more and more difficult to stay awake. It was not the exhilarating life that she had imagined.

Returning to the reserves, Yurlova immediately found an empty shed and began the task of de-lousing her clothes by singeing them by the fire, only accidentally to burn her underwear. When the lice kept coming back, Yurlova persuaded a Red Cross nurse to draw her a bath. She said that she was Kosloff's niece so as to avoid any questions about being in the camp.

During the latter months of 1914, the Russians were making little progress against the Turks. In fact Yurlova said that they were 'slowly retreating from an enemy whom we never saw ... our Cossacks were down-hearted ... the bravest of the brave, condemned to this life of idleness and inactivity.'[14] With food supplies running low, the soldiers took what they could find from the nearby Armenian communities. There was little love lost between the Armenians and the Cossacks. Yurlova said the men became drunk on a more regular basis and forgot to be careful of what they said in front of her as they regaled one another with stories of local prostitutes.

Reaching the River Araks, which is now called the Aras River and runs along the southern border of modern-day Azerbaijan, the Russians were being pushed back by the Turks into central Armenia. The Russians were greatly outnumbered. Seeing the Turks take position on the far side of the river, the Russian commander ordered that the main stone bridge across the river and several smaller wooden ones had to be blown up, and that way they could halt the Turks. Yurlova recalls with great drama that this was expected to be a suicide mission and Kosloff asked for volunteers to join him. According to Yurlova she was the only one to step forward and salute the general. Her action shamed about a dozen men into stepping forward. When the general insisted Yurlova join the group, she was humiliated when the soldiers complained that the operation would be further compromised if they had to babysit her at the same time. Given the proud military reputation of the Cossacks, it is unlikely that none of them volunteered, but it is likely that they would have seen little benefit in Yurlova tagging along.

Led by a sergeant with a small number of engineers, the group moved off into the dark. The sergeant deployed two small groups to set fire to the wooden bridges while he and the main party focused on the stone bridge. They separated out, following one after the other, with Kosloff telling Yurlova not to lose sight of him. Yurlova says her heart was pounding and she became more and more terrified. She was completely out of place on the mission, for when she heard gunfire, she instinctively stood up to see where it was coming from. Kosloff quickly pulled her back down to the ground. The Turkish soldiers had discovered the Russian plans and began to approach the bridge, firing ahead of them. When the sergeant engineer handed Yurlova the fuse, Kosloff took it from her and lit it himself, but in doing so he was fatally shot in the head. Horrified Yurlova scrambled to reach him, but she too was shot. As the bridges exploded one after the other, throwing flames up in the air, Yurlova crumpled and passed out.

The death of Yurlova's protector, and his ultimate sacrifice to save her, marked the end of her apprenticeship and gave her a desperate sense of guilt and a need to prove herself. Apparently the only survivor from the mission, Yurlova was awarded the Cross of St George. Both she and the other soldiers of Kosloff's company knew that she had simply been a bystander, a hanger-on, a burden to the mission. Yet Kurny, the Cossack who stepped up to take Kosloff's command, visited Yurlova in hospital and said he awaited her return. Maybe out of loyalty to Kosloff, he was prepared to accept her back.

However, before that future return to the ranks, Yurlova faced a more immediate battle: surviving hospital. She had been shot in the leg and her bandage had remained unchanged during her evacuation by cart and train to the hospital in Baku over 250 miles away. At the hospital a doctor examined Yurlova's leg, which had become swollen and black. Identifying gangrene, he declared that the leg would have to be amputated. The young girl was appalled and protested as she was taken through to the operating room to wait her turn. She continued to shout and demand a second opinion. Looking around the room, she was horrified to see body parts in buckets beside her bed. Hearing the fuss that she was making, an injured colonel stopped at the door of the operating room and insisted that the leg must be saved. Reaching out for her saviour, Yurlova said she held on to him throughout the operation to remove the bullet. She says that she refused general anaesthetic, terrified that the doctor would remove her leg when she was out cold.

Later, as she was recuperating in hospital, news spread that a young girl-soldier was in the wards and Yurlova received many female visitors. She was an object of interest, but one woman saw her as a lost soul and was determined to adopt her to save her from army life. Terrified at the thought, Yurlova appealed to the same colonel who had saved her from amputation and he helped organise her discharge from hospital and return to the front.

Yurlova returned to the front in the summer of 1915. By now she was only just fifteen years old and she rejoined the same company. Anxious about returning following the death of Kosloff, Yurlova found most of the men were not pleased to see her back. As far as they were concerned she hadn't actually helped blow up the bridges, she had simply survived. Yet Yurlova says that she took what they said to heart and was determined to prove herself to them.

Some time later, Yurlova was given instructions to wake the men for a night-time raid, but she was incredulous when they did not let her join them. So she ran, got her horse and followed them, falling in with the men at the back of the party who did not know her. The group split, with the idea that the first group would drive the enemy directly into the path of the second group (which Yurlova was in) and surround them. Suddenly Yurlova found herself in the midst of battle. Cossacks on either side of her drew their sabres, yelling at the top of their voices as they brought their swords down, again and again on each side. Yurlova drew her sabre and did her best to replicate their actions, her horse moving from side to side to avoid the men and horses that had been slain and had fallen to the ground.

In quick succession two Kurdish soldiers, one after the other, charged at Yurlova. Holding her sabre up in one of the basic drill positions, she prepared to defend herself, only for someone else to cut the soldiers down before they reached her. As the Russians declared victory, Yurlova realised that it had been Kurny who had saved her. He severely reprimanded her, but was pleased that she had survived the fight.

It was during the winter of 1915–16 that Yurlova, aged fifteen and a half, hit puberty. She was flummoxed when she began menstruating and became moody. She felt unable to confide in anyone: who would understand? She didn't want the men to think that she was homesick and so she tried to deal with it by herself. So that she would be seen as a soldier rather than a young woman, after eighteen months with the Cossacks she cut her hair.

By the beginning of 1916, the war was going badly for Russia. A year earlier, Russia had appealed for help from her allies against the Turkish Empire. In April 1915 the Allies decided to launch an attack on the Dardenelles Strait which provided Turkey with access from the Aegean Sea through to the Sea of Marmara, which in turn led to the Bosporus Strait past Istanbul into the Black Sea. The Gallipoli Campaign, as it became known, continued for eight months until January 1916, when the heavily defeated Allies were forced to retreat. Had the campaign been successful, it may well have taken Turkey out of the war. Then Russia could have diverted troops from the Caucasus region to the Eastern Front against Germany and Austria–Hungary (which in fact was Russia's western front). So in 1916 the Russians renewed their efforts and over the next six months made a significant (albeit temporary) advance into Turkey.

The dates and events in the following part of Yurlova's account become confused. She explains that during the 1916 advance into Turkey, the Hundred were in reserve. They were sent to Erzerum where Yurlova describes the aftermath of the battle which took place there from 11–16 February. She then says that they moved on towards Erzincan, describing the snow on the ground, but in fact the Russians did not seize Erzincan, the Turkish military headquarters, until July. As the Russians progressed further into Turkey they reached Sivas, about 150 miles to the west of Erzincan. Here, during the heat of battle, Yurlova and her company were tasked with moving guns and compiling an ammunition dump in a large dug-out whilst under enemy shell fire. Returning to the dump, the group found that the doorway was blocked by a large amount of earth thrown up by a shell that had exploded nearby. As Yurlova began to dig, another shell exploded.

Yurlova woke lying on her back, most of her body buried in the earth. Unable to move, and feeling strangely disconnected from the dull pain in her arm, Yurlova waited for help. She despaired that she would not be discovered until it was too late, but in due course a rescue party arrived. She tried to call out, but could make no noise – fortunately one of the men caught sight of her. Yurlova was taken to hospital in Tiflis (Tbilisi in Georgia). Here she spent at least two months recuperating in an officers' ward. She met a wounded pilot who suggested that she enrol in the local automobile school and train as a mechanic. Whilst in Tiflis, Yurlova was invited to an afternoon tea at the doctor's house. Wearing her uniform, she felt deeply uncomfortable compared to the society ladies dressed in the latest women's fashions. Overhearing various derogatory remarks from other guests, Yurlova decided to refuse all such future invitations.

Yurlova was accepted on to the automobile school's training course in the autumn of 1916 and was given accommodation in the local barracks. The students spent approximately three weeks in the classroom followed by a couple of weeks in the garage before learning to drive. Yurlova was a practical individual and learnt to drive quickly. As learners the students were given a petrol allowance, which they used to their advantage, offering to drive officers around and managing to earn sizeable tips. In the winter, after qualifying, Yurlova was assigned as a military driver in Erivan. She continued in this role until the summer of 1917 by which time Russia was in the midst of a political revolution.

In March 1917 the Russian population finally turned on the Tsarist regime and the first revolution took place, resulting in the Tsar's abdication. He named his uncle as his successor, but he refused the crown and so the Romanov dynasty came to an abrupt end. The war was putting the country and its people under considerable strain and hardship and they had lost sight of why they were at war. In a bid to take charge of the military situation, the Tsar had appointed himself commander-in-chief of the Russian army in September 1915, but this only resulted in him becoming the personification of Russia's military failures and its general suffering.

Following the March revolution, a provisional government was established which faced the difficult task of re-motivating a tired and demoralised army. Along the Eastern Front, the Russians had lost a considerable amount of land to the Germans and the Austro-Hungarians and the new government declared that the Russians had to defend their new-found liberty and drive the enemy out. However there was growing insubordination within the army and an increasing number of deserters. In the summer of 1917, the provisional government supported a new, decisive offensive across all fronts. It was during this time that Yurlova was employed as an ambulance driver. As she drove back and forth near the front, Yurlova's ambulance was hit by a shell and the resulting crash left her hospitalised for the following year, by which time the second Russian revolution in October 1917 had brought the Bolshevik party to power and Russia had descended into civil war.

Throughout her account, Yurlova stresses that she was seen as a child and treated akin to a drummer boy. She was an army volunteer carrying out supportive work, and the one time she describes being engaged in hand-to-hand combat she does not succeed in attacking the enemy and is unable to defend herself. Instead she has to be rescued. Importantly, she had protectors in the form of Koslof and later Kurny. With the rich military tradition of the Cossacks, Yurlova yearned to prove herself, and there was a certain sense of guilt that she didn't. As a young teenager she felt the lack of privacy acutely. Although she says that she decided to become a driver following the suggestion of another patient, it is possible that after turning sixteen and clearly no longer a child, it seemed a more appropriate role for a young woman than returning to the front. She was still able to wear a uniform, act in a masculine way and serve her country, but there were other female drivers, meaning she was no longer on her own amongst the men.

Princess Kati Dadeshkeliani

Princess Kati Dadeshkeliani described her decision to join the Russian army as an opportunity to escape from a deep depression brought on by a series of personal tragedies. Her father had been assassinated in 1909, then in 1914 her sister had committed suicide and her short-lived marriage had collapsed. According to Dadeshkeliani, the idea came about when she was invited to a small dinner party at a friend's house in March 1915. In an attempt to draw Dadeshkeliani out of her despair, her friend Madame Zulgadar insisted that she join her family and their guest Colonel Edik Khogandokov for dinner. Conversation moved on to the war and Madame Zulgadar joked that the colonel should take her to the front, but he replied that her responsibility was at home with her children. Dadeshkeliani said that she had no dependents and declared she wanted the colonel to take her. It seemed that he did not take much persuading, and he suggested that Dadeshkeliani would have to pose as his nephew. Consequently Princess Dadeshkeliani became Prince Djamal Dadeshkeliani.

While Dadeshkeliani saw army life as something to give her focus and rescue her from her depression, it is possible that the colonel viewed it as an amusing distraction. Also, he was not in great health and Dadeshkeliani would provide him with a degree of companionship. In the same way that Kosloff acted as a protector for Marina Yurlova, the colonel was to look after Dadeshkeliani. We can only speculate about the nature of their relationship and whether or not it was more than friendship. It may be that Dadeshkeliani skimmed over the details so as not to damage her social standing. Whatever the precise nature of the relationship, Dadeshkeliani was nonetheless a woman of status and privilege, and she used her connections to travel to the front and assume the role of an officer, an opportunity that would have been unavailable to the majority of Russian women.

In the opening months of the war along the Eastern Front, strategists on both sides looked back at Napoleon's invasion of Russia and his defeat after overstretching his supply lines, looking to learn important lessons. However, the first month of fighting is described as 'a museum piece of nineteenth-century warfare rather than an expression of the new possibilities open to twentieth-century soldiers.'[15] To their horror, the cavalry regiments realised they were no match for the new mechanised artillery. During the nineteenth century, when armies had staged large pitched battles, it was not unusual for wives of officers to travel and be close to their husbands. Often they would reside in a nearby town and on the day of battle join a party of observers on a suitable hill to watch events unfold. It could be that Dadeshkeliani's decision to go to the front was more in keeping with the old ways, yet so as not to be banished, she assumed a male disguise.

Dadeshkeliani recalls with almost childish enthusiasm that she only had three days to learn how to be a man. Conveniently, Madame Zulgadar's nephew was a subaltern and showed her how she should walk, salute and other basics. She then describes with great drama how she prepared her new appearance, saying that the hairdresser refused to cut her hair as he had cut her sister's hair short after her death and thought it would bring bad luck. So Dadeshkeliani demanded his assistant cut it:

> The assistant gave my long hair a close cut, and then I proceeded to don my Caucasian uniform: long dark grey riding-coat with belt (cherkesa), black blouse (beshmet), little light grey fur cap, light grey hood (baslilik), soft leather boots, Caucasian sword, dagger and revolver.[16]

During the long journey from Petrograd to the Austrian front, Dadeshkeliani says she invited the two daughters of a general to join her, and succeeded in fooling them that she was in fact a young male soldier. Yet despite this, Dadeshkeliani continued to worry that she would be recognised by officers with whom she had socialised in Petrograd. Seeing one of these men, whom she had only met briefly, she prepared herself and saluted, only for him to walk straight past her without looking. Yet the colonel acknowledged her concerns and brought together six officers that Dadeshkeliani knew and took them into his confidence. When they all swore that they would not reveal Dadeshkeliani's true identity she was called into the room to present herself as Prince Djamal. In her memoirs, Dadsehkeliani presents her experiences as an adventure, a successful ruse in which she posed as a man, and describes how wonderful it was that she fooled everyone, while the men that knew her secret protected her honour. Although she undertook a series of trips into the firing line, the colonel kept her close by, and most of the time she undertook auxiliary roles rather than combat duties.

Dadeshkeliani recalls that one of her earliest tasks was to take a message from the colonel to a regiment in the trenches. A skilled rider, she eagerly set off on horseback, but as she approached the rear trenches she found her route under enemy shell fire. Although 'a new and disagreeable sensation',[17] Dadeshkeliani was determined not to turn around or dismount. She did not want to be deemed a coward. Despite the danger, she successfully made her way there and back without being wounded. It was her first real experience of the war zone.[18] Next, Dadeshkeliani was sent to a field hospital and from there she went on to one of the hospitals further behind the lines. The experience made her feel nauseous and filled her with horror. It was not somewhere that she wished to stay. Instead, she declared, 'I was vexed at not being sent to the trenches, and began to show a sullen face to my Colonel.'[19]

Noticing that something was upsetting her, the colonel confronted Dadeshkeliani. She said that he was too protective of her, and he agreed to organise for her to go to the trenches. But once there, she was deeply unhappy. She quickly became disenchanted and said that there were plenty of men there who were more capable than her:

> I knew I could be of no assistance to them, and it was a humiliating thought. No, a woman is not in her place in the fighting ranks.[20]

Next, Dadeshkeliani worked with an ambulance unit. Although she maintained her disguise as Prince Djamal, she felt more comfortable in what she considered a naturally feminine role. After spending two tedious hours on outpost duty, and then accompanying a cavalry patrol in which nothing happened, Dadeshkeliani chose to return to ambulance work. Then, in August 1915, the colonel had to return to Petrograd due to ill health and Dadeshkeliani spent three months as a quarter-master for a hospital in Kamenetz-Podolsk. She then returned to Petrograd for the winter of 1915–16, a privilege denied the thousands of men ordered to remain in the frozen, snow-filled trenches. It was during this period that Dadeshkeliani met the Dowager Empress Marie as Prince Djamal.

The colonel soon recovered and was promoted to the rank of general. Together Dadeshkeliani and the general returned to the front, and in April 1916 she began work as the assistant to the head of an ambulance unit. Duties involved supervising parties of stretcher-bearers, tracking down supplies and mechanical parts that had gone astray, and assisting with the evacuation of a hospital near the front when it came under aerial attack. Dadeshkeliani had found a role in which she was content to remain, undertaking similar work to the women on the Western Front who worked for the First Aid Nursing Yeomanry as voluntary aid detachments, and for the other independent groups. Yet unlike the members of those organisations, Dadeshkeliani continued to pose as a man.

Three months later, Dadeshkeliani was out riding in a group when a horse struck her leg, breaking it badly. The true sex of a number of the women who posed as men in the Russian army was discovered when they were injured and given medical treatment. Dadeshkeliani was apparently lucky on this count because, when she arrived at the hospital, she was recognised by a friend who was working there as a nurse, who helped conceal the truth. Despite the odds they seemed to have succeeded, or the general helped avert any scandal, as after three months of recovering, Dadeshkeliani returned to the ambulance in November 1916. She remained with it, taking on administrative duties until the summer of 1917 when political events forced her into exile and to resume her life as Princess Kati.

Dadeshkeliani's story seems to be more about finding a place for herself and some sort of escape from her life, rather than being driven by a deep patriotic desire or an ambition to prove women capable of combat. Instead, she admitted that she did not think herself suited to life in the trenches and questioned whether it was a suitable role for women at all.

Maria Bochkareva

Maria Bochkareva is the most famous of Russia's female soldiers in the First World War. Born in 1889 into what was reported as a life of poverty, her actual family circumstances must be treated with some caution. As Russia was moving towards industrialisation, recent scholars, including Sergei Pushkarev and Jerome Blum, have questioned whether Russian conditions were actually as harsh as those portrayed in Soviet accounts of the period, and the American scholar Paul Gregory has demonstrated that living conditions were actually improving considerably during the period of Bochkareva's childhood. Nonetheless, she was born into what by contemporary standards would be regarded as considerable poverty.[21] Her family settled in Tomsk in Siberia where their life was hard, but made worse by her drunken father who became physically abusive. However Bochkareva was a survivor and retained hope that one day she would find a way out. Her escape came in the form of a young soldier returning from the front called Afanasi Botchkarev. He was serving in the Russo-Japanese war (February 1904–September 1905) and after a brief courtship, he proposed to fifteen-year-old Maria, for whom 'anything seemed preferable to the daily torments of home.'[22] Yet neither of them had any money, so they worked as manual labourers to earn a living:

> Hard work never daunted me, and I would have been satisfied, had it only been possible for me to get along with Afanasi otherwise. But he also drank ... and intoxication invariably brutalised him.[23]

Having escaped her father, Bochkareva now found herself in an abusive marriage of her own. In her memoirs, against a life of domestic violence,

Bochkareva presents herself as a loud, dramatic individual with a hot temper. Several times, finding herself in dire circumstances, Bochkareva declared with great drama that she attempted suicide. Other times she recalled screaming for attention, essentially throwing a tantrum to get her way. This is in contrast to Yurlova who portrayed herself as a wilful child, and to the aristocratic Princess Dadeshkeliani who was careful to retain a certain level of decorum and propriety. Bochkareva, on the other hand, is a hardened individual with no social grace or refinement. Yet she demonstrated that she could work hard and had a degree of intelligence. Bochkareva and her husband spent two years working for an asphalt business, laying roads and floors. She was promoted and given charge of a team of workers, while Afanasi was not, which created more conflict between them.

Still a teenager, Bochkareva left Afanasi and went on to meet a butcher called Yasha, and they lived as man and wife for three years. They had a good life together, but Yasha had a criminal past, and in the spring of 1912, when he helped conceal an escaped convict, he was arrested and imprisoned. Eventually Yasha was sentenced to four years' exile in Siberia, but Bochkareva was able to elect to go with him. This required her to spend two hellish months in the women's wing of the prison where Yasha was held, until, in the spring of 1913, when the snows had melted, they were released for the trek to outer Siberia. They ran a butcher's shop together, but Yasha's depression at his situation, his growing addiction to gambling and his jealousy of other men, meant their relationship broke down and became abusive. As their situation continued to deteriorate, Bochkareva once more looked for a way out. In the late summer of 1914, news of war reached Siberia:

> Day and night my imagination carried me to the fields of battle, and my ears rang with the groans of my wounded brethren. ... My heart yearned to be there, in the seething caldron of war, to be baptized in its fire and scorched in its lava. The spirit of sacrifice took possession of me. My country called me. And an irresistible force from within impelled me.[24]

In September, Bochkareva succeeded in getting permission to return to Tomsk, her family home, to contribute to the war effort. She cut her hair short and travelled in men's clothes. It took Bochkareva several months to reach Tomsk, where she learned that Afanasi had been sent to the front and was now a prisoner under the Germans.

Bochkareva said that is was only after a degree of soul-searching that she settled on becoming a soldier. She wanted to fight. The 25th Reserve Battalion had their headquarters in Tomsk, and with her mind made up,

Bochkareva went to enlist. She told the clerk that she wanted to speak to the commander. When she told him she wished to enlist, the man burst out laughing, calling for others to come and share the joke. But Bochkareva persevered and once more asked for the commander. Instead, she was met by his adjutant, who explained that women were not permitted to enlist because it was against the law. But once more Bochkareva asked to see the commander who simply repeated what the adjutant had said, saying that army regulations would not allow it. Besides, he argued, women were too weak. Yet he was impressed by Bochkareva's refusal to take no for an answer. He recommended that she send a telegram to the Tsar himself to express her determination to fight and to request permission to enlist. In a matter of days, the commander received a reply instructing him to accept Bochkareva. Her parents did not share her excitement. They were old and wanted Bochkareva to stay and care for them.

News of Bochkareva's enlistment spread, and many soldiers came to look at the new recruit as she arrived at the headquarters to join the 4th Company of the 5th Regiment. She was issued with her regulation uniform and a rifle, and had her hair clipped close to her scalp. Presenting herself in her uniform, Bochkareva had no time to get used to her new identity, as she was met with even more staring and further outbursts of laughter.

For Bochkareva's first night in the barracks, she dared not sleep. Her parents had warned her that, as the only woman amongst so many men, she would simply become a prostitute. She was placed in a general dormitory and the men were ordered to leave her alone, but they assumed that she was a 'woman of loose morals' and she spent the night fighting off their advances, actually hitting and kicking them as they tried to grope her.

To become accepted and seen as a soldier rather than a woman it would take time, and Bochkareva would have to prove herself:

It was slow work to establish proper relations with the men. ... I continued to mind my own business and never reported the annoyances I endured from the men. Gradually I won their respect and confidence. The small group of volunteers always defended me.[25]

It was common for the soldiers to adopt nicknames, and Bochkareva called herself Yashka, in honour of her lover, Yasha. Like Flora Sandes did in Serbia, Bochkareva made a point of getting involved in the social side of army life. She would join in with card games and story telling, and began to form friendships.

The new recruits were trained relentlessly over a period of three months. Bochkareva excelled in rifle training, earning both a commendation and further respect. Then, in February 1915, the company received their orders to go to the Polish front. Granted a week's leave the men intended to make the most of their last days of freedom and headed to the whore house. For their amusement they persuaded Bochkareva to go with them, if she wanted to be a proper soldier:

> Our group was ... promptly surrounded by the women of the place, and one of them, a very young and pretty girl, picked me out as her favourite to the boundless mirth of my companions. There was drinking, dancing and a great deal of noise. Nobody suspected my sex, not even my youthful sweetheart, who seated herself in my lap and exerted all her charms to entice me. She caressed me, embraced me and kissed me. I giggled, and my comrades gave vent to peaks of laughter.[26]

Then suddenly an officer burst into the room to round up the men that had broken their curfew. Most of them managed to escape and return to the barracks, but to their great amusement Bochkareva was arrested by the officer and spent the night in the military gaol.

At the end of the week, Bochkareva and the men set off to the front. The men were transported in vans while the officers sat in passenger cars. The officers invited Bochkareva to join them, but she insisted on staying with the men: she did not want to undermine the respect she had earned amongst them.

Meanwhile, in March 1915, Italy, seeing an opportunity to benefit from the conflict, declared war on its long-term adversary, the Austro-Hungarian Empire. Germany was concerned about its ally facing war on another front and began to take control of the Empire's army, placing German officers in charge of Austro-Hungarian soldiers. Until this point, the Germans and the Austro-Hungarians had failed to co-ordinate their offences on Russia. Now they managed to make significant progress and throughout the course of the year pushed the Russians further and further back along the Eastern Front.

Bochkareva and her fellow soldiers occupied a series of run-down trenches about 5 miles from the frontline. They could hear the heavy guns firing up ahead and watched the numerous wounded come past as they were taken to the hospitals in the rear. Within a few days, they were ordered further forward where they came under regular shell fire. The Russians had been firing heavily on the German positions in anticipation of a major offensive in which Bochkareva would take part:

> The front trench was a mere ditch, and as we lined up along it our shoulders touched. The positions of the enemy were less than three-quarters of

a mile away, and the space between us was filled with groans and swept by bullets. It was a scene full of horrors. Sometimes an enemy shell would land in the midst of our men, killing several and wounding more. We were sprinkled with the blood of our comrades and spattered by the mud.[27]

The attack took place at night, under the cover of darkness. Describing going over the top, Bochkareva said that her head was full of thoughts of family, of her past and of life and death, only to be replaced by confusion as men either side of her fell, either wounded or killed. 'Forward!' they were ordered to push on in the face of heavy enemy fire, but on reaching the Germans' barbed wire defences they found that the wire had not been cut by the earlier Russian bombardment. When this became apparent, the order came to retreat, but less than half of Bochkareva's company made it back. Many lay in no-man's-land calling out in pain and shouting for help. Their cries were torturous for Bochkareva and the others to hear. Unable to stand it any longer, Bochkareva made the decision to go and rescue the wounded:[28]

I climbed out of the trench and crawled under our wire entanglements. There was a comparative calm, interrupted only by occasional rifle shots, when I would lie down and remain motionless, as though I were a corpse. There were wounded within a few feet of our line. I carried them one by one to the edge of our trench where they were picked up and carried to the rear. The saving of one man encouraged me to continue my efforts till I reached the far side of the field. Here I had several narrow escapes. A sound, made accidentally, was sufficient to attract several shots, and I only saved myself by at once lying flat upon the ground. When dawn broke in the east, putting an end to my expeditions through No Man's Land, I had saved about fifty lives.[29]

For her bravery, Bochkareva was recommended for an award. Then the Russians tried to mount a second major offensive on the German positions, again during the night. This time the wire had been cut and the soldiers fixed their bayonets to their rifles and descended into the German trenches, but Bochkareva was shot in the leg and collapsed in no-man's-land. There she lay in the dark, surrounded by others calling out into the night as her company routed the enemy. In the early hours of dawn, to her great relief, she was collected by the stretcher-bearers and eventually transported to hospital in Kiev. Arriving there during Easter 1915, Bochkareva remained in hospital for about two months before returning to her regiment. Bochkareva says that towards the end of the summer of 1915 her company moved to a relatively quiet section of the front. Her main tasks were joining raiding groups or going out with observation parties who would man advanced listening-posts. They would sleep during the early part of the day and, as with the offensives, carry out their work at night.

Observation parties were typically made up of four soldiers. Located at approximately 50ft intervals along the front, each post was simply a place close to the enemy line, hidden in the undergrowth, maybe behind a tree or in a hole in the ground where the party could remain concealed. The party would crawl out to the post under the cover of darkness as quietly as possible so as to remain undetected by the enemy. The soldiers had to listen out for any unusual noise or movement, perhaps a surprise attack or enemy raid. As was standard practice, the parties would be relieved every two hours. On one occasion Bochkareva said she heard what she thought was a friendly patrol so she called out the password, but the men failed to give a reply so her observation party opened fire. Rather than fire back, the Germans dropped to the ground and waited silently for what Bochkareva estimated to be about two hours. They then crawled towards the post and attacked Bochkareva's party. One threw a grenade, which missed and exploded behind the listening post and then the two groups then began firing at one another. Out of the eight members of the German patrol, Bochkareva says they killed two, wounded four and the two others escaped.

Bochkareva also volunteered for scouting parties, for which each member would be armed with grenades. Apparently it wasn't unusual for opposing scouting parties to meet one another in no-man's-land. Either there would be a fight, or if one party had the advantage of not being seen by the other, it would bide its time and attack the others from behind with the hope of capturing the enemy.

In August 1915, the Germans bombarded the Russian trenches where Bochkareva and her company were stationed. The artillery succeeded in tearing apart the Russians' barbed wire defences. Bochkareva says that the sound of the guns was deafening, the very ground shook and men were buried alive by earth thrown up by the shells. Then, at 6 a.m., the Germans left their trenches. The Russians shelled no-man's-land and the German trenches heavily, while the men in the Russian trenches waited for orders. When the Germans were within 100ft, the soldiers directed concentrated rifle fire at them. Then they were ordered to leave their trenches and drive the Germans back.

Following the Russian counter-attack, Bochkareva was once again amongst those who volunteered to help the overwhelmed medical staff. She was recommended for the Cross of St George, but unlike Marina Yurlova, she was told that as a woman she could not receive it, although she was convinced that she had heard of some Red Cross nurses who had done. During the attack, Bochkareva had been shot in the arm, and after a short recovery period she was attached to an advanced first aid post as a medical assistant for most of Autumn 1915. She was recommended for a gold medal of the second degree for her medical work.

In late October 1915, Bochkareva was fully recovered from her arm wound. Accepted back in the ranks, she was promoted to corporal and given charge of eleven men. Unlike Flora Sandes, Bochkareva shared her experience of what it was like to make the decision to save one's own life by taking another. On one particular occasion she volunteered to take part in a large scouting party of thirty soldiers. The party set off through some woodland, convinced there was an enemy patrol hidden there, but it reached the Germans' barbed wire without being attacked. The soldiers realised all too late that the Germans had let them pass only to attack them from behind. The Russians were outnumbered and they were so close that there was a danger they might shoot one another, so they fixed their bayonets and charged:

> I found myself confronted by a German, who towered far above me. There was not an instant to lose. Life or death hung in the balance.
>
> I rushed at the German before he had time to move and ran him through the stomach with the bayonet. The bayonet stuck, and the man fell. A stream of blood gushed forth. I made an effort to pull out the bayonet, but failed. It was the first man that I had bayoneted; and it all happened with lightening-speed.[30]

Unable to use her rifle or bayonet to defend herself, Bochkareva was pursued by another German soldier. Instinctively she ran back to her trenches, stumbling as she went, disorientated and trying to find her way back through the wire. Remembering that she had several grenades, she lobbed one behind her into the path of her pursuer and ducked for cover to shield herself from the blast. Exhausted, she made it back to her own trenches.

Alongside these particular episodes that stood out in Bochkareva's memory, she recalled that as the winter progressed the front became less active and the soldiers' daily routine became tediously repetitive. As the snow increased and the temperature plummeted, conditions became tougher and the Russians' food supplies ran dangerously low. Frustration grew and the soldiers longed for battle, a major offensive that would end the conflict and allow them to leave the trenches forever. Men froze to death and at the end of the year Bochkareva, like many others, was hospitalised with severe frostbite. For the majority this resulted in amputation, but like Yurlova, Bochkareva was determined not to lose her foot and succeeded in keeping it. Afterwards she took great care of her feet, but it was difficult when the soldiers' boots simply fell apart, their clothes deteriorated into rags and there was a long waiting list for replacements. When the snow began to melt in spring 1916, the soldiers had to contend with wading through icy muddy water. Bochkareva was injured again in March 1916 when she was shot in the leg and the bone shattered. This time she was sent to hospital in Moscow until early June 1916. By the time she rejoined her regiment, the winter had long passed and they were now at the mercy of a swelteringly hot summer. Yet the Russian army was now making progress. In December 1915, the Allies had met at Chantilly and discussed launching simultaneous offensives on both the Western and Eastern Fronts during the following summer in order to apply considerable pressure to the Germans. The Russians were under a certain amount of strain and needed help. With the Tsar as its new commander-in-chief, Russia wanted to prove to the Allies that it could turn its fortunes around. Equally, France and England needed Russia to remain in the war. Russia also asked that, despite the invasion of Serbia by the Central powers, the Allies maintain their military base at Salonika on the Macedonian front and keep the Bulgarians occupied.[31]

The Allies began to plan a large offensive for the summer, which became the Battle of the Somme. However, in February 1916, the Germans launched their own offensive on the Western Front at Verdun, which took the French by surprise. Now it was the French who needed the Russians to act to take the pressure off them. The following month, the Russians decided to attack the Germans near Belarus, but it was a total failure. It wasn't until June when they launched what was known as the Brusilov offensive (after General Brusilov), that the Russians began to have major success along the Eastern Front.[32]

During this period Bochkareva was again wounded, however, this time badly, when a shell exploded close by. She had pieces of shrapnel lodged in her back. She was sent to Lutzk where the doctors said that they did not have the expertise to treat her, so she was then sent to Kiev, but the hospitals there were inundated and she lay for several hours in her stretcher in the street. Finally, she was sent to Moscow. The shrapnel was lodged in Bochkareva's spine causing paralysis and the surgeons were unsure how to proceed. Ultimately it took four months before she began to regain some movement, and then she worked hard to get back to her old self. Before Bochkareva could return to the trenches she had to learn how to walk again. All in all, her recovery took six months.

In December 1916 Bochkareva returned to her regiment once more, but she sensed a definite shift for the worse in morale. Yet she continued as before and was promoted to Senior NCO. However, by March 1917, there was growing discontent amongst the men and rumours of revolution at home in the cities, with stories that the Tsar had abdicated. This led to insubordination within the ranks and an increasing number of men deserting. The new provisional government tried to take control of the military situation, declaring that Russia was now fighting the Germans to protect its newly-won liberty. However, after three years in the trenches, the men were demoralized and unwilling to keep fighting. Alexander Kerensky, a member of the Duma who had had a significant role in the revolution, was appointed war minister and in July 1917 he became the prime minister of the provisional government. Following his success the previous year, Kerensky placed General Brusilov in charge of the Russian army and hastily they planned a new offensive that they hoped would re-galvanize the army. Yet, compared to the months of planning that had gone into the 1916 offensive, this time Bruslilov only had a matter of weeks. What was called the 'Second Bruslilov Offensive' or the 'Kerensky Offensive' was launched on 1 July 1917 and it was initially a success. But by 16 July the offensive had collapsed and several days later the Germans launched a large counter-attack, leaving the Russians in a worse position than they had been before.

The Women's Battalion of Death

Meanwhile, in May 1917, the new Russian government came up with another idea to boost morale. The president of the Duma, Michael Rodzianko, visited the front where Bochkareva and her fellow soldiers were organised for review. For Rodzianko, Bochkareva offered a wonderful opportunity for generating pro-war propaganda, and after being introduced to her, he asked her to return with him to Petrograd.[33] Back on the home front, the Russian women's organisations that had been supporting the war effort now began to petition the government to be allowed to form militia groups.[34] The government planned to use Bochkareva as the figurehead for a new female combat battalion. As with the publicity stunt in France in 1914, when the Scottish-American opera singer Mary Garden dressed as a young man and tried to enlist in the French army,[35] the aim with the female battalion was to shame the men back into fighting. However, rather than declaring their undying patriotism and then returning to suitable roles such as nursing, Bochkareva's women would be trained and sent into the trenches. The women were to be held up as examples to the rest of the country.

Bochkareva became a celebrity. She had her photograph taken and was surprised to see her image staring back at her from posters across Petrograd. She was made to speak publicly at the Maryinski Theatre promoting the battalion and inviting women to register that very evening. Newspaper reports followed, which encouraged yet more women. Over 2,000 women applied and were instructed to report to the Kolomensk Institute for medical examinations and enlistment. The institute became the battalion's barracks. The recruits hailed from a range of social backgrounds: there were dressmakers, servants, factory workers, peasants, aristocrats and university students.[36] The medical examinations were more lenient than for men and a number of the medical team were female doctors. Bochkareva gave a speech to her new recruits, warning them that 'there will be strict discipline, and any offence will be severely punished. ... It is the purpose of this Battalion to restore discipline in the army. It must, therefore, be irreproachable in character'.[37] She concluded by telling the new recruits that they were 'no longer women, but soldiers'.[38] The new battalion was called the Women's Battalion of Death, a shock battalion designed to be extremely mobile and lead an aggressive assault intended to turn around Russia's fortunes in the trenches. The following day, the women were taken to the barber to have their hair cut short, something which provided an amusing spectacle for members of the public.

Historian Laurie Stoff has studied the accounts of Russian women who joined the army and says that the majority were given supportive roles, such as carrying ammunition like Marina Yurlova or helping with the wounded as Princess Dadeshkeliani did. Despite their lack of training, many were assigned medical roles and 'while all these activities required the women to put themselves in very dangerous situations and risk their own lives, few reports speak of women actually carrying out violent actions against others.' This may be the result of correspondents and observers choosing not to report on women taking life, which seems to be a consistent attitude across Europe at the time.[39] This is why Bochkareva's story and her account are so exciting and she became so well known, because she had a combative role and she discusses the act of killing in her memoirs. Here lay another problem, however: the government looked for experienced women soldiers around whom they could construct Bochkareva's and any additional women's battalions. They found they lacked female officers, and indeed Bochkareva was given twenty-five[40] male officers during the training of her battalion before appointing women for promotion. It was the opinion of American journalist, Florence MacLeod who reported for *Leslie's Weekly* from Russia, that the lack of female officers meant 'the movement was impossible from the first and was doomed to failure.'[41]

She believed that Bochkareva had sufficient character and leadership qualities to govern her battalion, but that the government would be hard pressed to find any others as great as her.

Certainly the women who enlisted may have heard stories from the front over the previous few years, but many, fuelled by patriotism and the desire to fight, found their grand vision of army life did not match reality. Bochkareva believed in discipline and was extremely strict, forcing the women out of bed in the early hours and dismissing them for the mildest flirtatious glance at a male officer. She would slap the women if they misbehaved.

In light of the new political age, Bochkareva's women campaigned for a committee, whereby they would be consulted on each decision and the duties of the battalion. Bochkareva objected strongly. As far as she was concerned, for the army to function and to act decisively, soldiers needed to respond immediately to any order. The decision taken by many soldiers to form committees and to challenge every order had effectively paralysed the Russian army, and this inertia only benefited Russia's enemies. Despite orders from the government to accept the women's request, Bochkareva refused, and as a result she lost a large proportion of her battalion and was left with about 300 women.[42] Aside from the political challenges the women faced, men would also gather outside the barracks and taunt them. They were criticised in particular by the growing number of supporters of the Bolshevik political movement who saw the women as prolonging the war they wanted to end. Antagonism between the battalion and the Bolsheviks came to a head when the battalion was asked to join a pro-government march planned to coincide with a Bolshevik demonstration on the Mars Field of Petrograd. A fight broke out and shots were fired. Bochkareva reported that ten of the women were wounded and she herself was struck unconscious and woke up in hospital. For Bochkareva, this was a demonstration of the battalion's loyal support for the provisional government and its first test.

Bochkareva's battalion also attracted attention from overseas. British Suffragette and founder of the Women's Social and Political Union Emmeline Pankhurst celebrated the March revolution and the Tsar's abdication. She had socialised with a number of Russian political refugees and had followed Russian politics from afar. Now she hoped that Russian women would seize the opportunity for political independence. She knew that the provisional government wanted to continue the war, but there was a growing campaign for peace, and she feared that with Germany in a position to dictate terms, Russian women's new-found chance for independence would be lost. When she heard that Ramsay MacDonald, the Labour Party leader, was going to Russia to advocate peace, she was determined to go there herself and encourage women to support the war. Echoing the war minister Kerensky, she believed that Russia needed to win the war in order to foster the new democracy.

Pankhurst arrived in Petrograd on 18 June and a day later the British House of Commons voted in favour of the female vote. Pankhurst conducted a series of talks to inspire the Russian women to follow the British example. She gave one such speech at a fundraising event for the new women's battalion at Petrograd's Army and Navy Hall, in which she referenced Bochkareva's battalion, saying 'I honour these women who are setting such an example to their comrades'.[43] Pankhurst went on to meet Bochkareva, who said, 'Mrs Pankhurst became a frequent visitor of the Battalion, watching it with deep interest as it grew into a well-disciplined military unit. We became very much attached to each other.'[44]

At the end of June 1917, the Women's Battalion of Death was sent to the front. It spent a week at Molodechno during which it was accompanied by two American journalists, Rheta Childe Dorr and Bessie Beatty, who stayed with the women, interviewing and sharing food and drink with them. Beatty's account[45] is overly dramatic and contradictory. On one hand she says that the women, with their short hair and their uniforms had left their femininity at home with their make-up. Yet at the same the way she describes the friendship and devotion amongst the group as if it were a novel about a group of young girls at boarding school, mothering one another and carefully sharing their rations. Occasionally there were outbursts of giggling, but like a strict housemistress Bochkareva quickly scolded them.

That entire week it rained and the women began to feel pent up, hoping that the next day they would enter the trenches. One evening a group of hostile men surrounded their barracks, shouting insults and smashing the windows. When Bochkareva threatened to order the battalion to shoot the men, they left. Later, when the battalion moved up closer to the front, they slept in a couple of barns, but soon another crowd of men surrounded them. Bochkareva says that they were not threatening the women, but were there out of curiosity. The demoralised men at the front did not receive the women well. They either insulted them and disliked what they represented, or viewed them as a spectacle but did not necessarily take them seriously. By now it was July and the area came under intense shellfire. As part of the 525th Regiment, the women's battalion moved into trenches, but when the signal came to go over the top no one moved. The men refused and deferred to their committees. The women saw their opportunity to impress the men and chose to advance with or without them. Supported by a few hundred male volunteers, they hoped that the rest of the men would soon follow their example. Eventually they were joined by about half of the 525th Regiment and succeeded in taking parts of the Nocoapasski Forest. Ultimately the women reached the third line of the German trenches, but not before stumbling upon some unexpected obstacles:[46]

> There was poison awaiting us in that second line of trenches. Vodka and beer were in abundance. Half of our force got drunk forthwith, throwing themselves ravenously on the alcohol. My girls did splendid work here, destroying the stores of liquor at my orders. But for that, the whole regiment would have been drunk. I rushed about appealing to the men to stop drinking.[47]

The Russian offensive was on the verge of collapse when the Germans launched their counter-attack using guns they had concealed deep in the forest. With little support, the women tried to hold their position, but when they ran out of ammunition they were forced to retreat. Bochkareva had been knocked unconscious by a shell and she and the other wounded were taken to Petrograd for treatment. The remnants of the battalion stayed at the front under the command of Bochkareva's adjutant, Magdalena Skrydlova.[48]

News of the Women's Battalion spread across Russia, the facts becoming embellished with every retelling. In August, Florence Farmborough, a British Red Cross nurse working at a first aid post on the Eastern Front, wrote in her diary:

> Last Monday, an ambulance-van drove up with three wounded women soldiers. We were told that they belonged to the Bachkarova [sic] Women's Death Battalion. We had not heard the full name before, but we instantly guessed that it was the small army of women recruited in Russia by the Siberian woman soldier, Yasha Bachkarova. Naturally, we were all very impatient to have news of this remarkable battalion, but the women were sadly shocked and we refrained from questioning them until they had rested. The van-driver was not very helpful, but he did know that the battalion had been cut up by the enemy and had retreated.'[49]

Once Bochkareva's battalion had been officially sanctioned by the government, women across Russia campaigned to be allowed to form similar groups. Not waiting for the government to make them official, some went ahead and formed unofficial units. In total, the government authorised sixteen female military units between May and October 1917, only four of which were combat units (the others provided auxiliary support). Bochkareva's battalion was the only one of these that went into active service. The other three combat units, the 1st Petrograd Women's Battalion, the 2nd Moscow Women's Battalion of Death and the 3rd Kuban Women's Shock Battalion were still in training when the Bolsheviks rose to power in October, and the second Russian Revolution of 1917 put an end to the scheme. In addition, the Russian navy established the 1st Women's Naval Detachment. However they only received a small number of recruits and the work was mostly cleaning and cooking, the women lacking the literacy skills to be clerks. The unit was officially disbanded in August 1917, only a month after it was set up, and the recruits were re-employed by the navy as hired labourers.[50]

Despite the women proving themselves capable of fighting, before the Bolshevik Revolution in October the provisional government had already decided that the experiment in shaming the men into fighting had largely failed. By the autumn, the government had lost interest in the scheme. Only a week after first writing of her excitement at meeting members of the Death Battalion, Florence Farmborough wrote a damning assessment of the battalion:

> It was true; Bachkarova [sic] had brought her small battalion down south to the Austrian Front, and they had manned part of the trenches which had been abandoned by the Russian Infantry. The size of the Battalion had considerably decreased since the first weeks of recruitment … Many of them, painted and powdered, had joined the Battalion as an exciting and romantic adventure; she [Bochkareva] loudly condemned their behaviour and demanded iron discipline. Gradually the patriotic enthusiasm had spent itself … In honour to those women volunteers, it was recorded that they did go into the attack; they did go 'over the top'. But not all of them. Some remained in the trenches, fainting and hysterical; others ran or crawled back to the rear. Bachkarova retreated with her decimated battalion; she was wrathful, heartbroken, but she had learnt a great truth: women were quite unfit to be soldiers.

Yet despite this lack of faith in the women's battalions, when tensions grew in Petrograd between the provisional government and the Bolsheviks, the 1st Petrograd Women's Battalion famously defended the Winter Palace. As the Bolsheviks armed themselves and prepared to take over the government, the battalion was ordered to come to the palace. Poised to go to the front, the women believed they were to be reviewed and given their orders, only to discover that they were there to aid the Cossacks in the defence of the provisional government. Yet, knowing that they were heavily out-numbered and unwilling to fight their own people, many of the Cossacks deserted and the women's commander was against it too, so he ordered the women to return to their camp, leaving behind only a small detachment. When fighting began, the defenders numbered approximately 2,500 against the 10–15,000 revolutionaries. The women were forced back and took up positions inside the palace before they ultimately surrendered.[51]

The very fact that nearly 1,000 women are thought to have served as individuals in the Russian army is outstanding. For outside observers like John Morse it was a cause for jest, a ridiculous concept, something that could not be taken seriously. Yet for campaigners like Emmeline Pankhurst and journalists Bessie Beatty and Rheta Childe Dorr, it was something to be celebrated and the women to be revered. The women who joined the army did so for a range of reasons, and came from a variety of backgrounds, from princesses to peasants. Russia went to war at a time when its political situation was precarious, and the conflict only served to erode public confidence in the Tsar. The unusual political climate created by the first revolution of 1917, and the demoralisation of Russia's army and insubordination amongst its ranks offered women a real chance to come together in a combative unit, rather than as individuals. Had the women been given more time to train, or had there been more individuals like Maria Bochkareva to take charge, it could have been more successful. However, for the provisional government, the women's battalions were an experiment which they believed had failed. Despite this, however, Russian women did not lose the fighting spirit which had driven them to enlist and there are records of women continuing to fight in the Russian Civil War that followed the second revolution in October.

Notes

1 Morse, John, *An Englishman in the Russian Ranks: Ten months' Fighting in Poland*, p.68.
2 Stoff, Laurie, *They Fought for the Motherland: Russia's Women Soldiers in World War I and the Revolution*, p.30.
3 Ibid.
4 'Higher Education for Women in Nineteenth- and early Twentieth Century Russia', p.30, in Noonan, Norma C. and Nechemias, Carol (eds), *Encloypedia of Russian Women's Movements*.
5 Richard Stites, 'Women and the Russian Intelligentsia', p.57, in Atkinson, Dorothy; Dallin, Alexander and Warshofsky Lapidus, Gail (eds), *Women in Russia*.
6 During the war, the Russians changed the name of St Petersburg to make it less German sounding.

7 Stoff, Laurie, *They Fought for the Motherland*, p.66.
8 Stone, Norman, *The Eastern Front 1914–1917*, p.18.
9 Serbia's independence was not officially recognised until the Congress of Berlin in 1878 in which the European powers attempted to reorganise the Balkans following the Russo–Turkish war of 1877–78.
10 McNeal, Robert H., *Tsar and Cossack 1855–1914*, p.21.
11 Yurlova, Marina, *Cossack Girl*, p.19.
12 Translated '*Sotnia*' means 'Hundred' and was the equivalent to a company.
13 O'Rourke, Shane 'Women in a Warrior Society: Don Cossack Women, 1860–1914' in Marsh, Roaslind (ed.), *Women in Russia and Ukraine*, 1996, p.45.
14 Yurlova, Marina, *Cossack Girl*, p.41.
15 Stone, Norman, *The Eastern Front 1914–1917*, p.45.
16 Dadeshkeliani, Princess, *Princess in Uniform*, p.75.
17 Ibid., p.93.
18 In her memoirs Dadeshkeliani says that riding to and from the trenches she drew rifle fire with bullets flying all around her, but it seems unlikely that the Colonel would send her on such a dangerous mission so early on.
19 Dadeshkeliani, Princess, *Princess in uniform*, pp.95–6.
20 Ibid., p.96.
21 Mironov, Boris, *The Standard of Living and Revolutions in Russia, 1700–1917*, pp.8–9.
22 Bochkareva, Maria, *Yashka*, p.17.
23 Ibid., p.18.
24 Ibid., pp.66–7.
25 Ibid., pp.77–8.
26 Ibid., p.80.
27 Ibid., p.88.
28 Ibid., pp.88–91.
29 Ibid., p.91.
30 Ibid., p.105.
31 This would in turn help the Serbians, as only months before the British had decided to withdraw from Salonika, but they remained as the Russians requested, providing the base for the Serbians and her Allies to take back Serbia.
32 Neiberg, Michael S. and Jordan, David, *The Eastern Front 1914–1920*.
33 Bochkareva, Maria, *Yashka*.
34 Stoff, Laurie, *They Fought for the Motherland*.
35 'Mary Garden tries to enlist in French Army as a Young Boy', *New York Review*, 21 November, 1914.
36 Beatty, Bessie, *The Red Heart of Russia*, p.100.
37 Bochkareva, Maria, *Yashka*, p.160.
38 Ibid., p.162.
39 Stoff, Laurie, *They Fought for the Motherland*, p.32.
40 Bochkareva, Marie, *Yashka*, p.162.
41 MacLeod, Florence, *Runaway Russia*, p.168.
42 Bochkareva, Maria, *Yashka*, p.205.
43 As quoted in Purvis, June, *Emmeline Pankhurst: A Biography*, p.295.
44 Bochkareva, Maria, *Yashka*, pp.165–6.
45 Beatty, Bessie, *The Red Heart of Russia*.
46 Stoff, Laurie, *They fought for the Motherland*, pp.109–10.

47 Bochkareva, Maria, *Yashka*, p.211.
48 Stoff, Laurie, *They Fought for the Motherland*, p.111.
49 Farmborough, Florence, *Nurse at the Russian Front: A Diary 1914–1918*, pp.302–3.
50 Stoff, Laurie, They Fought for the Motherland, pp.114–47.
51 Ibid., pp.151–7.

8

British Women's Services, from 1917

Every Waac who goes to France is like the pawn who attains the top of the chessboard and is exchanged for a more valuable piece. She sends a fighting man to his job by taking on the jobs that are really a woman's after all. For is it not woman's earliest job to look after man?

Fryniwyd Tennyson Jesse[1]

In Britain, 1917 was a hugely significant year for women's war work. Following years of debate and attempts by women to expand their wartime service through voluntary organisations, the War Office at last permitted the formation of an official women's corps: the Women's Army Auxiliary Corps. This was followed later in the year by the Women's Royal Naval Service and then by the Women's Royal Air Force in 1918. Unlike in Russia, women were not permitted to take on combat roles; instead they were to provide auxiliary support to the men's services, thereby releasing the men for combat duty. It was an exciting opportunity and represented a huge step forward for the recognition of Britain's female labour force, but each service was carefully controlled by the British military.

Since 1914, Katharine Furse had been head of Britain's voluntary aid detachment scheme. After taking the first group of VADs over to France and establishing rest stations in Boulogne, she returned to London where she set up an office at Devonshire House. The principal role of the VADs was to provide nursing support and establish hospitals in times of emergency. However, at the beginning, the VADs found it hard to earn the acceptance of the military medical authorities, which preferred professionally trained nurses such as those within the Army Nursing Service or the British Red Cross. The professional nurses also looked down on the VADs, considering them unqualified. The VADs had to undergo a series of short courses run by the St John Ambulance Association, but the professional nurses were trained for at least three years. Furthermore, the majority of

VADs were financially independent women who attended VAD meetings in their spare time. This was resented by those for whom nursing was a full-time occupation and a means of earning a living. Yet, by 1916 it was clear how successful the VAD scheme had become and that its support was vital in hospitals both overseas and at home. Unlike the situation in 1914, everyone now knew what a VAD was and the women were accepted.

Despite the initial troubles that VADs faced integrating with professional nurses, Furse continued to look for opportunities to expand the VAD service. She said, 'I felt strongly that our function should be filling all gaps wherever our help could ...'[2] So in 1915, Furse established the General Service VAD. In this role, women took over from men who had been working in hospital kitchens and in clerical roles, releasing them for active service at the front. The idea was first trialled at Wandsworth military hospital in August 1915. Furse then worked with Arthur Stanley (commissioner of the British Red Cross) to expand the scheme over the course of the following year.[3] However she was surprised to be met with significant opposition to these plans, from both outside and inside the VAD:

> To whatever it may have been due, the feeling persisted with regard to VAD work, the nursing side, especially where nursing the wounded was concerned, being put on a higher plane in some people's estimation than all the other work, which seemed to me just as important if sick and wounded were to get all the practical attention they needed.[4]

Part of the resistance within the VAD may have been to do with the social background of the majority of its female members. Those from the upper classes felt that nursing was a suitable occupation for wartime, but drew the line at cooking and cleaning. Ms Warner, who had been a VAD since 1912 and had established her own detachment, believed that the introduction of General Service VADs was 'awfully silly', but that Furse 'wanted to have everything'.[5] In the hospital wards the VADs enjoyed the same status as the nursing staff, which included admission to the officers' clubs. Yet the General Service workers would be treated as the equivalent to 'other ranks', which the nursing VADs worried would have a negative impact on their reputation. At first the General Service VADs only worked locally in Britain, but by 1917 they were being sent overseas.[6]

Meanwhile, as the VAD organisation was expanding, Britain was facing a serious shortage of manpower which it endeavoured to resolve through a series of schemes that would ultimately lead to the official employment of women by the army. Recruitment figures were falling: in April 1915 only 119,087 men enlisted, compared to 462,901 in September 1914.[7] So in the summer of 1915 the National Registration Act was passed whereby all adults, male and female, aged between fifteen and sixty-five were listed. This showed the War Office that there were over 5 million men of military age who were not currently serving in the armed forces. The War Office decided to continue with voluntary enlistment under the Derby Scheme[8], which in November 1915 called for all men aged between eighteen and forty-five to enlist, or at least to attest their willingness to enlist if requested. Ultimately, however, the scheme failed to raise the numbers hoped and in 1916 conscription became unavoidable.[9] The first act, passed in January that year, enforced the conscription of unmarried men aged eighteen to forty-one with no dependents. Yet Britain still needed more men, and in May a second act was passed extending conscription to married men. The army then began to look at ways in which it could release men already in the army from supporting roles to fighting at the front. Given the number of active women's groups in Britain and working overseas, there was a growing debate in 1916 about the necessity of female conscription. The British army was already employing cooks from the Women's Legion, formed in 1915, at home in Britain. However there were many conflicting opinions, with British women being criticised for either doing too little or for being too militarised and wearing khaki coloured uniforms which should be reserved exclusively for fighting men.[10] Whilst it appeared, after the War Office flatly refused to employ women doctors or accept medical organisations such as the Scottish Women's Hospital or the First Aid Nursing Yeomanry (FANY), that it was coming round to the idea of employing women, it would only do so on its own terms. In the same way that the British military had tried to exert its authority over the FANY and the Women of Pervyse on the Western Front, the War Office wanted to be in control.

So in 1916 the Women's Services Committee was established to investigate Britain's female labour force. VAD commander Katharine Furse was one of the committee members. The committee concluded that the organisation of women's labour needed to be centralised in order to make it more efficient, and advocated that women could replace men in non-combatant roles.[11] Next came the Lawson report. Lieutenant-General H.M. Lawson was instructed to review 'the number and physical categories of men employed out of the fighting area in France.'[12] In the course of compiling his report, Lawson visited a number of British army camps in France, including Calais, Abbeville, Boulogne, Étaples, St Omer and Paris. Lawson applied a lot of diplomacy to his work, explaining to the British military commanders in France that the proposal of female labour was based on women's success in taking on men's roles at the home front, working as clerks, ticket collectors on public transport, in the police force and in munitions factories amongst other things. He explained that the intention was to support the army rather than to criticise its current operations. Lawson said:

> It must be realised that the physical conditions on the Lines of Communication and Rearward Services generally, are much less severe than in the front line, where, in the addition to the actual stress of fighting, is involved the exposure to all kinds of weather, with its accompaniment of wet and mud. In the rear, the soldier is nearly always passably well accommodated and the strain on his mental and bodily power is very much less.

In response to Lawson's report supporting the use of women in France, Field Marshall Haig, the British army's Commander-in-Chief in France, advocated a policy of dilution. As with skilled workers on the home front, this meant that a skilled job was broken down into a number of semi-skilled or unskilled tasks, each of which could be carried out by a less skilled worker. The replacement workers, i.e. the women, would not require much training and therefore there would not be a significant delay or fall in production. At the same time, the role of the skilled (male) worker would be protected.[13] When discussing the structure of the new women's service in the Women's Services Committee, Furse was adamant that it should have a military-style structure, and all the women members agreed that the head of the service would have to be a woman.[14] Once the decision was taken to form a women's service for the army, the director of recruiting at the War Office, Brigadier-General Sir Auckland Geddes, contacted his sister and asked her to help. Mrs Mona Chalmers Watson was a prime example of the modern woman. Like her aunt Elizabeth Garrett Anderson and her cousin Louisa Garrett Anderson she had studied medicine and during the war she was working as a physician in Edinburgh. Chalmers Watson was happy to take on an administrative role, but as she had a young family, she did not want to be the one to go overseas as the commander of the new service in France. During her search for a suitable individual, Louisa Garrett Anderson, who by now was back in London working with the Women's Hospital Corps at their military hospital in Endell Street, introduced her cousin to a university friend, Helen Gwynne-Vaughan. Gwynne-Vaughan had recently lost her husband to illness and had since thrown herself into her job as a professor of Botany at Birkbeck College, London. Despite having been involved with Garrett Anderson in promoting women's suffrage at university, Gwynne-Vaughan was relatively conservative and had shied away from the Women's Social and Political Union, of which Louisa had been a member. Yet she was unable to resist the idea of leading a women's army corps. After a series of interviews, Gwynne-Vaughan was officially appointed on 19 February 1917. The War Office decided upon the name 'Women's Army Auxiliary Corps' or WAAC. Chalmers Watson and Gwynne-Vaughan were to be its chief controllers, with Chalmers Watson as the senior of the two and based in Britain, while Gwynne-Vaughan would be in France. Their equivalent rank would be that of lieutenant-colonel.[15] Chalmers Watson described the army council instruction that officially set up the WAAC as 'an advance of the women's movement and … a national advance'.[16]

Working quickly, the first group of WAACs received two weeks' training following their induction and arrived in France on 31 March 1917. They were to be cooks and waitresses employed at the officers' club at Abbeville, followed a week later by a group of twenty-two clerks.[17]

Chalmers Watson and Gwynne-Vaughan quickly became firm friends and proved to be a good team. Gwynne-Vaughan could be blunt and demanding, while Chalmers Watson was more gentle and tactful. More often than not, Chalmers Watson was obliged to expend a great deal of diplomacy on her colleague's behalf. Right from the start, Gwynne-Vaughan wanted the WAAC to be seen as a military organisation on a par with the men. When the two controllers went on a preliminary trip to France, Gwynne-Vaughan insisted that both women fix lieutenant-colonel badges to their new uniforms, which led to a few raised eyebrows. Once she was in France with the first recruits, Gwynne-Vaughan insisted the WAAC act as soldiers would, standing to attention, saluting and using the correct titles. When Chalmers Watson received various complaints that the militarisation of the women was making the men uncomfortable and that it was inappropriate, she tried to make Gwynne-Vaughan back down.[18] Since the WAAC had established its headquarters at Devonshire House alongside the VAD, however, it is possible that Gwynne-Vaughan had got to know and taken advice from Katharine Furse. Since the early days of the VAD, Furse had been a strict disciplinarian and insisted that the women act in a military manner so as to be irreproachable. She firmly believed that this had helped the VAD hold their own alongside the men. Now that she was in France, Gwynne-Vaughan learned that her job was to be purely administrative, to oversee the women while they were in France, and to organise their food, accommodation, clothes and pay. It seemed that the title of 'chief-controller' was merely a way of paying lip service to the women, while all the decisions were made by men.

Back in London, Chalmers Watson was charged with sorting through the applications and arranging interviews. Unlike the VAD or the FANY, the WAAC looked to the working classes for recruits – women who already had the practical skills and work experience the WAAC needed. In the same way that professional nurses had initially responded to the VAD nurses and those in the VAD had disapproved of the General Service section, there was some antagonism between the established women's organisations and the WAACs, brought about by the class divide and the nature of their work.[19] As with each organisation when it started, it took time for the women of the WAAC to establish themselves and create an identity, as can be seen from their individual testimonies.

Asked why she decided to join the WAAC, Annie May Martin said that there may have been an underlying sense of patriotism, but for her she always had a 'wanderlust'.[20] Martin previously worked at the Central Telegraph Office in London, and like other working class girls she had rarely had the opportunity, until she joined up, to travel overseas. The way she saw it, life in London was hard, subject to blockades, the subsequent food shortages and the increasing number of Zeppelin raids, so she felt she may as well go to France, for it couldn't be any worse.

Emmy Gaunt from Leeds enrolled in the WAAC for clerical work in early 1917. Passing her medical examination, she was administered the necessary vaccinations and inoculations. Gaunt was then given a railway warrant and instructed to go to the Connaught Club in London, which was being used as a training depot for the corps. Gaunt took an oath of allegiance and received her uniform, which was 'made of khaki gabardine in the coat frock style, and tailored knickers with large pockets to hold our paybook and identification papers. The hats were brown felt with badge.' [21] The new recruits completed their brisk training, including marching together around Hyde Park in their uniforms, and set off for France. Amongst one of the first drafts to be sent out, Gaunt said that when the corps arrived in Boulogne a woman officer gave them a memorable speech. She impressed upon the new recruits that the future success of the WAAC, and whether or not any more units would follow, depended on how well they did their work.[22]

The members of the WAAC were generally referred to as 'wacks' and the nickname stuck. Mrs Graham[23] was an officer in the WAAC and recalled an anecdote that Gwynne-Vaughan had told her during her service. When the name of the corps was under discussion, Gwynne-Vaughan quickly declared a preference for 'Women's Army Auxiliary Corps' over 'Women's Corps' as she did not want to be known as 'Chief WC'. Describing Gwynne-Vaughan, Graham says that 'from the start she followed meticulously the army method of correspondence, discipline and the way of life. So that we slept on hard mattresses known as "biscuits" under three army blankets, our lavatories were known as latrines whether they were indoors or out and we had no comfort of dressing tables or carpets.'[24] Later, Graham became Gwynne-Vaughan's staff captain and says that her commander 'had a wonderful brain and a lively temperament which reduced some officers to pulp. She did lots of inspecting of Companies in her staff car, clad in long laced brown boots and soft khaki cap.'[25]

The WAAC was organised in a rush and it wasn't until June that the War Office confirmed that members of the corps were to be enrolled rather than enlisted, the formal army council instruction for its incorporation not being finally passed until 7 July.[26] The 200 or so members already in France who, like Emmy Gaunt, had taken the oath of allegiance, were required to re-enrol. They were to be employed by the military, but legally they were civilians, subject to civilian law. During the negotiations that had led to this decision, Gwynne-Vaughan had argued strongly for the women to be given equivalent status to the men whose jobs they were doing, while Chalmers Watson had concentrated on improving their pay. Once more it was Chalmers Watson's tact that led to an agreement being reached.[27]

Throughout 1917, the WAAC expanded, providing telephonists, telegraphists, shorthand typists, pay clerks, waitresses and cooks. The WAAC also provided intelligence workers. Miss Watkins was looking for a job in a government office and had made various applications when she was contacted by the War Office asking her if she wanted to go to France. Watkins had a knowledge of German, so the War Office arranged for her and five other women to join the WAAC as officers and to become part of the 'Secret Six'. Arriving at Connaught House, 'I experienced the odd sensation of being called "Ma'am" and saw rows of "other ranks" springing to their feet when I passed.'[28] Watkins and the other women spent their first night in France in a WAAC hostel in Boulogne, where she was surprised to find that all of them were to share the same room and that there were no screens separating the beds. The next day, they went to St Omer where they were to be based. They arrived to find a large open space in which stood a collection of Nissen huts: portable prefabricated structures made from corrugated steel, which could be quickly assembled when more accommodation was required. Watkins explained that the sleeping huts were divided into 'four tiny compartments by wooden partitions open at the top. In each "bedroom" there was one shelf and five pegs, so our unpacking was simple.'[29] The accommodation was, without a doubt, better than the trenches at the front, but it was by no means luxurious.

The next morning, even though it was a Sunday, the women were called to report to the office at 9.30 a.m. to meet their commander, Captain

Hitchings. He revealed to the women that their job would be to try and decipher coded German messages, which were transmitted over the wireless and intercepted by the British. The women became known as the 'Hushwaacs':

> Many of the messages sent were trivial ... but occasionally they would supply really valuable information as to the movement of troops; it was therefore of great importance that the codes should be solved as quickly as possible. Three or four different codes would be in use at the same time on different sections of the Line and for each of these there was a room at an office, usually with an officer in charge. We were divided up amongst different rooms. There were also a few 'non-coms' or male clerks, mostly doing the mechanical side of the work ...[30]

Watkins had only just turned twenty-two when she arrived in France, and she said that because the women were so young they tended to take events too seriously and were forever anxious to prove the Hushwaacs were a worthwhile venture. Some of the women acquired more responsibility when they were given temporary leadership of one of the rooms, but they also had to do their fair share of monotonous work and endure long hours, including weekends. For the first seven months, the women were only entitled to one quarter-day off a week. Watkins said they were thrilled when, in May 1918, the rules changed and they were to be given a monthly quota of full days off.

Meanwhile Katharine Furse was becoming more and more frustrated with her command of the VAD, or lack of it. Unlike Gwynne-Vaughan, because Furse had managed to achieve so much in the early days of the VAD, she was slower to recognise that she too was a nominal female leader and that her power was limited. In June 1917, Furse was awarded an OBE and was heartened that her work had been recognised, but by the autumn she wanted to leave. Furse relentlessly campaigned to improve the lives of the VAD, arguing for improvements in accommodation, increases in pay and better status. She tried to organise for the General Service VAD section to be absorbed into the WAAC, so that women's labour could be employed more efficiently and that the two organisations would not be competing for recruits. However the Joint War Committee of the VAD's parent organisations, the British Red Cross and the St John Ambulance Association, refused. Furthermore, most VADs signed up for a six-month contract. Those that were happy with their work stayed and renewed their contracts. Those that were unhappy left and the VAD was obliged to spend more time and money finding replacements, as well as funding general recruitment. Furse tried to tackle the issues head-on, but in the end she conceded defeat. Writing about her decision to resign her post, Furse said:

> Quite frankly I have not, for a long time, been happy about many matters concerning the V.A.D.s and do not care to continue holding a post full of responsibility which I am not empowered adequately to fulfil. I should never have accepted had I not realised that one accepted them (Honours) as a figurehead representing an organisation which had won them.[31]

Her mind made up, Furse submitted her resignation in November, but at the same time she was contacted by Mrs Chalmers Watson. There was to be a second women's service, this time for the Royal Navy, and Chalmers Watson recommended that Furse apply for the head position. Furse was successful and her first task was to design the structure of the new service. Realising that she knew little about the navy, Furse says that she immediately sought out a book that might teach her everything she needed to know. Fortunately she was able to look at how the WAAC was run for guidance, believing that, like the WAAC, the new service also needed to have a military structure. A number of Furse's senior VAD staff had resigned at the same time as she did and she invited them to join her, knowing that they worked well together. When deciding upon a name for the organisation, Furse wanted to ensure it wasn't one that would conjure silly nicknames like 'Wacks' and she settled on the Women's Royal Naval Service, the WRNS or the 'Wrens'. By 29 November 1917, the WRNS was officially announced. As had happened with the formation of the WAAC, Furse was only given a short amount of time to get things up and running. She said that the navy was impatient and that once the women were in uniform they were expected to know everything. This time Furse's headquarters were in Westminster and the training of recruits took place at Crystal Palace. The women in the WRNS carried out many of the same roles in the navy as those in the WAAC did for the army, doing domestic work and working as telephonists and telegraphers and replacing paymasters. They also worked as signallers, coders and decoders and storekeepers, cleaned life-belts and fitted depth-charges, amongst other things. To work on a boat was the equivalent of an army combat position on the frontline, therefore all WRNS were stationed on shore, and they adopted the motto 'Never at Sea'.[32]

In 1918, Britain's two military air services, the army's aviation branch the Royal Flying Corps (RFC) and the navy's Royal Navy Air Service (RNAS) were combined to form the Royal Air Force (RAF). Furse anticipated that when this happened, the new air force would request its own women's corps. As part of the army, the WAAC had already provided units to the RFC, but what concerned Furse was those WRNS who were based at the navy's air stations supporting the RNAS. Would they remain WRNS or would they be transferred over to the new corps? Some of the RFC bases already employed women as clerks and drivers independently of the WAAC, but complaints were made that these women were not officially enrolled in the WAAC as they should have been. The reason was that the RFC feared that when the merger came, they would lose their female workers when the RFC was no longer part of the army. This was resolved by granting the RFC the authority officially to recruit women as of 28 December 1917. However this meant that the new Women's Royal Air Force (WRAF) would face the challenge of bringing together elements of the WAAC, WRNS and RFC women as well as finding new members.[33] The RAF was formed on 1 April 1918. If the WAAC and the WRNS had been formed under time pressure, the WRAF was considered by some to be a rushed afterthought, not properly thought through. The RAF was the priority and the WRAF of secondary importance.

As with the WAAC, women were enrolled into the WRAF rather than enlisted, so that they were effectively civilians in uniform. The women were given one month to decide whether they wanted to transfer into the WRAF or remain with the army or the navy. The men, too, were given a month, but this was increased to six months in the hope that more men would apply for the RAF. A number of the women who transferred were dismayed to find that their new roles resulted in a demotion from officer to ordinary member and were upset by the loss of status. One advantage that the WRAF did have, however, was that the relationship between the women transferring over and the men was already well established and the men valued the female workforce.[34] In May 1918, the WRAF acquired two celebrities as officers, which brought the corps a certain amount of positive publicity. Elsie Knocker (now Baroness T'Serclaes) and Mairi Chisholm, the two Women of Pervyse, were recuperating in England following the gas attack that had forced them to leave their first aid post on the Western Front. Both were looking for a new cause, and jumped at the recommendation of a friend to join the WRAF.[35]

The reputation of the women's corps was important to their leaders, and the publicity generated by T'Serclaes and Chisholm was invaluable. However, each of the three women's services faced significant problems. In January 1918 the WAAC started to receive negative press when rumours circulated of impropriety amongst the men and the women. For fear of being sent home, the WAACs in France were generally more disciplined than in Britain. As civilians, any significant disciplinary hearings had to go through a civil process rather than military court-martial, which in turn generated negative news coverage and assumptions about the women's behaviour in France. As a consequence, the WAAC saw their recruitment numbers drop significantly over the next three months. Then, in a case of bad timing, Chalmers Watson chose to resign as chief-controller to look after her seriously ill son, which only served to undermine public confidence further. The damage was such that a commission was sent out to France at the beginning of March, which to Gwynne-Vaughan's relief (and much as she expected) presented an extremely favourable report.[36]

The episode was then completely eclipsed when, on 21 March, the Germans mounted a massive offensive on the Western Front. Known as the Michael Offensive, the Germans concentrated over half their entire gun power along the Western Front in the region of the Somme. In less than a day, the British were forced to retreat and on that first day the Germans claimed approximately 98.5 square miles of British territory.[37] By the end of March, the Michael Offensive had largely run its course, but in April came the Georgette Offensive further north in Flanders. With the British army in retreat, a number of the camps where members of the WAAC were based came under threat. Gwynne-Vaughan did her best to resist pre-emptive plans to remove all women from France. Now was their opportunity to prove their value in very trying circumstances. The WAACS were applauded in the national press for their bravery and dedication to their service, replacing the more critical reports earlier in the year. In April, Queen Mary became the WAAC's commander-in-chief, which added a great deal of prestige to the organisation, and it was renamed Queen Mary's Army Auxiliary Corps.[38]

Furse said that fortunately in the WRNS they never faced a disciplinary case that required them to go to court, as the members 'loved the game of being in the Navy', and if there were any difficult cases the individual was simply discharged from service.[39] Furse says she never forgot how important the reputation of the corps and its women was, especially in its formative stages. Yet she had little to worry about. Under her leadership the VAD had earned the name 'the Starched Brigade' and the WRNS was called 'the Prigs and the Prudes' or 'the Perfect Ladies'. With regards to pregnancy amongst its members, Furse took a very liberal approach with the WRNS, choosing not to discharge the woman immediately, but to oversee the early stages of her medical care. Overall, there were very few pregnancies.[40] In the WAAC, Gwynne-Vaughan's approach to unexpected pregnancies was extremely pragmatic. She made sure each case was reported, providing both the date of conception and the dates of the woman's service and leave. In a number of cases she was able to prove that the baby had been conceived before the woman enrolled, or on other occasions that the individual was married and had conceived whilst on leave with her husband.[41] The issue of unplanned pregnancies had been addressed by the commission that investigated the WAAC in March 1918. It had concluded that the rate of unmarried pregnancies in the WAAC was lower than in civilian society.[42]

The WRAF, on the other hand, faced serious problems with its leadership, with three different commandants in the first six months. The first commandant was Lady Gertrude Crawford, daughter of the Earl of Sefton. Like Furse and Gwynne-Vaughan she soon realised that she, too, was merely a figurehead under the guidance of men. When she wrote and complained about her situation to the man who had appointed her, the Air Ministry's master general of personnel, Sir Godfrey Paine, he recommended that she resign.

The next commandant was the Honourable Violet Blanche Douglas-Pennant, daughter of Lord Penrhyn. She had experience of working on various committees for schools and hospitals and working as a commissioner in Wales for the National Health Insurance Commission. Taking up her role in June, she found that she too faced the same limited ability to effect any of the changes that she wished to impose. In the rush to form the WRAF, the corps did not have enough officers to manage the large number of airwomen. There was also a shortage of uniforms, the training the recruits received was poor and their living conditions were below par. The Air Ministry did not want the work of the WRAF to be hampered by another change in leadership and so Paine made attempts to appease the situation and granted Douglas-Pennant the status equivalent to brigadier.[43] Yet the troubles continued, and, unhappy with her leadership, Douglas-Pennant's three principal officers resigned in July 1918. The RAF had little time to deal with the women falling out with one another; they simply wanted an efficient and reliable auxiliary service at their disposal. To her credit, Douglas-Pennant did succeed in establishing a much-needed WRAF officer training centre in Eltham during the summer, but she had done this with little help from the Air Ministry.

Feeling that she was failing in her leadership, Douglas-Pennant once more offered Paine her resignation, but again he refused. Godfrey Paine was then replaced by Sefton Brancker who was less sure about Douglas-Pennant. He asked a number of people for their opinions of her and her leadership, not necessarily asking those who worked closest to her. Forming a fairly negative assessment of the situation, Brancker decided that the WRAF could not move forward until its problems were solved, and he decided to sack Douglas-Pennant because she was unpopular. As a result, Douglas-Pennant became a scapegoat for the uneasy start that the WRAF leadership had faced and she later went to great lengths to clear her name and restore her reputation. For now, Brancker needed to find a new commandant, and among those suggested were Furse and Chalmers Watson, while the War Office suggested Gwynne-Vaughan.[44]

Brancker interviewed Gwynne-Vaughan and they got on very well together, which helped enormously. Gwynne-Vaughan, although reluctant to leave the WAAC, brought a wealth of experience with her, and fortuitously, as she began her new role, the long-awaited uniforms finally arrived. In addition, she organised for the women to wear badges, to denote their equivalent ranks to the men. With a confidence that Douglas-Pennant had lacked, the knowledge of how to get things done in a predominantly male environment and the support of Brancker, Gwynne-Vaughan managed to turn the WRAF around.

Many of the girls who went to serve overseas found that they had to grow up very quickly, and that life in the war zone was not what they had expected. Grace MacPherson, a twenty-three-year-old Canadian, arrived in England in 1916 with aspirations to serve overseas. She applied to the VAD, but had to wait until the following year before she was given a position. In the meantime she undertook the required first aid courses and worked for the Canadian Pay Office in London. In 1917 she was at last selected to drive an ambulance for a Red Cross convoy in the coastal town of Étaples, France, which was 20 miles south of the hospital city of Boulogne. She arrived in April amidst unseasonable 'rotten, cold weather, snow, rain & wind'[45] and was thrown straight into work. The convoy was in charge of a fleet of ambulances and tasked with taking patients to and from the trains and the hospitals. MacPherson's first week was tough. She was assigned night shifts and recalled in her diary that this meant starting work at 11 p.m. At 1 a.m. she was allowed to take a break and to try and get some sleep before heading out again at 4.30 a.m. Aside from a quick cup of coffee at 7.30 a.m., she remained on duty until 9.30 a.m. Shortly after her arrival, the weather worsened and the ports were closed. This meant that the recovering patients could not be evacuated and sent to England, so the hospitals became full. The hospital trains continued further down the line and the women had a moment of respite. Despite the long hours, this was where MacPherson wanted to be, in a job she wanted to do. In her diary she declared, 'it was glorious to think at last I was actually driving an amb[ulance].'[46]

MacPherson had a good idea of what the work would entail, particularly after eight months living in London and hearing people's stories, but she had not anticipated the other drivers would cause her problems.

Writing an article about her experiences for *Gold Stripe* in 1919, she said, 'My first two months there were utterly miserable.' In a group of twenty, MacPherson was one of only three Canadian drivers and she found it difficult to get on with the British girls. It seems that MacPherson felt certain individuals were bullying her, making her life difficult, and that within the convoy there was a clique that treated her badly. After a month, the male commander of the unit called MacPherson to his office and severely reprimanded her. According to MacPherson, he said, 'that my whole attitude was wrong, that I didn't seem able to get into the swing of things, that I would not accept the discipline, that I was not taking interest in my work … and he did not think I was suited …'[47]

The exchange left MacPherson mortified and 'broken-hearted': she had never before received such a direct dressing-down. She sought one of the senior women, 'Chambers', and asked her whether she thought that she was as bad as the commander had said. Chambers replied that too often she had to reprimand MacPherson for doing the wrong thing, to which a desperate MacPherson replied:'I'm ready to accept any discipline, order or obedience going. I understood before I came over that things would be strict & I did not come from the other side of Canada to be sent home after 4 weeks for little things like this.'[48]

Chambers said that she had suggested to the commander that MacPherson was transferred to Boulogne and given a job in which she could be more independent. MacPherson thought that whilst Boulogne could prove more interesting she resolved 'just to stick it & show them I can.'

MacPherson confided in Chambers which girls were responsible for bullying her, but Chambers only offered a few comforting words and seemingly did little more. MacPherson said that the whole situation had reduced her to 'the most awkward, ungainly, self-conscious lump alive.' However, she managed to overcome it. As she said, she had not come all the way from Canada to turn back now. It helped that she made strong friendships with other Canadian women in the nearby hospitals, whom she came across on her daily rounds.

While the British tried to control the women it employed and restrict their work to the back theatres of war, along the lines of communication and outside of the fighting area, they could not hold back the expansion of the war zone. Particularly towards the end of the war, there were an increasing number of bombing raids, targeting areas behind the lines that were previously thought safe. The Germans generally concentrated their aerial attacks directly behind the frontlines, targeting the movement of troops and trains. They also launched further Zeppelin raids on England, in particular the south-east counties and east coast. London, Suffolk,

Norfolk and right up to Tyneside and even Scotland had been subjected to attacks. Paris, too, was subjected to aerial raids, but towards the end of 1917 there was an apparent shift in German policy. Germany began to target the allied base camps in France further behind the lines, using long range artillery. It was against the Geneva convention to attack hospitals, so medical staff hurried to paint red crosses on the roofs of their buildings so that they could be clearly seen from the sky. MacPherson recalled that in September 1917, she and the other drivers were told not to drive with their lamps on for fear of air raids that night. Then, that evening, she heard a series of loud bangs. It turned out that Camiers, a town 4 miles north on the road to Boulogne, had had an air raid, and the bangs that MacPherson had heard were the bombs exploding. In that attack, several people had been killed and others wounded. Immediately MacPherson and her team were tasked with evacuating the hospital in Camiers and bringing the casualties to Étaples.

With the massive German offensive of March 1918, the raids became more frequent and more intense. As the Germans advanced, they brought their long-range artillery with them. One of the worst raids occurred in Étaples on 19 May 1918. MacPherson says that, even though it was a clear moonlit night, the town received no advanced warning and all the town's lights were on. The members of the convoy had nowhere to seek refuge and were told to remain in their huts. The men's staff quarters at the nearby No.1 Canadian Hospital were badly hit, with over seventy killed. The nurses' quarters at the hospital were also hit and three nurses were killed. Other hospitals in the area were hit too, and after the raid three buildings were forced to close. In all, MacPherson estimated that there were 750 casualties. One of the German planes came down. The pilot survived and was immediately questioned. He deeply regretted that the hospitals had been hit, explaining that his orders had been to target the nearby railways and military supply trains.[49]

Other base camps were also targeted. WAAC Dolly Shepherd worked as a driver in the Dunkirk area. With both shells and bombs raining down around them, Shepherd was forced to pull over to change a tyre. The male officer whom she was driving insisted she ignore the tyre and drive on, but Shepherd knew she would be severely reprimanded when she returned the car to the garage. Ignoring the officer's protests, she insisted on changing the tyre and then continued on their journey to a depot, only to find it was no longer there. Less than an hour before, it had taken a direct hit and both Shepherd and the officer acknowledged their narrow escape.[50]

Kathleen Mary Allen was a clerk in Calais and kept an account of the air raids in her diary. In September 1917:

We had a rotten air raid last night and we lay under our mattresses; it lasted about one and a half hours. A piece of shell came through the roof of one of our huts but no-one was in it. ...

Sept. 6th 1917
We have had two more air raids – rotten ones both of them. Last night they came about three miles away but of course we did not see them. ...

Sept. 7th 1917
The Zeps kept away last night so we had a good night's rest. ...

Sept. 8th 1917
Had another good night. I think we began to dread going to bed because it is so terrible if they come.[51]

By 1917, it was impossible to deny the extent to which British women had contributed to the war effort, both at home and overseas. When the Imperial War Museum was founded in London in March that year, it established a Women's Work Committee to capture a full record of their activities. In March 1919, the British photographer Olive Edis was commissioned by the committee to travel to the Western Front and compile a photographic record of the women at work. Even though the war had ended, there was still a vast amount of work to be done, refugees needing to be rehomed, hospitals still with patients, graves needing tending and the army still needing support. As a studio photographer, Edis was used to a controlled environment, so this commission would provide her with an interesting challenge. She was the only official female war photographer and had a specially designed uniform.[52]

The British issued strict restrictions on newspaper journalists and photographers in order to control the information received by the public, which in turn could be used to inform the Central powers of Allied manoeuvres along the Western Front. Gradually the War Office grew to appreciate the power of photographs as propaganda and authorised several official war photographers such as Ernest Brooks, John Warwick Brooke and David McLellan. All the photographers were male. Many of the photographs of women were posed, generally portraying the more traditional, feminine roles of nursing. Yet there were a number of unofficial war photographers. For example, the Women of Pervyse, Elsie Knocker and Mairi Chisholm, went to Belgium with their own cameras. In the 1910s, more and more people owned their own personal cameras and to begin with, Knocker and Chisholm were merely keeping a personal record of their work and the things that they saw. Later on, when they had to raise funds to continue their work at their first aid post in Pervyse, they too discovered the power of photographs as propaganda. They returned to Belgium with more expensive cameras and began to take images with more purpose. Meanwhile, over in Russia, Florence Farmborough was also taking her own photographs. As mentioned earlier, Farmborough was working as a Red Cross nurse and worked with a field ambulance in the Galician region along Russia's border with Austria–Hungary. Despite moving back and forth with the Russian army, she took her large plate camera with her. She would transport it in a cart with the nursing staff's camp beds and other personal possessions. Farmborough had an unofficial agreement with a Russian liaison officer, who would take her undeveloped plates to Moscow, where her friends would have them developed. He would then return with the prints and more photographic supplies so that Farmborough could continue taking more.[53]

Without a doubt, the women who took up the men's jobs on the home front proved that women were capable of doing men's work and could be relied on. Meanwhile, groups like the VAD and independent organisations such as the First Aid Nursing Yeomanry, the Women of Pervyse, the Scottish Women's Hospital and the Women's Hospital Corps, demonstrated that women could also work in the war zone. Yet despite this, when the British military made the decision to establish the WAAC, WRNS and WRAF, these organisations were tightly controlled. As commander of the VAD, Furse had endeavoured to identify where help was needed and to provide the workers. However, with the three auxiliary services, the decisions were made by the War Office, the Admiralty and the Air Ministry, and the female commanders oversaw the administration, although both Furse and Gwynne-Vaughan showed that they were willing to play the system in trying to build their organisations and look out for the women as best they could. Certainly there was no serious consideration of the women forming combative units like Maria Bochkareva's Battalion of Death or the other Russian units, but as the back theatres of war became more and more vulnerable to attack, the initial reservations about sending a woman into an active war zone were no longer relevant.

Notes
1 Tennyson Jesse, Fryiwyd, *The Sword of Deborah: First-Hand Impressions of the British Women's Army in France*, p.59.
2 Furse, Katharine, *Hearts and Pomegranates*, p.553.
3 Furse, Katharine, 'Terms and Conditions in Relation to W.A.A.C.', relating to General Service VADs, Women at Work Collection, Imperial War Museum, document BRCS 10 6/3.

4 Furse, Katharine, *Hearts and Pomegranates*, p.553.
5 Warner, J., from author's transcription of Imperial War Museum tape interview, IWM Collection 997.
6 Dame Beryl Oliver, 'V.A.D. Members of the British Red Cross Society, and the Order of St John of Jerusalem', pp.37–8, in Wadge, D. Collett (ed.), *Women in Uniform*, pp.35–53.
7 Simkins, Peter; Jukes, Geoffrey and Hickey, Michael, *The First World War: The War to End all Wars*, p.98.
8 Named after Lord Derby who was at the time Director-General of Recruiting.
9 Simkins, Peter; Jukes, Geoffrey and Hickley, Michael, *The First World War: The War to End all Wars*, p.98.
10 Noakes, Lucy, *Women in the British Army: War and the Gentle Sex, 1907–1948*.
11 Ibid.
12 'Report by Lt Gen HM Lawson on the number and physical categories of men employed out of the fighting area of France' in the Women at Work Collection, IWM, document 'Army 3 3/2'.
13 Noakes, Lucy, *Women in the British Army*.
14 Jenny Gould, 'Women's Military Services in First World War Britain', in Higonnet, Margaret R. (ed), *Behind the Lines: Gender and the Two World Wars*.
15 Izzard, Molly, *A Heroine in her Time*.
16 BEU Monthly Record, November 1917.
17 Izzard, Molly, *A Heroine in her Time*, p.143.
18 Ibid.
19 Ibid.
20 Imperial War Museum taped interview with Annie May Martin, former WAAC. IWM Catalogue No. 42 transcribed by the author.
21 Gaunt, Emmy, 'Recollections of the Great War', p.1, National Army Museum archives, document number 1998-01-56.
22 Ibid.
23 She does not give her maiden name.
24 Graham, Mrs O.B., 'Notes on Experiencing During 1914-1918 War as a WAAC Officer', p.1, National Army Museum Archives, document number 1998-01-59.
25 Ibid., pp.1–2.
26 'Watson, Alexandra Mary Chalmers' in the Oxford DNB, http://www.oxforddnb.com/templates/article.jsp?articleid=67666&back=.
27 Izzard, Molly, *A Heroine in her Time*.
28 Watkins, G.E.G., 'Memories of a Hushwaac in France. St Omer Sept 1917 – Apr 1918; Paris Plage Apr 1918 – Nov 1918', National Army Museum Archives, p.1, document number 1998-01-110.
29 Ibid., p.2.
30 Ibid., p.3.
31 Furse, Katharine, *Hearts and Pomegranates*, p.556.
32 Ibid., p.569.
33 Escott, Squadron Leader Beryl E., *Women in Air Force Blue: The Story of Women in the Royal Air Force from 1918 to the Present Day*, p.14.
34 Ibid.
35 Atkinson, Diana, *Elsie and Mairi go to War*.
36 Izzard, Molly, *A Heroine in her Time*.
37 Willmott H.P., *World War I*, p.253.
38 Izzard, Molly, *A Heroine in her Time*.

39 Furse, Katharine, *Hearts and Pomegranates*, p.570.
40 Ibid.
41 Izzard, Molly, *A Heroine in her Time*.
42 Noakes, Lucy, *Women in the British Army: War and the Gentle Sex, 1907 – 1948*, p.60.
43 Escott, Squadron Leader Beryl E., *Women in Air Force Blue*.
44 Izzard, Molly, *A Heroine in her Time*.
45 MacPherson, Grace, 'Diary volume 1', CWM ARCHIVES / ARCHIVES DU MCG: Textual Records 58A 1 284.9.
46 Ibid.
47 MacPherson, Grace, 'Diary volume 2', CWM ARCHIVES / ARCHIVES DU MCG: Textual Records 58A 1 284.9.
48 Ibid.
49 MacPherson, Grace, 'Gold Stripe' 1919, CWM ARCHIVES / ARCHIVES DU MCG: Textual Records 58A 1 284.13.
50 Imperial War Museum taped interview with Dolly Shepherd, former WAAC, reel 11.
51 Personal diary of Kathleen Mary Allen as a clerk at Calais and Vendroux with the Women's Royal Auxiliary Corps, 1917-1919. National Army Museum. Archive number 2006-07-53.
52 Neale, Shirley, 'Olive Edis' in *Oxford Dictionary of National Biography*.
53 Imperial War Museum taped interview with Florence Farmborough (1975), reels 12 and 13, catalogue number 312.

9

Women in the American Military

We stood in front of him in our uniforms listening to every word of his eloquent speech; He said we had been good Marines and he was proud of us; Then, in his closing statement he said, 'We will not forget you. As we embrace you in uniform today, we will embrace you without uniform tomorrow.' All down the file of men standing at strict attention, the line broke, and everyone roared with laughter. The Secretary of the Navy forgot that he was talking to women.

Elizabeth Shoemaker, Marine (F)[1]

When war broke out in Europe in 1914, the United States of America declared itself neutral and provided humanitarian aid to both sides. Yet there was a growing antagonism between Germany and the USA, in particular concerning Germany's use of submarines to target shipping convoys in the Atlantic. The USA said that it would hold Germany responsible for any American ships that were sunk and demanded it restrict its submarine warfare policy. In the meantime, the USA was engaged in a series of border disputes with Mexico, so when the USA received evidence in early 1917 that the Germans were looking for an alliance with Mexico against the USA, this soured relations further. Shortly afterwards, the Germans recommenced unrestricted submarine activity, resulting in a complete breakdown in diplomatic relations between the two countries. This ultimately prompted the USA to join the war on the side of the Allies. With war looming, President Wilson ordered General Pershing to withdraw American troops from Mexico.

When the United States declared war on Germany on 6 April 1917, the British immediately demanded 500,000 men whom it could use to replenish its tired army. The French requested as many men as the USA could afford to spare. However, at that time, the US army only numbered 127,588 men with an additional 80,446 in the National Guard.[2] In order to take part in a large-scale European war in which manpower was at a premium, President Wilson realised he would have to sanction military conscription. Eventually the US army numbered over 4 million, more than half of whom served overseas with the American Expeditionary Force (AEF).[3]

Arriving in Washington DC straight from his service in Mexico, General Pershing was given command of the AEF. Like President Wilson, Pershing was well aware that in its current state, the US army was not yet ready to go to Europe. It had insufficient supplies and equipment, let alone enough men. As well as demanding men, the USA's new allies also requested that by the end of 1918 the US would provide over 4,500 aeroplanes and 5,000 pilots, but in 1917 the US army air service consisted of just sixty-five officers, of whom only half knew how to fly. Their equipment consisted of only fifty-five planes, all of which were old and only fit for basic training.[4] Therefore Pershing's first challenge was to build up the US army, to train up the conscripts and take to Europe whatever manpower he had available. However, he drew the line at integrating US soldiers into the British army and placing them under British command. He was determined that they would go overseas under American command.

Since the war began in 1914, the USA had the advantage of watching the impact of the conflict on women, to see how the different voluntary organisations operated, what they achieved and how, on the British home front, women took on men's roles. Therefore, when the US entered the war, the concept of a militarised woman was not entirely new. Dr Rosalie Slaughter Morton, who ran a successful practice in New York, had travelled to Britain, France and then on to Serbia to see women's voluntary hospital units in action. In London she saw the Women's Hospital Corps running a military hospital entirely staffed by women. In Serbia she saw the Scottish Women's Hospital treat casualties on the Macedonian front. In fact, Morton spent time with the 'American Unit', a Scottish Women's Hospital unit entirely funded by the American public. Morton even spent several months working voluntarily in one of the neighbouring hospitals along the front. After returning to her practice at the end of 1916, she became heavily involved in setting up America's own voluntary hospital units, staffed by women doctors.

The public read newspaper stories and books recounting stories of heroic women working in the trenches along the Western Front. Arthur Gleason, an American journalist, had gone to Belgium to cover the war in early 1914. His wife Helen, a renowned beauty, joined Doctor Munro's Flying Ambulance, the independent unit consisting of a small team of women who drove ambulances under a hail of shellfire in Belgium. These women had assumed their own military-style uniforms including breeches and laced-up boots. Arthur Gleason proudly wrote several books about Helen's experiences, which were published in America.[5] There were further reports of Knocker and Chisholm, the Women of Pervyse. Regular fundraising tours that came to the USA and the news from their Canadian neighbours raised awareness of the European conflict.

Following the events of March 1917, when the British army established the Women's Army Auxiliary Corps, complete with khaki uniforms, and sent the first women overseas, Newton D. Baker, the US secretary of war, was adamant that the American army would not enrol women, despite a desperate shortage of clerical staff.

However the secretary of the navy, Josephus Daniels, thought the complete opposite. He completely accepted that in order to make the navy an effective force in wartime he needed to solve its manpower shortage. To send men overseas would certainly require more labour and without a doubt would also generate a great deal of extra paperwork and administrative responsibilities. Referring to naval regulations, he determined that they were ambiguous and that there was nothing explicitly to say a woman could not serve as a yeoman.[6] This was in direct contrast to the women physicians who were campaigning for acceptance in the US Army Medical Corps. The women argued that recent legislation stipulated that, provided the individual had the correct qualification, a 'civilian' was eligible for commission within the corps, and that 'civilian' could mean either man or woman. However, in August 1917, a judicial ruling declared that at the time the legislation was written (1916), it was intended to be understood as 'male'.[7]

Daniels permitted women to enlist in the Naval Reserve Force, from which they would be selected for non-combative duties. Recruiting women aged between eighteen and thirty-five, the navy had 200 female recruits within a month, the total peaking at 11,000 in 1918.[8] The women were listed as 'yeoman (F)' to denote their sex, although they were popularly referred to as 'yeomanettes'. Daniels' decision to allow women was all the more extraordinary as they were allowed to enlist (rather than enrol as civilians like Britain's Women's Army Auxiliary Corps), which meant that they were subject to naval discipline, and upon discharge received honourable discharge and all a veteran's benefits. Furthermore, they were paid the same as the men.[9] The force's opposite number in Britain, the Women's Royal Naval Service, was not formed until November that year. The women in both corps were not permitted to serve on board naval vessels as this was a combative role. Instead they carried out administrative duties, working in such roles as telegraphists, telephone operators, draughtsmen and accountants. Many were recruited from these jobs in the civilian world, for the yeomanettes received no training other than what they learnt on the job, although some put themselves through night school. Only a handful went overseas to work, the majority remaining in the States.[10]

Over a year later, the US marines decided in August 1918 to recruit women. Heavy casualties meant they needed to release men for combative duty, but they chose to enrol the women as civilians rather than enlist them, although upon discharge they were still given full veterans' status. Also, like the navy, the marines ensured that the women received the same pay as the men. Historian Lettie Gavin believes that the reasons the marines took so much longer to employ women was because, despite initial resistance, they 'observed the change in the national attitude toward women at this time and hope to utilise the obvious public relations value of recruiting females.'[11] Secretary Baker still refused to permit women to serve in the US army, but General Pershing, commander of the AEF, demanded auxiliary workers. It was essential for the AEF for its telephone switchboards to be efficiently managed. These were of vital importance to the army as a means of relaying information and military orders between army headquarters and the men at the front. The situation was complicated by the language barrier between the French and the Americans: any misunderstandings and incorrect messages could have huge implications. Finally, in November 1917, the War Department relented and instructed the American Telephone and Telegraph Company to recruit and train the required women, who would operate as part of the Army Signal Corps. Intending to select women from within the company, the AT&T found there were not enough bilingual speakers and so it issued a public appeal. It received 7,000 applicants.[12] After these applicants had been vetted and carefully selected, there remained some who possessed the required language skills, but had no idea how to operate a switchboard, and so they had to be trained. The first group of women were sent out in March 1918 and were followed by five more groups, meaning that by the conclusion of the war in November that year there were 233 women serving overseas with the US army, deployed in a total of seventy-five different French towns and cities.[13] When American soldiers first dialled the telephone exchange and were met with a 'hello' from a fellow American, they were overjoyed. Life would be much easier now the 'Hello Girls' were there.[14] The Hello Girls won respect and did a wonderful job, even when they were under pressure manning the lines during a major offensive, or when most of the equipment in a telephone exchange was destroyed by a bombing raid.[15] However, their longest battle came after the war, when, like the women in the navy and the marines, they expected to be discharged with full veterans' status, only to be denied.

When the women signed up they believed that they had enlisted in the army, but the War Department claimed that they had been enrolled as civilians and that they had served their contract. The dispute between the women and the War Department was not resolved until 1977, nearly sixty years later.[16] However it took two more years for the statute to be processed, meaning the surviving women were not awarded their discharge certificates and veteran status until 1979.[17]

Even with the Hello Girls, the US army still needed more help. The AEF employed English-speaking French and Belgian women, and also employed some women who were already serving in France in the British Women's Army Auxiliary Corps (WAAC).[18] Emmy Gaunt was one of the WAACs instructed to work for the US army. It was Easter 1918 and she had spent a year working in Boulogne before being asked to work for the Americans. The WAACS were sent to Tours in the Loire Valley where they were to look after the AEF's archives, part of the American Central Records Office, which after three months relocated to Bourges, which was about 75 miles further inland. In the office they kept index cards corresponding to each soldier serving in the AEF, which they had regularly to update so that they could answer any enquiries from friends and relatives as to the status of a particular soldier. If the soldier was killed, they had to provide the next of kin with the grave details. General Pershing visited the offices and Emmy Gaunt remembers him stopping to say a few words to them. To start with, Gaunt said that there was something of a culture clash between the English and the Americans: 'We found it much more difficult to accustom ourselves to the ways and habits of the American men and women, than to those of our French Allies. The Americans certainly put themselves out to entertain us after office hours.'[19]

The USA's armed forces were also supported by several voluntary organisations, which Pershing was quick to bring under military control. These were the American Red Cross, the Salvation Army, the Young Men's Christian Association and the Young Women's Christian Association.

As with its sister organisations across the world, the American Red Cross (ARC) originated from the ideas of the Swiss humanitarian Henry Dunant in the 1860s to found the International Red Cross Society, a neutral organisation for the treatment of war wounded. Regardless of America's neutrality, the ARC sent out medical missions to work for both the Allies and the Central powers. When the United States entered the war, the ARC responded by expanding dramatically. By the beginning of 1919 approximately one-third of the population of the United States (22 million adults and 11 million children) had become members[20], 6,000 of whom worked overseas.[21]

Many American women travelled to Europe in order to help prior to 1917, and the majority did so as nurses. For example, Emily Simmonds, a qualified nurse, went to London where she was recruited by fellow American Mabel Grouitch to join a group of nurses sent to Serbia to aid relief efforts in Serbia. She worked tirelessly in terrible conditions and was forced to use her knowledge as a surgical nurse to perform small, but life-saving operations when there were no doctors to hand. Later, when Serbia was invaded and occupied by the Central powers (Germany, Austria–Hungary and Bulgaria), she assisted with the evacuation of the refugees. Mary Dexter, also a nurse, took up an unpaid position at an American hospital in Paignton, Devon, in September 1914. The project had been founded by a number of wealthy Americans living in Britain at the time, including Lady Randolph Spencer, the American mother of Winston Churchill, then Britain's Lord of the Admiralty. In 1915, Dexter decided to go to Belgium and worked at the Belgian Red Cross hospital at La Panne. Then, at the end of 1917, she joined an independent ambulance organisation, the Lowther-Hackett Unit.[22]

Both Barbara Lowther and Norah Hackett had been running canteens for the French army when they decided to form the ambulance unit. They managed to raise the money to buy ambulances and they employed women drivers from Britain, Ireland, France and America. They were officially attached to the French army, and both Lowther and Hackett were given the rank of lieutenant. Their finest hour was working with the French Army Ambulance Corps along the front at Compiègne, clearing casualties under shellfire.[23]

Dr Marguerite Cockett is credited with forming an American ambulance unit, which was attached to the French army prior to 1917. As well as serving in France, the unit also went with the Red Cross to Serbia. Cockett and her colleague Miss Butler also worked with the American Fund for French Wounded.[24] This was just one of the many charities set up by Americans living in France when the war began in the summer of 1914.

The Salvation Army was established as a charitable Protestant organisation in London in 1865, and like the Red Cross it expanded throughout the latter half of the century as countries established national branches. Compared to the Red Cross and the Young Men's Christian Association, the Salvation Army was the smallest organisation, however its contribution to the First World War had a lasting effect. Organised around a military structure, its members were given ranks and led by Commander Evangeline Booth, the daughter of the original founder of the Salvation

Army, William Booth. General Pershing authorised Booth to send out a small group to France and it duly arrived in August 1917. Pershing arranged for its members to be fitted with uniforms in Paris and assigned each individual the rank of private in the army.[25] As with the Hello Girls, Pershing believed that bringing the workers under military discipline (and control) would ensure that they worked hard and did their utmost to support their fellow countrymen.

The group established a Salvation Army hut in Demange, which provided the men with a canteen and an area where they could read and write and relax playing games. Later they added a piano. In addition to its aid work, the Salvation Army became famed for bringing the doughnut to the Western Front. This was credited to Salvationist Ensign Helen Purviance who wanted to conjure up something different for the troops to eat at the canteen. She went to acquire what ingredients she could and came back with everything she needed to make a dough. At first, Purviance made crullers, but then, realising how it would please the men to eat something that would remind them of home, she decided to shape doughnuts. Immediately the doughnuts became hugely popular, with men forming long queues to get them.[26]

Under General Pershing's orders, the third organisation, the Young Men's Christian Association (YMCA), was in charge of entertainment, which consisted of organising for celebrities to perform to the troops. In addition, the YMCA provided canteens and hostel accommodation. The YMCA was responsible for a total of 828 professional entertainers being sent overseas, and of these, 561 were women.[27]

Vaudeville star Elsie Janis was one of the famous singers who toured France with the YMCA. Prior to going to France, she had helped with recruitment drives and selling Liberty bonds. She also sang for benefits and to her great amusement she tried to knit garments for the American troops. Janis wanted to contribute to the war effort, but she was the first to admit that she would not have cut it as a nurse. She was encouraged to take her talents overseas and to perform for the troops there, so she decided to go to Paris. Janis still had an outstanding contract to perform in the French capital, which gave her a genuine excuse to travel. Janis and her mother set off together, for they were inseparable, and took a hotel room in Paris, which they used as their base. Within a day of her arrival, two members of the YMCA called on Janis to discuss a possible tour. They brought with them a map of the country and showed Janis all the different places that she could perform. In her biography, Janis explained that she didn't want to join any kind of organisation, not least because she didn't want to have her activities dictated to her by anyone else or be obliged to wear a uniform. Initially,

Janis refused to commit to the YMCA, but regularly having to fill out per-mits and justify her reasons for staying on in Paris irritated her and so she decided that the YMCA would give her a suitable *raison d'être* and that life on the road would be far more fun than appearing in the same old theatres night after night. Before leaving Paris, Janis was at a dinner party one even-ing when the alarms sounded for an impending air raid. Janis was amazed when the hostess's butler calmly entered the room and announced, 'Les Gothas sont arrivés, Madame' and the hostess merely turned to her guests and offered them more drinks before taking them into the next room and switching the gramophone on.[28]

Once on tour, Janis kept up a fast pace, performing for two weeks straight before returning to Paris for a short break. Some days she per-formed up to seven times, and on occasion gave additional impromptu performances. The 'stages' varied dramatically. At Mailly the men had constructed their own camp theatre; at a British flying school in Vendôme they had gone one further and had their own props, scenery and lights. Other times Janis performed on tables and whatever spaces were avail-able. Janis described one concert at Molleins-le-Bois where the stage was not up to her wild performance style:

> They had built a platform in the heart of the woods. They had a band that played 'Ragtime Strutters Ball' as I never had heard it played. At the end of my show I went quite wild, leading it and dancing at the same time. The platform had reckoned without my cartwheels and gave way beneath me. I was fished out and put back into action. A moment later a whistle blew. Here and there a man jumped to his feet, yelled, 'So long, Elsie!' and ran. In the distance I saw them lining up, fastening on gas masks and other front-line 'weight' and I knew that once more I was an 'Overture' to a real show! I quickly asked the band to change from 'Beale Street Blues' to 'Over There,' and the men marched away singing it as I stood on what was left of the platform leading that marvellous band![29]

Janis was keen to get closer to the front if possible and the YMCA arranged for her to travel to an American section of the warzone at Toul. She recalled it as a particularly exciting day, for she was shown where the Americans had concealed their heavy artillery guns in the woods just behind the front. Janis says that she was allowed to fire one of the guns at the German trenches.

Taking a brief trip to England, Janis was stopped at Southampton and interrogated. Her belongings and her person were searched: 'my vanity case, handbag, and even lipstick were examined.'[30] Finally she was released and allowed to find her mother, who had been left waiting for her. At the time, Janis was outraged by the very notion that she could be a spy. Once in London, she received a personal apology from British Intelligence and they asked her not to mention the matter. There was concern that if it got out that the British had arrested the 'Sweetheart of the AEF', it would irrevocably damage British–US relations.

The YMCA was also responsible for employing the first black women to work overseas on behalf of the United States army. Mrs James L. Curtis, Addie W. Hunton and Kathryn M. Johnson all travelled to France. Curtis was sent to St Sulpice, near Bordeaux, where there was a large concentration of male black troops working in auxiliary roles. Later, all three women worked at the port of St Nazaire, again a place where a large number of black troops worked, for the rest of the war. The women had to deal with racism even within the YMCA, and even though at times they questioned why they had come to France, they took a great deal of pride in their work.[31]

Outside of these organisations, there was another group of American women who were determined to go to Europe and establish a name for themselves. During the war, over twenty American female journalists and writers travelled overseas.[32] Despite the restrictions placed on the press along the Western Front and attempts to discourage women from the front, most of these women were much more successful than Dorothy Lawrence, the young British woman who dressed up as a soldier in 1915 and spent ten days on the front in order to create a sensational headline.

By the 1910s, women were more firmly established in the US press than in Britain and they were not all confined to covering women's topics, instead writing about politics and legal trials. George Horace Lorimer, the editor of the *Saturday Evening Post* was extremely successful in raising his paper's circulation, identifying the types of articles that his readers wanted and employing women to get the stories. In August 1914, Lorimer dispatched Irwin Cobb to cover the front, but because of the restrictions on travel, Cobb was unable to get near the Allied side, so instead he travelled with the German army as they progressed through Belgium. A second writer, Samuel Blythe, was to cover Europe's capital cities. As an established author, Mary Roberts Rinehart asked Lorimer to send her to Belgium to report for the *Post*. Lorimer agreed, but as Rinehart's husband was against her going she delayed,[33] so instead Lorimer employed Corra Harris to go to London.

Harris was an interesting choice, given her anti-British sentiments. She arrived in London at the end of September and immediately complained that the British were not taking the war seriously enough. She had hoped to see grand demonstrations of patriotism – flags waving, men marching and women crying – but by now Britain had already been at war for two months. She immediately investigated the different voluntary organisations including the Women's Emergency Corps. Although she described its members as 'aloof' she was critical of Lord Kitchener (who was Britain's Secretary of State for War) for being unwilling to send them overseas. In mid-October she then travelled over to France where she was determined to get close to the front, because she was a war correspondent after all. Along with an interpreter, Harris set off in a carriage to Senlis, north of Paris, from where the initial German advance had been pushed back. From there they tried to go on to Soissons where they would be in range of the Germans' heavy artillery, but they could only get passes as far as Compiègne, several miles away. Harris tried unsuccessfully to persuade their carriage driver to continue the last few miles on to Soissons. Harris' nerves then got the better of her, as she became increasingly worried that her attempts to get to the front would result in her being arrested and accused of being a spy. Whilst in London, Harris had seen a porter at her hotel arrested for espionage, and now in the Compiègne Forest she and her interpreter found themselves being trailed by a French soldier. When asked what he was doing he replied that he was on the lookout for spies. For Harris it was the last straw and she gave up her attempts to reach the front. She returned home to the US in December. It was only then that she began to regret her decision and after much thought resolved to return and this time succeed. However, by that time Lorimer had replaced her with Mary Roberts Rinehart, whose husband had finally relented and given her permission to go.[34]

Rinehart was much more forceful and proactive in her bid to get to the front. Lorimer provided her with letters of introduction to his contacts in London, including Lord Northcliffe, the powerful media magnate behind many British papers, including the *Times* and the *Daily Mail*. Lord Northcliffe then provided Rinehart with more letters of introduction, in this case to the senior members of the Belgian army and government. Northcliffe was opposed to the British government's policy to ban the press and enforce censorship, believing it facilitated German propaganda, so he was more than happy to aid the American press. He helped Rinehart in her bid to secure interviews with Queen Mary of England and the King and Queen of Belgium who were currently residing at the coastal resort of La Panne in the small remaining section of unoccupied Belgium.[35]

Even with Northcliffe's help, Rinehart knew it would be difficult to get across to Belgium as a journalist, let alone to the front. So she decided to go as a member of the Red Cross, because in the 1890s, before she had married, Rinehart had qualified as a nurse. She appealed directly to the head of the Belgian Red Cross, Dr Depage (founder of Edith Cavell's nursing school in Brussels) while he was over in London. She was direct, explaining that it was important that the Americans understood the true situation in Belgium and that it could result in aid and support.[36] Depage agreed and organised for a car to collect her from Calais and take her on to his hospital in La Panne. When Rinehart published her account of her adventures in Belgium she said that as a member of the American Red Cross it was her duty to investigate the true situation of the hospitals near the front and report back to America.[37]

Once Rinehart was at La Panne she managed to organise a night-time trip into the Belgian trenches near Dixmude, the same area in which Doctor Hector Munro's Flying Ambulance was stationed and the two Women of Pervyse, Mairi Chisholm and Elsie Knocker, ran their first aid post. Rinehart was closely supervised by a group of soldiers who led the way. In her writing, Rinehart described the inhumane condition of the shallow trenches, the mud and the foul smell from the flooded Yser canal. As it was relatively quiet that night, Rinehart pressed the soldiers to take her further into the trenches. They moved forward in pairs, and Rinehart persuaded her guide, a Belgian lieutenant, to take her to an outpost, a ruined building situated in no-man's-land. The captain leading the group looked back to check their progress and was horrified to see what they had done, but Rinehart says he dared not call out for fear of drawing German fire. Reaching the outpost, Rinehart found herself only 600ft from the German trenches. The party then continued further along the line towards Nieuwpoort, wading through pools of water and mud. Despite the restrictions on the press, Rinehart declares that she was always very open about the purpose of her visits, carrying her notebook with her wherever she went.

Rinehart then continued with her tour of the Western Front, relying on her network of contacts and letters of introduction. She visited the section of Ypres controlled by the French and met General Foch before continuing on to a British airship station. It was here, in February that she encountered Chisholm and Knocker, just after they had been awarded the Order of Leopold for their first aid and ambulance work along the Belgian frontlines. The women invited Rinehart and one of the British officers to join them that evening for dinner at their first aid post. Chisholm warned Rinehart that the village was regularly shelled, but hoped that she wouldn't mind. When Chisholm and Knocker left, the officer explained to Rinehart:

Of course they have no business there ... It's a frightful responsibility to place on the men at that part of the line, but there's no question about the value of what they are doing, and if they want to stay they deserve to be allowed to. They go right into the trenches, and they take care of the wounded until the ambulances come up at night. Wait until you see their house and you will understand why they got those medals.[38]

Rinehart and the officer were driven to Pervyse, and as they approached the trenches they had to turn off the headlamps. About a mile from their destination the car skidded and became stuck. A group of soldiers who were passing tried to move it for them with no luck. They were then rescued by an armoured vehicle, only to become stuck again and leaving the chauffeur with the car, Rinehart and the officer continued on foot, in the rain. They arrived in time for food, which Rinehart recalled with some shock was placed on the table in the pans in which it was cooked. Her feet were sore from walking and she was grateful to be able to rest and to warm herself in front of the fire, but she was unable to relax fully. She looked up at the sagging ceiling, fearing imminent collapse, and, looking over at the mantelpiece, she saw an arrangement of various pieces of shrapnel. Later on, the chauffeur arrived with the car, which had been pulled back on to the road and towed to Pervyse because it ran out of petrol. It looked unlikely that they would be able to get any more fuel, so Chisholm and Knocker offered Rinehart a bed for the night. She thanked them, but was extremely wary of the idea, as they anticipated heavy bombardment that evening. Meanwhile, visitors from the trenches dropped in to heat themselves by the fire and smoke their pipes. The group even had an impromptu concert using the beaten-up piano in the corner of the room. Then, much to Rinehart's relief, the chauffeur reappeared with a can of petrol and announced that they could leave before the guns started.[39]

During her time in Europe, Rinehart generated a great deal of work. In addition to her royal interviews, she met with the British field marshal and commander of the British Expeditionary Force Viscount French, who showed her the British position along the front at Béthune. She also interviewed Winston Churchill, who was then First Lord of the Admiralty. Compared to her experience of the Belgian trenches, Rinehart's diary suggested that she found the tour of the British and French trenches relatively disappointing. Although she was provided with plenty of information from her guides, the tours were more controlled.[40] Rinehart returned to the United States in March 1915 and later that year she published her book chronicling her experiences. In it she included an entire chapter entitled, 'How Americans can help'.

Not all the women who travelled to Europe supported the war. Inez Milholland, a qualified lawyer, was an active suffragist and a pacifist.

Having spent time in London, she had seen the Pankhursts' militant Suffragettes, the Women's Social and Political Union, in action. Frustrated in her attempts to practise law she campaigned vocally for female equality. With many friends in the press, she understood the power of propaganda. So when, in 1915, Milholland's ex-fiancé, the Italian inventor Guglielmo 'Billy' Marconi, was appointed by the Italians to oversee their military radio operations, she saw an opportunity to promote her views of pacifism. She decided to travel to Italy with Marconi in May that year as a freelance correspondent for the *New York Tribune* and *Collier's Weekly* magazine. It is likely that Milholland would have read Rinehart's articles from France and Belgium and hoped that her own work would bring her the professional success she so desired. Milholland settled in Rome where she applied for press accreditation from the Italian Ministry of the Interior to go on official press tours of the front, but she was unsuccessful. Like Rinehart she hoped to interview the royal family, which would earn her a sizeable fee. However, she had no letters of introduction and the Italian government refused her request.

Looking for a story, Milholland travelled to Bologna, which was close to the war zone. She spoke to officers on the train *en route* and then visited a military hospital in the city, where the head of the nursing staff was a fellow American. Yet, like many of her articles, her account of the trip to Bologna remained unpublished. Ultimately Milholland was not a trained journalist and her writing was basic and far too subjective. The *New York Tribune* did publish several of her articles, but *Collier's Weekly* didn't publish any.

Finally, she was granted permission to visit the war zone in the Dolomites. The trenches were empty, as the Front had moved further forward. She travelled to Brescia full of excitement, only for it to turn into great disappointment. While the male journalists in the party were allowed to go on, she was held back on account of being a woman. Apparently the other American correspondents had protested at a woman being included in the group and she was then ordered to return to Rome. Outraged at the insult to her sex, she complained directly to the Italian prime minister who explained that it was her pacifist views which the Italians objected to rather than her gender and she was asked to leave the country. Shortly afterwards, Italy imposed a ban on all correspondents from neutral countries.[41]

Away from the Western Front, political events in Russia attracted a number of female correspondents keen to witness the dawn of a new democracy. Florence MacLeod, Bessie Beatty, and Rheta Childe Dorr were among those who went. MacLeod, a reporter for *Leslie's Weekly* spent time in Petrograd watching the repercussions of the first Russian revolution unfold. She then decided in April 1917 to leave Petrograd and head to the front, but first she had to find someone willing to give her the correct permits to travel. Like Rinehart had done in order to get to Belgium, MacLeod chose to join the Red Cross. She spoke with Colonel Eugene Hurd, an American in charge of a Red Cross field ambulance, who dealt with the Russian Red Cross on her behalf. She then travelled with Hurd as he returned to his field hospital and he instructed her that as far as anyone else was concerned, she was a nurse and she needed to earn her keep. One of the nurses was suspicious of MacLeod and ordered her in Russian to bandage a man's foot before walking off. In order to maintain the pretence, MacLeod said that Hurd walked over and told her what to do in English, which the nurses did not understand, all the time giving the impression they were simply chatting. Next, Hurd got MacLeod to assist him with an amputation. MacLeod had already spent time visiting hospitals while she had toured France, and to her relief she got through the operation without fainting or being sick: in fact it fascinated her. MacLeod remained at the field hospital for three months, regularly travelling with Hurd to other first aid posts near the front. There were some dangers – occasionally enemy planes flew overhead – but the hospital proudly displayed the Red Cross in the hope that it would protect them. Whenever there was a gas attack on the nearby front, the hospital had to close all windows and doors and everyone had to keep their gas masks close to hand.[42]

At the end of June, MacLeod returned to Petrograd to find that the British Suffragette, Emmeline Pankhurst was there, and that the Russian government had raised a combat battalion of women. Pankhurst's visit was an attempt to demonstrate good relations between Britain and Russia. America was keen to support a new democracy and the women's battalion was a propaganda experiment by the Russian government to shame its fighting men and get the country's army back on track. Both Bessie Beatty and Rheta Childe Dorr covered Pankhurst's visit and then spent nearly two weeks with the women's battalion travelling up to the front. Beatty was working for the *San Francisco Bulletin* and Dorr for the *New York Evening Mail*.

After Russia, Dorr travelled to France, where her son was serving in the American Expeditionary Force. Sent there as a war correspondent to report on the conditions faced by the American soldiers, she unsurprisingly found it a personal and emotional experience. Empathising strongly with all the thousands of other mothers back home in the USA, she spent three months in France researching her next book, which she entitled *A Soldier's Mother in France*.

Eunice Tietjens was another American journalist who went to France following America's entry into the war. She arrived in Paris in October 1917 and worked for the *Chicago Daily News*. Her chief Paul Scott Mowrer proved an ideal boss. Whilst the male correspondents were given the 'heavy work' reporting on the military and politics, Tietjens was officially designated to cover the human side of war; the soldiers on leave, the French population and the refugees. Yet Tietjens didn't posses any desire to write 'women's stories' and understanding this Mowrer allowed her to dig out her own stories.[43]

> For the most part I was in Paris, though from time to time I went on trips to the little towns behind the lines, in what was loosely called 'the front.' These trips lasted from a few days to several weeks, and were arranged for me by Mowrer with infinite red tape through the various military channels. I was sometimes with the French army, sometimes with the American, and once through a fluke for a couple of weeks with the British. The British did not encourage women behind their lines. Only once did I get to the front-line trenches, near enough to the enemy to see the German soldiers with a telescope – they usually stopped me at the light artillery line – but I had plenty of exciting adventures.[44]

As well as writing articles about the communities living close to the front, Tietjens actively participated in charitable causes. For example over Christmas and New Year, she campaigned to raise funds with the Red Cross to buy presents for the Parisian children and then helped distribute them.

Like others who were living behind the lines, Tietjens was unable to escape the increasingly regular bombing raids. When the sirens sounded, she and those who lived in nearby apartments in Paris's Latin quarter would hurry down into the neighbour's cellar. Here she spent many evenings with an artistic group of painters and their muses until the all-clear sounded.

Tietjens explained that the newspaper office became a sort of tourist information bureau for Americans in Paris. On one occasion, two soldiers came in despairing that they could not remember where their hotel was, and that they had left all their kit and money there. Mowrer's secretary helped them work out which hotel it was, only for them to return the next day asking where they could get tattoos done.

In October 1918, Tietjens received her orders to return home. The end of the war was in sight and her paper was reducing the number of correspondents in Paris. However Tietjens chose to stay a little longer, and joined the American Red Cross, working for them until January 1919. Before she left the *Chicago Daily News*, Tietjens had applied for another trip to the

French front. When the papers came through, the Red Cross granted her leave to go. What was intended to be a straightforward, controlled press tour ended in a horrendous tragedy that, despite everything she had seen in her year in France, gave Tietjens an insight into the true horrors of trench warfare. The group of women was under the charge of a French lieutenant, assisted by Mademoiselle de la Vallette, a female chaperone from the French government. Tietjens was joined by another female correspondent, Cecil Dorrian of the *Newark Evening News*, the author Elizabeth Shepley Sergeant, and finally Sergeant's friend, the wife of an American officer. The group set off toward Rheims and reached the battlefield of Mont de Bligny in the afternoon. The lieutenant cautioned the women to pay attention, to be meticulously careful and not touch anything, looking out for unexploded shells and grenades. Tietjens set off in one direction with Vallette whom she knew from previous trips, while the others spread out across the site. It was quite common to collect souvenirs of war, and despite the lieutenant's warning, Tietjens found a German copy of the New Testament, which she picked up, while Vallette picked up 'a wooden stick with a cylindrical metal head from which hung a number of strings of white tape'.[45] Vallette asked Tietjens what she thought it was, when she said that she did not know, Vallette went to take it to the lieutenant for inspection:

> At the same moment Cecil Dorrian … called to me to come and look at the view, thereby saving my life. For I turned away and walked in another direction.
>
> Afterwards I learned that Mademoiselle went to the lieutenant and asked him the same question she had asked me. He replied, terror-stricken, 'Put it down, mademoiselle, put it down quickly!' She leaned down to do so, but in some fashion she must have pulled one of the strings, or set it down too roughly in her confusion, for it exploded, killing her instantly, tearing off an arm of the lieutenant, and wounding Elizabeth Sergeant in the legs.[46]

Tietjens describes the shock of seeing Mademoiselle Vallette's half naked body and the extent of her internal injuries and then after a moment she heard the screams of the lieutenant. Elizabeth Sergeant, on the other hand, fell noiselessly to the ground. Dorrian stayed with the group, while Tietjens ran to alert the French soldiers who had accompanied the group and were waiting for them a short distance away.

Sergeant was severely wounded and spent the next two years in hospital. While Sergeant was driven to hospital, Dorrian and Tietjens persuaded the French soldiers to remove Vallette's body from the battlefield, but they left her lying by the roadside. Due to military protocol, they had been reluctant to move her at all until a French officer could certify her cause of death, but an officer was unlikely to be available until the following day. Tietjens did not want Vallette to lie there overnight, so as Tietjens was dressed in her official correspondent's uniform, which was the same as an officer's, she used all the authority she could muster and ordered the soldiers to place Vallette's body in one of the cars. Dorrian and the American officer's wife took the train back to Paris while Tietjens remained with the body. When the French military authorities refused to take responsibility for the body, Tietjens made up her mind to return Vallette to Paris herself. She paid the soldier who was their chauffeur to drive her through the night back to the capital. When he refused, fearing court marshal, she pointed to her correspondent's uniform and said that he had been under the lieutenant's command. Now that he had been wounded, she was second-in-command and the chauffeur must do as she said. Avoiding the main roads, they managed to reach Paris in the early hours of the morning and broke the news to Vallette's shocked family.[47]

While American newspapers were prepared to employ female journalists, the US army refused to give them the same military accreditation that it awarded to official male correspondents. Despite this, Peggy Hull was determined to earn herself a legitimate role as a war correspondent with full accreditation from the US army. In the late 1800s, in order to break into the world of newspapers, budding female journalists performed 'stunts' to generate big stories and win the front headlines, much as Dorothy Lawrence had tried to do. The American Nellie Bly (Elizabeth Jane Cochrane) was famous for this. In 1887, she feigned insanity and was committed to a mental asylum where she spent three months undercover, investigating allegations of maltreatment. In 1889 she embarked on a round-the-world trip in a bid to beat Jules Verne's fictional character Phileas Fogg and complete it in under eighty days. She succeeded.[48]

Before joining the Allies in April 1917, the US army was engaged in a conflict along the Mexican border from March 1916 until February 1917. There, General Pershing, the future commander-in-chief of the American Expeditionary Force during the First World War, was victim to Hull's own stunt, with a little bit of help from her fellow correspondents. The conflict over, General Pershing led the US troops out of Mexico. Suddenly Hull rode up alongside him on a white horse (to be sure that she would stand out in any black and white photos), carrying a large bouquet of flowers. The press photographers seized upon the moment and the picture of Hull and Pershing went global 'carrying the headline: "American girl correspondent leads troops out of Mexico with General Pershing."'[49]

Hull was pleased when the *El Paso Morning Times* gave her the press credentials she so desired. However, despite the number of American women working overseas as reporters, the American War Department still refused official military accreditation to women. Hull then followed Pershing to France in the summer of 1917 and, like Tietjens, she wore a feminised version of the official war correspondent's uniform made up of 'a trim officer's tunic, calf-length skirt, polished boots, Sam Browne belt and campaign hat'.[50] During the Mexican conflict, Hull had struck up a friendship with General Peyton C. March and reported on his troops whilst in France. Hull sold articles to the *Chicago Tribune*, but the male war correspondents working with the AEF protested about her being there, forcing Hull to defend her position. Family illness forced Hull to return home in the autumn, but her battle was not over. The following summer, she went to Washington DC and with General March's help won military accreditation. She began her career as an official war correspondent by travelling to Siberia to cover the US army's role in the Russian Civil War.

The United States provided substantial support, both through raising funds and by sending individuals and voluntary organisations to Europe long before it entered the war in 1917. By then, there was plenty of evidence demonstrating to the United States military the value of women's contribution to the war effort. When the British armed services established its three female auxiliary services, the Women's Army Auxiliary Corps and the Women's Royal Naval Service in 1917, followed by the Women's Royal Air Force a year later, it was done according to its own terms and conditions. Many arguments followed between the female commanders of the women's corps and the heads of each service to clarify and improve the status, pay and welfare of the women. This makes the actions of the United States army and navy all the more interesting. None of the American women's services had a female commander; instead they reported directly to the male officers. In this sense the United States's approach to employing women in the military was even more controlled than in Britain. However, Daniels' decision to allow the yeomanettes to enlist, and for both they and the women marines to receive equal pay to the men was hugely significant for campaigners of female equality in the workplace. It established a valuable precedent for any future debates on the matter.

The contrast of Secretary Baker's reluctance for the army to employ women with Daniels' progressive actions demonstrates the extent to which opinion was still divided in the United States regarding the appropriate role of women in wartime. Despite Pershing's persistent requests for auxiliary workers, the War Department only permitted him to have the Hello

Girls. The very fact that Pershing was obliged to employ local civilians and members of Britain's Women's Army Auxiliary Corps shows how serious the shortage of manpower was. If the Hello Girls hadn't been organised under duress it may be that their status would have been less ambiguous and it would have saved both the army and the women a lengthy legal battle. Had Baker been more like Daniels, it is interesting to think how many more women would have been employed by the army and how many more American women would have gone overseas to serve for their country. Pershing was quick to bring the major voluntary organisations under military control and to use them as efficiently as possible. He put a great trust in both the men and the women that the honour of working for the United States army would ensure their hard work and dedication, and it did.

The female journalists were all very career driven and, as shown by both Mary Roberts Rinehart and Florence MacLeod, they were not adverse to using women's traditional role in nursing to get their headlines. Even if the military wasn't allowing women to take up combat roles, they were determined to get to the front to show that they were just as good as the men. They provide an insight into America's transition from neutral observer to patriotic ally. Although many of them wanted to steer away from human interest stories and report on the military action, the female reporters brought a certain empathy to their observations, which was rarely seen in the work of the male correspondents.

Notes

1 Taken from interview with Mrs Elizabeth Linscott (née Shoemaker) in the Springfield Sunday Republican (February 1960 p.42) reproduced in Hewitt, Linda, J., *Women Marines in World War I*, p.41.
2 Lacey, Jim, *Pershing*, p.88.
3 Henry, Mark, *The US Army of World War I*.
4 Lacey, Jim, *Pershing*, p.93.
5 In his books Arthur Gleason awarded most of the credit for the first-aid post established at Pervyse to his wife Helen. Following the publication of his book, this claim was hotly disputed by Elsie Knocker and Mairi Chisholm, who in fact established the post, although Helen did help them in the early stages. Whether or not it was factually accurate, Gleason's books still made an impact.
6 Gavin, Lettie, *American Women in World War I*.
7 Bellafaire, Judith and Herrera Graf, Mercedes, *Women Doctors in War*, p.33.
8 Gavin, Lettie, *American Women in World War I*.
9 Ibid.
10 Ibid.
11 Ibid., p.25.
12 Schneider, Dorothy and Carl J., *Into the Breach: American Women Overseas in World War I*, p.178.
13 Ibid., pp.177–8.

14 Gavin, Lettie, *American Women in World War I.*
15 Ibid.
16 Schneider, Dorothy and Carl J., *Into the Breach.*
17 Gavin, Lettie, *American Women in World War I.*
18 Zeiger, Susan, *In Uncle Sam's Service.*
19 Gaunt, Emmy, 'Recollections of the Great War', National Army Museum
    Archive, document 1998-01-50.
20 Irwin, Julia F. 'Making the World Safe: The American Red Cross and the
    Nation's Humanitarian Awakening
21 Schneider, Dorothy and Carl J., *Into the Breach*, p.154.
22 Dexter, Mary, *In the Soldier's Service: War Experiences of Mary Dexter
    1914–1918.*
23 Kanner, Barbara Penny, 'Lowther, Barbara (Toupie)' in *Women and War*, vol. 2,
    edited by Bernard A. Cook.
24 *Home Front Heroes – A Biographical Dictionary of Americans During Wartime,*
    Vol 1, edited by Benjamin F. Shearer.
25 Schneider, Dorothy and Carl J., *Into the Breach.*
26 Gavin, Lettie, *American Women in World War I.*
27 Schneider, Dorothy and Carl J., *Into the Breach*, p.154.
28 Janis, Elsie, *So Far so Good! An autobiography*, p.154.
29 Ibid., pp.180–1.
30 Ibid., p.186.
31 Gavin, Lettie, *American Women in World War I.*
32 Burger Johnson, Katherine, 'Journalists, American Women, During World War I'
    in *Women and War: A Historical Encyclopedia from Antiquity to the Present,*
    Bernard A. Cook
33 Cohn, Jan, *Improbable Fiction: The Life of Mary Roberts Rinehart.*
34 Talmadge, John E., *Corra Harris: Lady of Purpose.*
35 Cohn, Jan, *Improbable Fiction.*
36 Ibid.
37 Rinehart, Mary Roberts, *Kings Queens and Pawns: An American Woman at the
    Front.*
38 As reported in Rinehart, Mary Roberts, *Kings Queens and Pawns*, p.234.
39 Rinehart, Mary Roberts, *Kings Queens and Pawns.*
40 Cohn, Jan, *Improbable Fiction.*
41 Lumsden, Linda J., *Inez: The life and times of Inez Milholland.*
42 MacLeod, Florence, *Runaway Russia.*
43 Tietjens, Eunice, *The World at My Shoulder*, p.141.
44 Ibid., pp.141–2.
45 Ibid., p.161.
46 Ibid., p.161.
47 Ibid.
48 Ross, Ishbel, *Ladies of the Press.*
49 Belford, Barbara, *Brilliant Bylines*, p.190.
50 Ibid., p.190.

10

The Foundations for Women in Wartime

The First World War saw the militarisation of women on an unprecedented scale. The women's movement had succeeded in giving women more confidence, allowing them to assert themselves and ultimately helping them to assume new responsibilities in wartime. The fight for suffrage brought women with similar views together and demonstrated the power of the collective voice, even if not everybody agreed with what they had to say or how they went about it.

Whenever there was a debate about the proper role of women in wartime, the argument kept coming back to the principle that women were life-givers, not life-takers. Professional nursing had only emerged in the latter half of the nineteenth century, and by the early 1900s it had become an acceptable role for women. It fitted the perception of life-giver and was suitably feminine. So therefore it is not surprising that the majority of voluntary organisations that ventured out to the Continent in the first months of the war provided some form of medical care. However, these voluntary groups went beyond nursing: they pushed at the boundaries of what was deemed acceptable. Women began driving ambulances, they set up mobile canteens and adopted military-style khaki uniforms as they edged closer to the front. Both Marie Marvingt, the French aviatrix, and Briton Flora Sandes, began the war as nurses, before Marvingt joined the French infantry and Sandes became a soldier in the Serbian army. The American journalist and writer Mary Roberts Rinehart used her nursing qualification to join the Red Cross in order to travel to Belgium in 1915. Fellow American journalist Florence MacLeod did not have any medical training when she persuaded the commander of an American Red Cross unit in Russia to employ her so that she could get closer to the action on the frontline.

As the war continued and the opposing armies became entrenched, the women's voluntary organisations also became more established. In France large hospital bases were established behind the lines in towns like Boulogne, Étaples and Rouen, and consequently more and more nurses were sent overseas to tend the wounded.

In addition to satisfying their strong sense of patriotism, professional women hoped that the war would provide them with valuable experience with which to advance their careers. Journalists hoped that by proving themselves as war correspondents they could access the front and make headlines. Medical women of many nations hoped that the need for doctors would mean that their respective armies' medical corps would welcome them, but instead they were turned down and met with strong opposition. They presumed that their qualifications would distinguish them from the rest of the female workforce. Russia was prepared to employ its female doctors from 1914 onwards, but these women were restricted to hospitals behind the lines. They held a lower status and were paid less than their male peers. When women doctors were finally accepted to work for the British and the United States armies it was as contract workers, so that they too could be paid less and were of lower status than the male doctors.

In the early stages of the war, the armies, particularly the British, tried to ban women from the front. Then in 1916 the War Office changed tack and instead tried to assert authority over women's groups such as the First Aid Nursing Yeomanry and the first aid unit run by the Women of Pervyse. Yet each group succeeded in retaining its independence. So as with the medical contract workers, when Britain decided officially to form a women's auxiliary service, it ensured that the War Office had ultimate control over the corps.

The years 1916–17 were the turning point that led Britain, France, Russia and the United States seriously to consider using the female workforce, by forming auxiliary corps for their armed services. The different nations on both sides of the conflict were experiencing an acute shortage of manpower; conscription alone was not enough and they had to release men from support roles so that they could be sent to the front. While the early voluntary groups had been for the most part made up of women from the upper classes who were independently wealthy, the auxiliary services introduced women from the middle and working classes to war work.

Each of the British services, the Women's Army Auxiliary Corps, the Women's Royal Naval Service and the Women's Royal Air Force, had a female commander-in-chief, but in terms of power and authority men remained the decision-makers. These female commanders, despite battling hard to improve the status, pay and the living standards of their women, found that they were ultimately figureheads. The women who worked for the United States army, navy and marines came under even more direct control because they did not have a female commander and instead reported directly to male officers. Yet the US navy and marines made a point of ensuring that women had equal pay. Russia was the only country that actually formed a women's combat unit. Russia already stood apart from the other countries in the war owing to the number of women who fought in its army either dressed as men like Princess Dadeshkeliani or enlisted as women like Maria Bochkareva. Yet the decision to form the women's combat battalions was less about rewarding the women for their military prowess and more of a desperate attempt at shaming their men into fighting. It was an experiment that was considered to have failed, even though Bochkareva's battalion did reach the front and they did go over the top.

Throughout the war, the militarisation of women varied enormously. Some women were properly enlisted, some were enrolled, others were employed on contract and some were given rank and status, but very few actually saw combat. There were many inconsistencies. In the United States, women doctors challenged the wording of the legislation for acceptance to the Medical Corps, arguing that it was ambiguous. The United States army responded by declaring that it was intended to mean men only, while the naval secretary Daniels interpreted the law to mean that women were allowed to enlist in the navy.

When the United States joined the war, it was taken aback by the scale of men and equipment its allies demanded. President Wilson and General Pershing understood that in order to provide the Allies with a significant force, they would have to increase the size of the army through conscription. Pershing was adamant that, to achieve this, women would be needed, but he was not supported by Newton D. Baker, the secretary for war. He was eventually permitted to employ women in the signalling corps – the 'Hello Girls' – but he had to employ local women as well, as members of Britain's Women's Army Auxiliary Corps. Another of Pershing's achievements was fully to appreciate the value of voluntary organisations such as the Salvation Army and the Young Men's Christian Association. Unlike the British army, he asserted immediate control over these organisations and designated them important roles in looking after his men. This was an acknowledgement of the wider support network that his army needed in order to operate in this large-scale conflict.

While various individual women and voluntary groups were trying to get closer to the front, there were women who suddenly found themselves unexpectedly and unwillingly in the war zone, civilians living in areas occupied by the enemy. The heroic actions of the resistance networks and their women experienced a different type of combat role as they risked their lives time and time again. In the same way that 1916–17 was a turning point for the armed services' employment of women, it also marked a change in life in the occupied zone. Anti-espionage units became more sophisticated and the borders were more tightly controlled and heavily defended. In response, new underground networks such as the White Lady had to be more organised and these adopted a military-like structure with their members enrolling as soldiers and pledging oaths of allegiance. They wanted to be able to say that they had done what they could to have served their country in its time of need.

With significant technological advances, warfare changed dramatically at the beginning of the twentieth century and continued to do so throughout the First World War. Not only was greater manpower (or woman-power) required, but the war zone expanded. Long-range artillery and aerial bombings meant that places that had previously been safe weren't any longer. The hospital cities and military bases behind the lines came under attack and Zeppelins targeted the British east coast and the southern counties. Realistically it wasn't possible to keep women out of harm's way, so in such circumstances, shouldn't they too be allowed to defend their country?

When the war ended, many of the women who had been involved remained working in Europe. The First Aid Nursing Yeomanry, the Voluntary Aid Detachments and the Red Cross continued to work, as did the three British auxiliary services, before they were disbanded (the Women's Royal Naval Service in 1919, the Women's Royal Air Force in 1920 and the Women's Army Auxiliary Corps in 1921). At the end of the war, the United States also disbanded its women's auxiliary services. The employment of women on the home front during the war seemed to have a larger impact on women in general and their place in society than the efforts of those returning from service overseas.

Certainly in France, now that the war was over the soldiers seemed keen to return to life as it was, to reset the gender balance. With the world now at peace, there were no longer exceptional circumstances. For example in Britain's industrial sector the employment of women dropped significantly when the war ended, with 750,000 women being made redundant. The press also changed its stance on female workers: after praising them during the war it became more critical. However the post-war years saw a decrease of women employed in service and an increase of women in clerical roles and in relatively new industries such as those working with chemicals and in engineering.[1] In France, women found that more universities offered women medical training during the war, but at the end of the war closed their doors once more. The newly qualified doctors now found themselves with little experience compared to medics returning from war and fewer employment opportunities. The quest for employment equality was far from over.

Yet the place to look for the lasting effects of the militarisation of women in the First World War is not 1919 but twenty years further on, in 1939. As war looked increasingly likely during the 1930s, Britain formed the Auxiliary Territorial Service (ATS) in 1938. The First Aid Nursing Yeomanry was invited to form a transport corps within the ATS. This service became the equivalent of the Women's Army Auxiliary Corps, overseeing the employment of women by the army throughout the Second World War. Both the navy and the Royal Air Force re-established their auxiliary services straight away in 1939; the Women's Royal Naval Service and (with a slight name change) the Women's Auxiliary Air Force. In 1941 Britain passed legislation for female conscription into the three services. Other countries followed suit. Both Australia and New Zealand formed three auxiliary services, and in 1941 Canada formed the Canadian Women's Army Corps, followed a year later by the Canadian Women's Auxiliary Air Force and the Women's Royal Canadian Air Service.[2] After joining the conflict in December 1941, the United States formed the Women's Army Auxiliary Corps in 1942 (it became the Women's Army Corps the following year), and women's services for the navy, the coast guard and the air force. Although restricted to flying stateside, the United States permitted women to fly air force planes. In Britain, women in the Air Transport Auxiliary – including the record-breaking aviatrix Amy Johnson – worked as pilots to deliver planes to male RAF squadrons. As in the First World War, Russia, now the Soviet Union, employed women in combat roles. Marina Raskova, a famed female pilot, had flown in the Soviet Air Force as a navigator since the early 1930s. She was given permission by the Soviet leader Joseph Stalin to form a regiment of female pilots during the Second World War.[3] The Soviet army also employed women snipers, believing that their relatively slim build and patience made them ideal. Two famous women snipers were Nina Alexeyevna Lobkovskaya and Mila Mikhailovna Pavlichenko. Lobkovskaya's company claimed over 3,000 targets whilst Pavlichenko had an individual score of over 300.[4]

Indeed in the Second World War, each country undertook espionage on a much larger scale. Amongst the most famous female agents were Violette Szabo, Noor Inayat Khan, and Odette Hallowes of the Special Operations Executive. All three women were also members of the First Aid Nursing Yeomanry during the early 1940s and Khan had also been an officer in the Women's Auxiliary Air Force.[5]

The women of the First World War had succeeded in laying the foundations that led to women being fully accepted in the armed forces. Despite great danger, and in the face of great resistance, received wisdom and male expectations, they proved that they were capable of operating effectively in the war zone and thereby established a much more extensive role for women in wartime.

Notes
1 Beckett, Ian F.W., *Home Front 1914–1918: How Britain Survived the Great War.*
2 Brayley, Martin, *World War II Allied Women's Services.*
3 Goodpaster Strebe, Amy, *Flying for her Country: The American and Soviet Women Military Pilots of World War II.*
4 Axell, Albert, *Russia's Heroes.*
5 Foot, M.R.D., *SOE: An Outline History of the Special Operations Executive 1940–1946.*

Bibliography

Primary sources

Allen, Kathleen Mary, Personal papers, National Army Museum Collection, document 2006-07-53

Gaunt, Emmy, *Recollections of the Great War*, National Army Museum Collection, document 1998-01-56

Graham, Mrs O.B., Personal papers, National Army Museum Collection, document 1998-01-59

Greg, E.A., *Getting Out*, MS in private papers of Miss E.A. Greg, Imperial War Museum, documents 8337

Hutchinson, Beryl, Personal papers, Liddle Collection, Leeds University, document LIDDLE/WW1/WO/057

MacPherson, Grace, *Personal papers and diaries* held by the Canadian War Memorial Archives. Call numbers:

CWM ARCHIVES / ARCHIVES DU MCG : Textual Records 58A 1 21.12

CWM ARCHIVES / ARCHIVES DU MCG : Textual Records 58A 1 256.16

Pemberton, E.B., *Private papers of Miss E B Pemberton OBE*, Imperial War Museum, documents 3684

Watkins, G.E.G., *Memories of a Hushwaac in France*, St Omer, Sept 1917–Apr 1918; Paris Plage Apr 1918–Nov 1918. National Army Museum Collection, document 1998-01-110

Recorded interviews

Farmborough, Florence, Recording of interview, 1975, Imperial War Museum, document 312

Martin, Annie May, Recording of interview, 1973, Imperial War Museum, document 42

Shepherd, Dolly, Recording of interview, 1975, Imperial War Museum, document 579

Warner, J., Recording of interview, 1977, Imperial War Museum, document 997

Newspaper articles

'Emergency Women – Aiding the nation in many ways', in *Daily Chronicle*, 9 March 1915
'Letter to the Editor', in *Votes for Women*, 28 August 1914

Bibliography

Aldridge, Olive, *The Retreat from Serbia through Montenegro and Albania* (London: Minerva Publishing, 1916)

Antier, Chantal, Walle, Marianne and Lahaie, Olivier, *Les Espionnes dans la Grande Guerre* (Rennes: Editions Ouest-France, 2008)

Atkinson, Diane, *Elsie and Mairi go to War: Two Extraordinary Women on the Western Front* (London: Preface Digital, 2009) (Random House Group)

Axell, Albert, *Russia's Heroes* (London: Constable, 2001)

Bates, Christina, Dodd, Dianne and Rousseau, Nicole, *On all Frontiers – Four Centuries of Canadian Nursing* (Ottawa: University of Ottawa Press, 2005)

Beatty, Bessie, *The Red Heart of Russia* (New York: The Century Co., 1918)

Beauchamp, Pat, *Fanny Goes to War* (London: John Murray, 1919)

Beckett, Ian F.W., *Home Front 1914–1918 – How Britain Survived the Great War* (Kew: National Archives, 2006)

Beckett, Ian F.W., *Territorials – A Century of Service* (Plymouth: DRA Publishing, 2008)

Belford, Barbara, *Brilliant Bylines: A Biographical Anthology of Notable Newspaperwomen in America* (New York: Columbia University Press, 1986)

Bellafaire, Judith and Graf, Mercedes, *Women Doctors in War* (College Station: Texas A&M University Press, 2009)

Bochkareva, Maria, trans. by Levine, Isaac Don, *Yashka: My Life as Peasant, Exile and Soldier* (London: Constable and Co., 1919)

Brayley, Martin, *World War II Allied Women's Services* (Oxford: Osprey, 2001)

Burger Johnson, Katherine, 'Journalists, American Women, During World War I' in Cook, Bernard A., *Women and War: A Historical Encyclopedia from Antiquity to the Present* (California: ABC-CLIO, 2006)

Chandler, Malcolm, *Votes for Women, c. 1900–28* (London: Heinemann, 2001)

Charbonnier, Alain, 'History, Facts, Anecdotes and Legends – Women Secret Agents who Acted in the Risorgimento', in *Online Gnosis Italian Intelligence Magazine*, 2011, issue 1. (http://gnosis.aisi.gov.it/Gnosis/Rivista26.nsf/ServNavigE/25 accessed 2nd May 2013)

Clark, Linda L., *Women and Achievement in Nineteenth-century Europe* (Cambridge: Cambridge University Press, 2008)

Cohn, Jan, *Improbable Fiction: The Life of Mary Roberts Rinehart* (Pittsburgh, PA: University of Pittsburgh Press, 2006)

Cook, Bernard A., *Women and War: A Historical Encyclopedia from Antiquity to the Present* (California: ABC-CLIO, 2006)

Cordier, Marcel and Maggio, Rosalie, *Marie Marvignt – La Femme d'un Siecle* (Sarreguemines: Editions Pierron, 2000)

Crofton, Eileen, *The Women of Royaumont: a Scottish Women's Hospital on the Western Front* (East Linton: Tuckwell Press, 1997)

Croy, Princess Marie de, *War Memories* (London: Macmillan, 1932)

Dadeshkeliani, Princess Kati, trans. Ashton, Arthur J., *Princess in Uniform* (London: G. Bell & Sons, 1934)

Darrow, Margaret H., *French Women and the First World War* (Oxford: Berg, 2000)

Dexter, Mary, *In the Soldier's Service: War Experiences of Mary Dexter; England – Belgium – France 1914–1918* (Boston and New York: Houghton Mifflin Company, 1918)

Dudgeon, Ruth A., 'Higher Education for Women in Nineteenth- and early Twentieth Century Russia', in Rule, Wilma and Noonan, Norma C., *Russian Women in Politics and Society* (Westport, CT: Greenwood Press, 1996)

Dyhouse, Carol, *Students: A Gendered History* (London: Routledge, 2006)

Elston, M.A., 'Anderson, Elizabeth Garrett (1836–1917)' in *Oxford Dictionary of National Biography* (Oxford: Oxford University Press, 2004; online ed., Oct 2005) (www.oxforddnb.com/view/article/30406, accessed 21 Feb 2014)

Emslie Hutton, Isabel, *With a Woman's Unit in Serbia, Salonika and Sebastopol* (London: Williams & Norgate, 1928)

Escott, Squadron Leader Beryl E., *Women in Air Force Blue: The Story of Women in the Royal Air Force from 1918 to the Present Day* (Wellingborough: Stephens, 1989)

Farmborough, Florence, *Nurse at the Russian Front: A Diary 1914–18* (London: Constable, 1994)

Farnam, Ruth, *Nation at Bay: What an American Woman saw and did in Suffering Serbia* (Indianapolis: Bobbs-Merrill, 1918)

Finzi, Kate John, *Eighteenth Months in the War Zone – The Record of a Woman's Work on the Western Front* (London: Cassell, 1916)

Fletcher, N. Corbet, *The St. John Ambulance Association: Its History, and its Part in the Ambulance Movement* (London: St John Ambulance Association, 1931)

Foot, M.R.D., *SOE: An Outline History of the Special Operations Executive 1940–1946* (London: Folio Society, 2008)

Frost, Elizabeth and Cullen-Du Pont, Kathryn, *Women's Suffrage in America – An Eyewitness History* (New York: Facts on File, 1992)

Furse, Dame Katharine, *Hearts and Pomegranates: The Story of Forty-five Years, 1875 to 1920* (London: Peter Davies,1940)

Gavin, Lettie, *American Women in World War I* (Colorado: University of Colorado, 1997)

Glaze, Robert L., 'Tompkins, Sally Louisa (1833–1916)' in Tendrich Frank, Lisa (ed.), *An Encyclopedia of American Women at War: From the Home Front to the Battlefields* (California: ABC-CLIO, 2013)

Goodman, Susan, *Gertrude Bell* (Leamington Spa: Berg, 1985)

Goodpaster Strebe, Amy, *Flying for her Country: The American and Soviet Women Military Pilots of World War II* (Oxford: Harcourt Education, 2007)

Gordon, Winifred, *A Woman in the Balkans* (London: Thomas Nelson, 1918)

Gould, Jenny, 'Women's Military Services in First World War Britain' in Higonnet, Margaret R. (ed.), *Behind the Lines: Gender and the Two World Wars* (New Haven, CT: Yale University Press, 1987)

Hacker, Barton C. and Vining, Margaret (eds), *A Companion to Women's Military History* (Boston: Brill, 2012)

Hacker, Carlotta, *Indomitable Lady Doctors* (Toronto: Clarke Irwin, 1974)

Hallam, Andrew and Hallam, Nicola (eds), *Lady Under Fire on the Western Front: The Great War Letters of Lady Dorothie Feilding MM* (Barnsley: Pen & Sword, 2010)

Harris, Kirsty, *More than Bombs and Bandages, Australian Army Nurses at Work in World War I* (Newport, NSW: Big Sky, 2011)

Harrison, Mark, *The Medical War: British Military Medicine in the First World War* (Oxford: Oxford University Press, 2010)

Henry, Mark R., *The US Army of World War I* (Oxford: Osprey, 2003)

Hewitt, Linda J., *Women Marines in World War I* (Washington D.C: History and Museums Division, U.S. Marine Corps, 1974)

Holmes, Rachel, *The Secret Life of Dr James Barry: Victorian England's Most Eminent Surgeon* (Stroud: Tempus, 2007)

Howarth, Janet, 'Fawcett, Dame Millicent Garrett (1847–1929)', *Oxford Dictionary of National Biography* (Oxford: Oxford University Press, 2004; online ed., Oct 2007) [http://www.oxforddnb.com/view/article/33096, accessed 29 Oct 2012]

Hutton, Marcelline, *Russian and West European Women 1860–1939: Dreams, Struggles and Nightmares* (London: Rowman & Littlefield, 2001)

Hutton, Marcelline, 'Women in Russian Society from the Tsar to Yeltsin', in Rule, Wilma and Noonan, Norma C., *Russian Women in Politics and Society* (Westport, CT: Greenwood Press, 1996)

Irwin, Julia F., *Making the World Safe: The American Red Cross and a Nation's Humanitarian Awakening* (Oxford: Oxford University Press, 2013)

Izzard, Molly, *A Heroine in her Time – A Life of Dame Helen Gwynne-Vaughan 1879–1967* (London: Macmillan, 1969)

Janis, Elsie, *So Far, so Good! An Autobiography* (London: Long John, 1933)

Jenson, Kimberly, *Mobilizing Minerva: American Women in the First World War* (Urbana-Champaign, IL: University of Illinois Press, 2008)

Jenson, Kimberly, 'Volunteers, Auxiliaries and Women's Mobilization: The First World War and Beyond (1914–1939)' in Hacker, Barton C. and Vining, Margaret (eds), *A Companion to Women's Military History* (Boston: Brill, 2012)

Jordan, David, *The Balkans, Italy & Africa, 1914–1918: From Sarajevo to the Piave and Lake Tanganyika* (London: Amber Books, 2008)

Kanner, Barbara P., 'Lowther, Barbara (Toupie)' in Cook, Bernard A., *Women and War: A Historical Encyclopedia from Antiquity to the Present* (California: ABC-CLIO, 2006)

King, Hazel, *One Woman at War: Letters of Olive King 1915–1920* (Melbourne: Melbourne University Press, 1986)

Krippner, Monica, *The Quality of Mercy: Women at War, Serbia 1915–18* (Newton Abbot: David and Charles, 1980)

Lacey, Jim, *Pershing* (Basingstoke: Palgrave Macmillan, 2008)

Ladoux, Georges, trans. by Dawson, Warrington, *Marthe Richard, The Skylark: The Foremost Woman Spy of France* (London: Cassell, 1932)

Landau, Henry, *Spreading the Spy Net: The Story of a British Spy Director* (London: Jarrolds, 1938)

Landau, Rom, trans by Dunlop, Geoffrey, *Piludski: Hero of Poland* (London: Jarrolds, 1930)

Lawrence, Dorothy, *Sapper Dorothy – The Only English Woman Soldier in the Royal Engineers 51st Division 79th Tunnelling Co. During the First World War* (Milton Keynes: Leonaur Ltd/Oakpast, 2010)

Lee, Janet, *War Girls: The First Aid Nursing Yeomanry in the First World War* (Manchester: Manchester University Press, 2005)

Leneman, Leah, *Elsie Inglis – Founder of Battlefield Hospitals Run Entirely by Women* (Edinburgh: NMS Publishing Limited, 1998)

Leneman, Leah, *In the Service of Life* (Edinburgh: Mercat Press, 1994)

Leneman, Leah, 'Medical Women in the First World War – Ranking Nowhere' in *British Medical Journal*, Vol. 307 No. 6919 (18–25 December, 1993) pp.1592–4

Lumsden, Linda J., *Inez: The Life and Times of Inez Milholland* (Bloomington: Indiana University Press, 2004)

MacLeod Harper, Florence, *Runaway Russia* (New York: The Company Co., 1918)

Macnaughtan, Sarah, *My War Experiences in Two Continents* (London: John Murray, 1919)

Manson, Cecil and Manson, Celia, *Doctor Agnes Bennett* (London: Michael Joseph, 1960)

Martin, William, *Verdun 1916* (Oxford: Osprey, 2001)

Matthews, Dr Caroline, *Experiences of a Woman Doctor in Serbia* (London: Mills & Boon, 1916)

McDougall, Grace, *Nursing Adventures. A F.A.N.Y. in France* (London: William Heinemann, 1917)

McGregor Hellstedt, Leone, *Women Physicians of the World: Autobiographies of Medical Pioneers* (London: McGraw-Hill, 1978)

McKenna, Marthe, *I was a spy!* (London: Queensway Library, 1934)

McNeal, Robert H., *Tsar and Cossack, 1855–1914* (London: Macmillan, 1987)

Micheletti, Laura Marie, 'Co-education' in Martinez Aleman, Ana M. and Renn, Kristen (eds), *Women in Higher Education: An Encylopedia* (California: ABC-CLIO, 2002)

Miles, Rosalind and Cross, Robin, *Warrior Women: 3000 Years of Courage & Heroism* (London: Quercus Publishing, 2011)

Miller, Louise, *A Fine Brother: The Life of Captain Flora Sandes* (Richmond: Alma, 2012)

Mironov, Boris, *The Standard of Living and Revolutions in Russia, 1700–1917* (New York: Routledge, 2012)

Morrison, Dr Lt-Col J.T.J., *Experiences in Serbia 1914–1915* (London: 1915)

Morse, John, *An Englishman in the Russian Ranks: Ten Months' Fighting in Poland* (London: Duckworth, 1915)

Murray, Flora, *Women as Army Surgeons – Being the History of the Women's Hospital Corps in Paris, Wimereux and Endell Street, September 1914–October 1919* (London: Hodder and Stoughton, 1920)

Neale, Shirley, 'Edis, (Mary) Olive (1876–1955)' in *Oxford Dictionary of National Biography* (Oxford: Oxford University Press, 2004) online edition: [www.oxforddnb.com/view/article/54348 accessed 17 Aug 2013]

Neiberg, Michael S. and Jordan, David, *The Eastern Front 1914–1920: from Tannenberg to the Russo-Polish war* (London: Amber, 2008)

Nicolai, Walter, trans. by Renwick, George, *The German Secret Service* (London: S. Paul, 1924)

Noakes, Lucy, *Women in the British Army: War and the Gentle Sex, 1907–1948* (London: Routledge, 2006)

Norris, Geoffrey, *The Royal Flying Corps: A History* (London: Frederick Muller, 1965)

Oldfield, Audrey, *Woman Suffrage in Australia – A Gift or a Struggle?* (Cambridge: Cambridge University Press, 1994)

Oliver, Dame Beryl, 'V.A.D. Members of the British Red Cross Society, and the Order of St. John of Jerusalem' in Wadge, D. Collett (ed.) *Women in Uniform* (London: Sampson Low, Marston & Co., 1946)

O'Rourke, Shane, 'Women in a Warrior Society: Don Cossack Women 1860–1914' in Marsh, Rosalind (ed.), *Women in Russia and Ukraine* (Cambridge: Cambridge University Press, 1996)

Paget, Dame Louise, *With our Serbian Allies* (London: Serbian Relief Fund, 1915)

Pantelic, Ivana, 'Liocic (Liotchich-Milosevic), Draga (1855–1926)' in de Haan, Francisca, Daskalova, Krassimira and Loutfi, Anna A. (eds), *Biographical Dictionary of Women's Movements and Feminisms: Central, Eastern and South Eastern Europe, 19th and 20th Centuries* (Budapest: Central European University Press, 2006)

Piggott, Juliet, *Queen Alexandra's Royal Army Nursing Corps* (Barnsley: Leo Cooper, 1975)

Pilsudski, Joseph, trans. and ed. Gillie, D.R., *Joseph Pilsudski: The Memories of a Polish Revolutionary and Soldier* (London: Faber, 1931)

Pohl Lovejoy, Esther, *Certain Samaritans – The Story of the American Women's Hospitals* (New York: Macmillan, 1927)

Popham, Hugh, *The F.A.N.Y. in Peace and War: The Story of the First Aid Nursing Yeomanry 1907–2003* (Barnsley: Leo Cooper, 2003)

Proctor, Tammy M., *Female Intelligence: Women and Espionage in the First World War* (London: New York University Press, 2003)

Purvis, June, *Emmeline Pankhurst: A Biography* (London: Routledge, 2002)

Rédier, Antoine, trans. Hall, Olive, *The Story of Louise de Bettignies* (London: Hutchinson, 1926)

Richer, Marthe, trans. Griffin, Gerald, *I spied for France* (London: John Long, 1935)

Rinehart, Mary Roberts, *Kings, Queens and Pawns: An American Woman at the Front* (New York: George H. Doran, 1915)

Van Rokeghem, Suzanne; Aubenas, Jacqueline and Vercheval-Vervoot, Jeanne, *Des Femmes dans L'Histoire en Belgique Depuis 1830* (Brussels: Luc Pire, 2006)

Ross, Ishbel, *Ladies of the Press: The Story of Women in Journalism by an Insider* (London: Harper & Bros, 1936)

Sandes, Flora, *An Autobiography of a Woman Soldier: A Brief Record of Adventure with the Serbian Army, 1916–1919* (New York: Frederick A. Stokes, 1920)

Sandes, Flora, *An English Woman-Sergeant in the Serbian Army* (London: Hodder and Stoughton, 1916)

Scardino Belzer, Allison, *Women and the Great War: Femininity under Fire in Italy* (Basingstoke: Palgrave Macmillan, 2010)

Schneider, Dorothy and Schneider, Carl J., *Into the Breach: American Women Overseas in World War I* (New York: Viking, 1991)

Schneider, Jean-Jacques, *Nicole Mangin: Une Lorraine au Coeur de la Grande Guerre – L'unique Femme Médecin de L'armée Française (1914–1918),* (Nancy: Editions Place Stanislas, 2012)

Shearer, Benjamin (ed.), *Home Front Heroes: A Biographical Dictionary of Americans during Wartime, Vol. 1* (Westport, CT: Greenwood Press, 2007)

Shipman, Pat, *The Femme Fatale: Love, Lies, and the Unknown Life of Mata Hari* (London: Weidenfeld & Nicolson, 2007)

Silverstone, Rosalie and Ward, Audrey, 'Mary Anne Elston' in *Careers of Professional Women* (London: Croom Helm, 1980)

Simkins, Peter; Jukes, Geoffrey and Hickey, Michael, *The First World War: The War to End all Wars* (Oxford: Osprey, 2003)

Slaughter Morton, Rosalie, *A Woman Surgeon – The Life and Work of Rosalie Slaughter Morton* (London: R. Hale & Co, 1937)

Souhami, Diana, *Edith Cavell* (London: Quercus, 2010)

Steinback, Susie, *Women in England, 1760–1914: A Social History* (Brighton: Wheatsheaf Books, 1984)

Stites, Richard, 'Women and the Russian Intelligentsia' in Atkinson, Dorothy; Dallin, Alexander and Warshofsky Lapidus, Gail, *Women in Russia* (Hassocks: Harvester Press, 1978)

Stobart, Mabel St Clair, *Miracles and Adventures: An Autobiography* (London: Rider & Co., 1935)

Stobart, Mabel St Clair, *The Flaming Sword in Serbia and Elsewhere* (London: Hodder and Stoughton, 1916)

Stoff, Laurie S., *They Fought for the Motherland: Russia's Women Soldiers in World War I and the Revolution* (Kansas: University Press of Kansas, 2006)

Stone, Norman, *The Eastern Front 1914–1917* (London: Penguin, 1998)

Talmadge, John E., *Corra Harris, Lady of Purpose* (Athens, GA: University of Georgia Press, 1968)

Tennyson Jesse, Fryiwyd, *The Sword of Deborah: First-hand Impressions of the British Women's Army in France* (New York: George H. Doran, 1919)

Terry, Roy, 'Watson, Alexandra Mary Chalmers (1872–1936)' in *Oxford Dictionary of National Biography* (Oxford: Oxford University Press, 2004), online edition: [http://www.oxforddnb.com/view/article/67666 accessed 27 Oct 2012]

Thuliez, Louise, trans. Poett-Velitchko, Marie, *Condemned to Death* (London: Methuen, 1934)

Thurstan, Violetta, *Field Hospital and Flying Column: Being the Journal of an English Nursing Sister in Belgium & Russia* (London: G.P. Putnam's Sons, 1915)

Tietjens, Eunice, *The World at my Shoulder* (New York: Macmillan, 1938)

Van Til, Jacqueline, *With Edith Cavell in Belgium* (New York: H.W. Bridges, 1922)

T'Serclaes, Baroness, *Flanders and Other Fields: Memoirs of the Baroness de T'Serclaes* (London: Harrap, 1964)

Tsui, Bonnie, *She Went to the Field: Women Soldiers of the Civil War* (Guilford, CT: Globe Pequot Press, 2006)

Turnbull, Michael T.R.B., *Mary Garden* (Portland, OR: Amadeus Press, 1997)

De Vries, Susanna, *Complete Book of Heroic Australian Women: Twenty-one Extraordinary Women Whose Stories Changed History* (Pymble NSW: Harper Collins, 2010)

Ward, Irene, *F.A.N.Y. Invicta* (London: Hutchinson, 1955)

Whitehead, Ian R., *Doctors in the Great War* (London: Leo Cooper, 1999)

Willmott, H.P., *World War I* (London: Dorling Kindersley, 2003)

Yurlova, Marina, *Cossack Girl* (Somerville MA: Heliograph, 2010)

Zeiger, Susan, *In Uncle Sam's Service: Women Workers in the American Expeditionary Force* (London: Cornell University Press, 1999)

Zeni, Luisa, *Briciole: Ricordi di una Donna in Guerra 1914–1921* (Rome: Eredi cremonese,1926)

Index